The AMERICAN
HERITAGE
Book of GREAT
HISTORIC
PLACES

The AMERICAN HERITAGE *Book of*

HISTORIC

GREAT
PLACES

By the Editors of AMERICAN HERITAGE

Narrative by RICHARD M. KETCHUM

Introduction by BRUCE CATTON

Published by AMERICAN HERITAGE PUBLISHING COMPANY, INC., New York

Book Trade Distribution by McGRAW-HILL BOOK COMPANY

AMERICAN HERITAGE
PUBLISHING CO., INC.

PRESIDENT AND PUBLISHER
Paul Gottlieb

EDITOR-IN-CHIEF
Joseph J. Thorndike

SENIOR EDITOR, BOOK DIVISION
Alvin M. Josephy, Jr.

EDITORIAL ART DIRECTOR
Murray Belsky

GENERAL MANAGER, BOOK DIVISION
Kenneth W. Leish

———

Staff for this Book

EDITOR
Richard M. Ketchum

EDITORIAL ASSISTANTS
Helen Augur
Caroline Backlund
Robert Cowley
Margaret Di Crocco
Hilde Heun
Jean Leich
Joan Wharton

SPECIAL ADVISER
Francis S. Ronalds

ART DIRECTOR
Irwin Glusker

ART ASSISTANT
Trudy Glucksberg

ORIGINAL MAPS
Harold Faye

———

Library of Congress Catalog Card Number:
57-11274

International Standard Book Numbers:
07-034413-2, regular; 07-034414-0, de luxe

This wooden Indian surveys Old Sturbridge's village green from a lookout on the front porch of Grant's General Store.

Sturbridge: Eighteenth-Century Community

There are few places in the country where one can see so well what life was like in the eighteenth and early nineteenth centuries as in Old Sturbridge Village. Built alongside the gentle Quinebaug River in south central Massachusetts, Sturbridge was the creation of two industrialists named Wells, who devoted years to collecting and restoring more than thirty buildings in the community, and furnishing them with the authentic implements and appurtenances of the period. It was not their purpose to re-create an actual town, but to reconstruct a typical, functioning community where one can see what life was like then.

There is a traditional village green, a meeting-house, school, country store, sawmill and gristmill, a blacksmith shop, and houses ranging in style from a simple one-room cottage to an imposing Georgian mansion. Most of these buildings house collections of early New England crafts and tools, and Old Sturbridge Village is a working community where cabinet-maker, miller, potter, weaver, and coppersmith carry on trades as their forbears did.

A convincing background for the skill, ingenuity, and thrift of New England's preindustrial days, Old Sturbridge Village is a place of unusual educational interest, where the eighteenth century and the remarkable contributions of its inhabitants are handsomely preserved for posterity.

Corn meal and buckwheat flour are still ground at the Wight Gristmill (left), powered by a huge undershot water wheel.

The interior of the Hitchcock Boot Shop is fitted out with the tools which cobblers used in the late eighteenth century.

49

Provisions for the Peddlers

For a time sea and river sufficed as the high roads of colonial commerce but, because of the perverse way men had of moving constantly toward the western sky, the day came when a better means of supplying the families of the interior had to be devised. The Yankee peddler was the answer.

Loaded down with more dead weight than most of us would care to lift—much less carry—these men slogged through torrential rains, blistering heat, ankle-deep mud, and were bitten by dogs, snakes, and every known kind of insect in their appointed rounds. For nearly two hundred years these "damn Yankees from Connecticut" and other parts of New England plied their trade, visiting every house and settlement in the remote, lonely interior. What they did required little knowledge or capital, and for most of them it spelled opportunity.

They supplied housewives with tinware, pins, gingham, and bits of ribbon; husbands with nails, jack-knives, and tools; children with candy sticks, jew's-harps, and trinkets. In return they received the honey, coonskins, beaver pelts, and hand-carved furniture that were the farm families' sole currency. Several million people depended on these shrewd, inquisitive men to bring them the articles they needed (and some they didn't know they needed), and as fast as the Yankee peddler sold his wares the mills of the Northeast worked to replace them.

Early in our history New Englanders began to take advantage of the rocky hills and tumbling streams God had given them, it seemed, instead of topsoil. By 1650 there was, at Saugus, Massachusetts, an ironworks which was the wonder of its day. It had a rolling and slitting mill that compared with the best in Europe, from which came iron to be made into nails, guns, cooking utensils, chains, hardware, and farm implements for the burgeoning frontier. Out of home and mill came rope, candles, earthenware, leather goods, glass, paper, and a host of other products in increasing numbers.

There are still many places where New England's industrial beginnings can be seen. At Saugus, for example, the entire ironworks has been reconstructed into a working museum where visitors may inspect the ingenious mechanisms devised by their forebears. Just up the hill from the ironworks is the old iron-master's house—a dark seventeenth-century remnant of the Elizabethan style which is one of the finest surviving examples of this type of dwelling, and one of the earliest frame houses in America.

On Nantucket a windmill continues to produce corn meal, as it has since 1746. Near the village of Wickford, Rhode Island, with its concentration of eighteenth-century houses, is the old snuff mill operated by Gilbert Stuart's father. Farther north, in a town the Indians called Pawtucket, or "the place by the waterfall," Samuel Slater built a textile mill in 1793 which still stands. When President Madison decided to enhance the prestige of American cloth, he gave it his approval by wearing a suit of Pawtucket woolen at his inauguration.

At Simsbury, Connecticut, John Higley minted the first copper coins in the colonies, stamping them with the charming inscription: "I am good Copper—Value me as You Will." No such happy thoughts ever graced the bowels of Newgate Prison, in nearby East Granby, where the ore was mined. Here, seventy feet below the grim ruins, are caverns where circles were worn in the rock floor by the pacing feet of chained prisoners—Tories, thieves, and debtors forced to work in iron collars, handcuffs, and leg irons.

In an elm-shaded glen in New London, Connecticut, there is a low, gambrel-roofed gristmill established in 1650. Although the overshot wheel is a replica of the first one, the beams, gears, and grinders of the original mill remain.

The old stone mill in Newport has been the subject of controversy for years. Often attributed to Norsemen, it is more probably the ruin of a windmill built by Benedict Arnold's great-grandfather, the first governor of Rhode Island. The mill owes its preservation to Judah Touro, a son of the first regular rabbi of Jeshuat Israel Congregation in Newport, who lived and made a fortune in New Orleans and served with Andrew Jackson in the War of 1812. When he died he left $500,000 to churches and other institutions of many faiths, and gave the city of Newport $10,000 to buy and improve the grounds around the old mill.

In the painting above, a Yankee peddler has descended from his wagon to extol the virtues of a coffee grinder to a matronly assemblage. The Eastham windmill pictured at right is still in operation. Once a common sight along the Massachusetts coast, windmills were used for the grinding of corn. Shown below is the restored Saugus Ironworks. From left to right are the wharf and warehouse, the blast furnace, the forge, and the rolling and slitting mill. Partly hidden among the trees is the ironmaster's house, built in the seventeenth century.

Emerson's grandfather watched the battle at North Bridge from his study in the Old Manse. Scarcely changed since 1769, it was the home of Emerson, and later of Nathaniel Hawthorne, who wrote *Mosses from an Old Manse* here.

New England's Literary Heritage

The flowering of what we often call "literary New England" was the impact of the poet on the Puritan spirit. What these writers had to say can be understood much more readily if it is measured against the surroundings that colored their work.

It is all very well to visit the Vassall-Craigie House in Cambridge and think that this was where Henry Wadsworth Longfellow lived when he taught at Harvard. But if we remember that the house had been there since 1759, in the heart of those origins the poet so wanted to make into a national tradition for his countrymen, his poems come to life a little bit more.

Maybe Thoreau would be better understood if he were read on the banks of Walden Pond, where he stated the belief that man need not be hampered by civilization's material things. And to visit the quiet old village of Concord is to understand better how Emerson, back from his travels to think, to walk, and to observe life, found that "The purpose of life seems to be to acquaint every man with himself." Parts of Concord are unchanged since the time when he found in them a philosophy of individualism that seemed to set men free and provide them with a new energy.

If you walk along Highland Avenue in Salem as the sun goes down, Gallows Hill stands out in stark relief as it did for Nathaniel Hawthorne, one hundred years ago. And in the House of the Seven Gables and Witch House there are still memories of the grim Puritan past which both fascinated and repelled him.

There is Seamen's Bethel, in New Bedford, where Herman Melville sat and heard sermons which he united with his knowledge of the sea and the whale hunt to produce what has been called "the perfect and final result of the Puritan's desperate three-century-long struggle with the problem of evil."

One of the many other places with long memories is the serene brick house in Amherst that harbored Emily Dickinson from the world and its confusions and allowed her to discover something of the human soul. And in Portsmouth, New Hampshire, and South Berwick, Maine, you can see the beautiful homes of Thomas Bailey Aldrich and Sarah Orne Jewett, which were scenes of their delightful New England stories.

Morning mists rise from Walden Pond where Thoreau came to escape a way of life which made men "tools of their tools."

Henry David Thoreau

Ralph Waldo Emerson

Nathaniel Hawthorne

Roger Williams

Conformist and

In nearly all the old towns of New England, facing the village green or common, are the towering white spires of Congregational churches which are lineal descendants of the early Puritan meeting-houses. Of all these, perhaps only one really dates back to Puritan times—the Old Ship Church in Hingham, Massachusetts, built in 1681, and now a Unitarian church. Plain to the point of severity, it is a fine example of its makers' deliberate indifference to aesthetics which resulted so often in dignity and simple beauty.

The beginning of religious liberty in the United States was largely the story of those folk who fled the intolerance of the Massachusetts Bay Colony. Roger Williams left Salem for Rhode Island, determined to "hold forth a lively experiment that a most flourishing civil state may stand and best be maintained with full liberty in religious concernments." For years the Baptists who found refuge there had no church, meeting under a tree or in a member's house; but finally, in 1775, they erected in Providence the First Baptist Meetinghouse "for the publick worship of Almighty God." And although Baptists in those days frowned on frivolities, they nevertheless hung a bell in their place of worship which bore the inscription:

For freedom of conscience the town was first planted,
Persuasion not force, was used by the people:
This church is the eldest and has not recanted,
Enjoying and granting bell, temple and steeple.

In Newport, the Central Baptist Church has withstood time's ravages since 1733, and the Newport Historical Society has preserved the lovely interior

With its classic portico and high, graceful steeple, the Congregational Church in Litchfield, Connecticut, displays the best qualities of New England church architecture.

George Whitefield

Thomas Hiscox

Jonathan Edwards

Cotton Mather

Nonconformist

of the Seventh Day Baptist Church, oldest of that denomination in the country. Newport is also the site of the Touro Synagogue—oldest synagogue building in America—built by descendants of Sephardic Jews who arrived in 1658.

Perhaps if Massachusetts Bay Colony had been governed by a William Penn instead of a Cotton Mather, those terrible months of the witchcraft craze would never have occurred. (Penn's answer to a charge that a Pennsylvania woman went riding on a broomstick was to state caustically that Pennsylvania had no law against riding on broomsticks.) But such was not the case, and Penn's New England brethren suffered much at Puritan hands. Despised, often whipped, mutilated, or hanged (if they succeeded in gaining entrance to the colony), the Quakers had already survived some years of persecution by the time Penn established his "Peaceable Kingdom" in 1681. One landmark of their survival still stands on the Great Road, near Saylesville, Rhode Island. An ell of this plain wooden meetinghouse, built from hand-hewn timbers mortised together with pegs, dates back to 1703.

One of the most interesting of the lesser religious denominations that flourished in New England was known as "The United Society of Believers in Christ's Second Appearing"—or the Shakers. Their celibacy and a belief in separation from the world led to their gradual decline; but near Canterbury, New Hampshire, one may still see, clustered about a white meetinghouse built in 1782, the sparsely furnished frame houses of those who protested against the adornments of a vain world.

Newport's Touro Synagogue, dedicated in 1763, is the oldest in America. Slim Grecian columns, chandeliers, and wainscoted seats adorn its red, white, and blue interior.

John Quincy Adams   Brooks Adams   John Adams   Henry Adams   Charles Francis Adams

The Adamses of Quincy

One day in 1945, Henry Adams was taking a friend through the Adams house in Quincy, Massachusetts. When they reached the study, he pointed to an old chair and remarked, "There is the chair in which John Adams was stricken." He paused for a moment, then turned to his friend. "Do you know how I know?" His guest shook his head. Adams turned the chair over and showed him a piece of paper tacked to the bottom. There, in a fine script, were these words: "Father was seated in this chair when he was stricken July 4, 1826. [signed] John Quincy Adams."

The big comfortable house in Quincy which so many generations of Adamses knew as the "Old House" is not particularly distinguished architecturally. In terms of history, however, it is one of the great American homes. It was purchased in 1787 by John Adams, the ambitious young lawyer, who, with his cousin Sam, was referred to contemptuously by Governor Shirley as "this brace of Adamses." John believed in the law, and demonstrated it by defending the British troops who fired on the Americans in the Boston Massacre. He believed in freedom, and helped make it by signing the Declaration of Independence. He was largely responsible for Washington's appointment as commander in chief when the Revolution broke out. He served abroad from 1778 to 1788, became first envoy to the Court of St. James, Vice President under Washington, and, in 1797, the second President. And in one of those strange and wonderful coincidences of history, he and Thomas Jefferson died on July 4, 1826—the fiftieth anniversary of that Declaration of Independence they both signed and did so much to preserve.

On a hill not far from this house John's wife, Abigail, held the hand of their little boy, John Quincy Adams, and listened to the British guns firing on Breed's Hill. That boy was the sixth President of the United States when his father died, and in 1831 he was elected to the House of Representatives—something achieved by no other President. There he remained for literally the rest of his life. In 1848 he collapsed at his desk and died two days later.

The next owner of the house was John Quincy's son, Charles Francis Adams, who became Lincoln's minister to Britain during the Civil War. Upon his death the mansion passed to his sons, among them Henry, Charles Francis II, and Brooks, the famous writers and historians. Through the years in which this one family made and lived American history, they brought to the "Old House" its fascinating relics—portraits of George and Martha Washington which John Adams paid Edward Savage $46.67 to paint (the receipt is still on the back of the canvas); a cradle that rocked two United States Presidents; and the great collection of books in the library (facing page). Under the lid of John's desk, used when the house was the summer White House, is an index to his personal filing system, with headings such as "From Secretary of War and Navy," "Drafts of Speeches," and "Letters from General Washington."

**Four generations of famous Adamses made the
"Old House" in Quincy their summer home.**

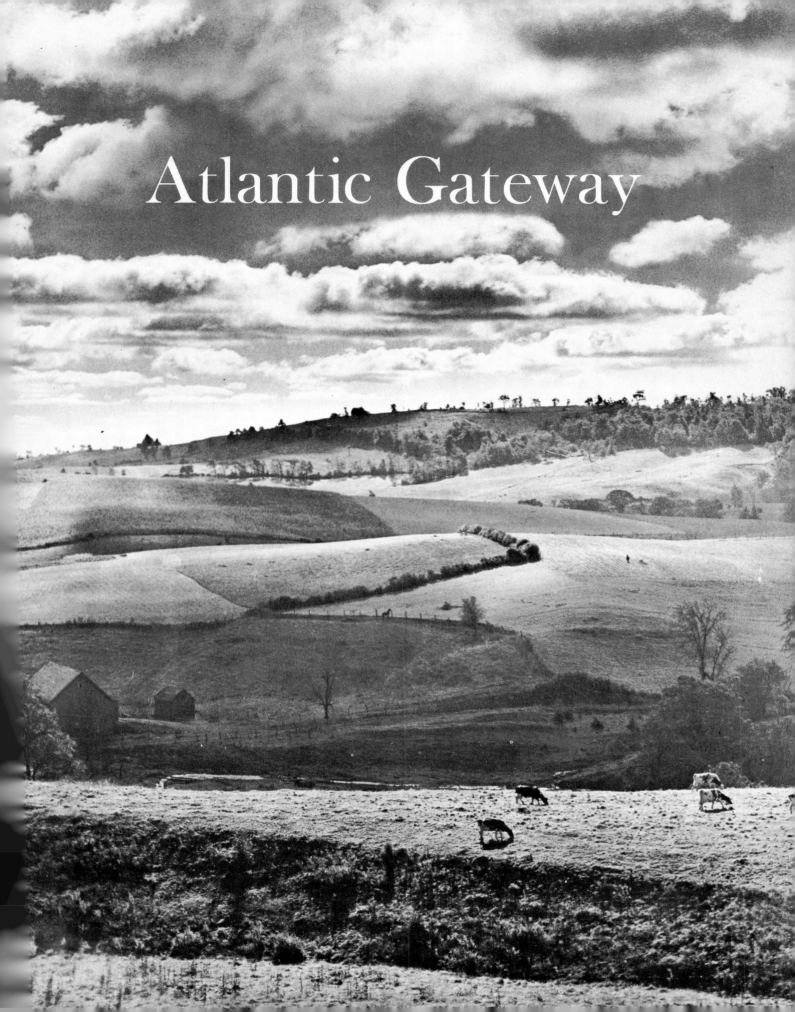

Atlantic Gateway

Peter Stuyvesant

The Hudson River Valley

From the east bank, Ichabod Crane paused to look out over the great river. As he watched, "The sun gradually wheeled his broad disk down into the west. The wide bosom of the Tappan Zee lay motionless and glassy, excepting that here and there a gentle undulation waved and prolonged the blue shadow of the distant mountain. . . . A slanting ray lingered on the woody crests of the precipices that overhung some parts of the river, giving greater depth to the dark-gray and purple of their rocky sides. A sloop was loitering in the distance, dropping slowly down with the tide, her sail hanging uselessly against the mast; and as the reflection of the sky gleamed along the still water, it seemed as if the vessel was suspended in the air."

This was the way Washington Irving remembered the Hudson in 1819. So unchanged is the picture that he could have been describing the "mighty deep-mouthed river" seen by Giovanni da Verrazano in 1524, Henry Hudson and the crew of the *Half Moon* in 1609, or the visitor today. On a rocky peak in the Adirondacks which the Indians called "the cloud splitter" lies Lake Tear-of-the-Clouds, from whose waters a little brook begins. Joined by others, the deepening

stream flows southward for over 300 miles, past Storm King, Bear Mountain, and the awesome cliffs of the Palisades, past the great piers of Manhattan Island, and then channels a deep undersea canyon that extends into the vast Atlantic more than 135 miles beyond Ambrose Lightship and nearly a mile and a half below the surface of the ocean.

In the little towns along its banks once stood the whitewashed or yellow brick houses, overhung with trees, where broad-hatted burghers sat with their *vrouws* to smoke an evening pipe. And from Hell Gate to Albany, every cove and crag of the river had its legend. At Hell Gate, a man known as the Pirate's Spook, whom Peter Stuyvesant had killed with a silver bullet, appeared in stormy weather in his little boat. The ghost of Rambout Van Dam, a resident of Spuyten Duyvil who was cursed forever for defying the Sabbath, rowed with muffled oars back and forth across the Tappan Zee. Men heard the eerie chant of a ship's crew at midnight when the moon was up near Point-no-Point, and captains of all real Dutch ships used to lower their peaks when they approached Thunder Mountain, in deference to the goblin in a sugar-loaf hat who was keeper of the mountains.

All these legends persisted when Washington Irving made his first trip up the Hudson in 1800, and as he grew up around Tarrytown and Sleepy Hollow he absorbed the magic of the old Dutch life, as well as the knowledge of those people on whom his charming distortions were based. Katrina Van Tassel of "The Legend of Sleepy Hollow," for example, was actually the belle of the Van Alen family, whose portrait hangs in their old house near Kinderhook. And Ichabod Crane was modeled after a cruel schoolmaster who taught where the present Crane School now stands, near Rensselaer.

The place that mirrors both the legends of Irving and the patroon system that determined the character of the Hudson Valley for more than two centuries is Philipsburg Manor, in North Tarrytown. In 1683 Frederick Philipse built this establishment in the center of his 25,000-acre estate, and the visitor who crosses the footbridge over the milldam once pic-

Iroquois Indians paddled out to meet Henry Hudson's *Half Moon* as it sailed up the river named for the explorer.

The restored gristmill and the stone milldam of Philipsburg Manor look much
like the original ones which Currier & Ives pictured a hundred years ago.

tured by Currier and Ives can see the house that was
home, office, and fortress for the Lord of the Manor.
The stone walls of the house are two feet thick, with
gun ports in the cellar walls to protect the manor
against river pirates. A ramp which was used to take
cattle indoors to safety during raids leads to the cellar,
which has a dairy, a storeroom for a year's supply of
food, and a slave kitchen with an enormous fireplace.
Also in the house are the Lord of the Manor's office,
and a secret passage which enabled Philipse to eaves-
drop on his indentured servants. Furnished in the
Dutch tradition—which was to buy what the owner
liked and to use it in the most comfortable fashion—
the Manor has the earliest tablecloth in America; what
is thought to be the first painting of New Amsterdam;
a lovely, blue-curtained cabinet bed; and a rare collection of candelabra and candlesticks.

Not far from the old Manor are the slave house and
the smoke house. The old mill, built by the first Lord
as part of his industrial settlement, looks out over the
wharf where Philipse's ships once landed their cargoes.
Tenant farmers brought their grain to the mill, paid
their rents, then made their purchases at the trading
post. Down the road from the mill is the Sleepy Hollow Church, built by Philipse, where everyone for

miles around worshiped. It was "the sequestered situation of this church" that made it seem to Irving "a
favorite haunt of troubled spirits. . . . To look upon
its grass-grown yard, where the sunbeams seem to sleep
so quietly, one would think that there at least the dead
might rest in peace."

The Philipsburg Manor dining room is Dutch style, with
pewter, delft, and a brass chandelier brought from Holland.

John Quidor painted the terrified Ichabod Crane and his horse "Old Gunpowder" fleeing from the Headless Horseman through Sleepy Hollow woods.

It was "the very witching time of night" when Ichabod Crane passed the spot where Major André was seized, and neared the "deep black part of the stream, not far from the church, [where] was formerly thrown a wooden bridge; the road that led to it, and the bridge itself, were thickly shaded by overhanging trees, which cast a gloom about it even in the daytime, but occasioned a fearful darkness at night." Today, there is a bridge near the place where Ichabod saw the Headless Horseman, and it is a fittingly short walk to the place where Washington Irving is buried, near the ghosts of the river he loved so well.

There are, of course, other survivals of the Dutch. Fort Crailo in Rensselaer is an old brick building built about 1705 and used as a fortress against the Indians. It was here that Dr. Richard Shuckburgh is supposed to have written the words of "Yankee Doodle," while seated on the curb of an old well in the garden. One entire street in Hurley is practically a museum of these early eighteenth-century houses, and Fishkill, one of the most attractive villages along the Hudson, has the Hendrick Kip House and a Dutch Reformed Church built about 1784. Nearly all the old Hudson Valley towns have one or more examples of the Dutch heritage. Two houses which conjure up an image of the patroon system are Van Cortlandt Manor at Croton-on-Hudson and the Van Rensselaer Manor House at Claverack. Another is Albany's Schuyler Mansion, the scene of Alexander Hamilton's marriage, and "Gentleman Johnny" Burgoyne's con-

finement after Saratoga. There are more modest buildings, too—homes of simpler folk which preserve the medieval flavor of their prototypes in Holland. The typical house was a two-story-and-loft building, usually made of Holland bricks, with an entrance stoop and stepped gable which faced the street. Washington Irving's elaborate Sunnyside at Tarrytown, which he described as "full of nooks and corners as an old cocked hat," is actually constructed around the ruins of a simple farmhouse built about 1690. Other good examples are the William Stoutenburgh House in East Park, with its low-pitched gable roof, and the Jan Pieterse Mabie House at Rotterdam Junction, one of the Mohawk Valley's earliest Dutch dwellings.

On Staten Island is the Voorlezer's House, believed to be the nation's oldest elementary school building. A *voorlezer* was a layman hired to teach children and conduct limited religious services, and he lived as well as worked in this house. At Broadway and 204th Street in New York City is the Dyckman House, built in 1783, which is now a museum. Another old Dutch house is the Senate House at Kingston, built in 1676 by Colonel Wessel Ten Broeck and partially burned by the British in 1777.

Although the Dutch tradition has been fastened to the Hudson Valley, this is unfair to the far more

Washington Irving is buried in the old Sleepy Hollow graveyard which Ichabod Crane passed on his legendary ride.

The first successful steam packet on the Hudson was Fulton's *Clermont*, shown here on its maiden voyage in 1807.

The variety of architecture along the Hudson is remarkable. At top are two colonial buildings, the Hasbrouck House (left) from the New Paltz Huguenot settlement and the Livingston family manor, Clermont. A pair of curiosities are shown below. Octagonal houses like the one at left were a fad a century ago; Bannerman's Castle, however, is unique, no doubt inspired by the river's Rhine-like setting. At bottom are two homes with a Gothic flavor: Martin Van Buren's Lindenwald (left) and Washington Irving's villa, Sunnyside.

numerous and influential groups from other nations who followed them. The British fleet which claimed New Netherland in 1664 for James, Duke of York, was the advance agent of thousands of English who eventually dominated the area. The Billopp House on Staten Island and Fraunces Tavern in lower Manhattan, where Washington said farewell to his officers in 1783, are two fine examples of the pre-Revolutionary period. British enthusiasm for the valley kindled the desire of families from all over Europe to settle there, and in 1710 a thousand people poured into New York in one week, and eighteen languages were spoken in the city.

In 1677 a small group of French Protestant refugees had settled in New Paltz, and there are still six fieldstone houses from this Huguenot village grouped along a ridge overlooking the Wallkill River. But in most cases, immigrants who came into the valley found no means of obtaining land from the manor

lords whose vast holdings lined the banks of the river. The British had perpetuated the Dutch patroon system by granting huge estates to families like the Livingstons and Schuylers, and at the end of the Revolution, when tenant farmers expected to take over confiscated Tory property like the Philipse lands, they found that patriot manor lords had already snapped them up. Largely for this reason, the valley was never heavily populated between New York and Albany.

Although whaling was once a big and profitable business for Hudson River ports, with Hudson the principal center, this industry was largely the property of Sag Harbor, on Long Island. Salt breezes still blow past the picturesque houses built by whalers 150 years ago, and the town is full of reminders of a time when life centered around the Long Wharf and one of the largest whaling fleets in the country dropped sail there.

The whaling industry never recovered from the Panic of 1857, but new activity took its place on the Hudson. In 1807 Robert Fulton had steamed upstream in the *Clermont,* and his wife's powerful relative, Chancellor Livingston, soon controlled a monopoly on the building and operating of all boats propelled by "force of fire or steam." Fulton's "folly" was christened in honor of the house which still stands near Germantown. Built in 1729-30 by Robert Livingston, it was rebuilt by his son's widow after the British burned it in 1777, and it was here that Fulton married the great-granddaughter of the original owner.

Two monuments to the era of opulence are the Vanderbilt Mansion at Hyde Park and the Ogden Mills Mansion at Staatsburg, both built in the 1890's. The fifty-room Vanderbilt palace, with its elaborate carving and tapestried walls, is surrounded with magnificent old trees and shaded drives which command a majestic view of the great river. During the twentieth century, most of the great manorial estates along the Hudson beween New York and Albany were gradually turned over to institutions. Although the tenant farmers who dreamed of owning land along its banks never fulfilled their dream, today thousands of people live on the river in monasteries, schools, colleges, and in homes for the aged and orphanages which have taken over the great manors.

The sidewheeler *Mary Powell* was the most elaborate of all the "floating palaces" once so numerous on the Hudson.

William Penn's Plantation

William Penn was no industrialist, and if he could return today to discover that his next-door neighbor was a gigantic steel mill he would undoubtedly find this product of man's ingenuity a remarkable thing to behold. But whether he would find it surprising is open to question. The view of U.S. Steel's Fairless Works from the lawn at the reconstructed Pennsbury Manor is not an aesthetic one, but it is, somehow, a tangible reminder of the faith William Penn had in his fellow man. Because of him, men found in Pennsylvania a climate of freedom—an atmosphere which extended into many fields of endeavor—so that Henry Adams, describing the United States of 1800, could judge Pennsylvania the "only true democratic community." It was the "ideal American State, easy, tolerant, and contented," Adams thought, and "had New England, New York, and Virginia been swept out of existence in 1800, democracy could have better spared them all than have lost Pennsylvania." A good deal of the credit belongs to William Penn.

When Penn and 100 followers set sail for the New World in September, 1682, George Fox had a *bon voyage* message for them: "My friends that are gone, and are going over to plant, and make outward plantations in America, keep your own plantations in your hearts, with the spirit and power of God, that your own vines and lilies be not hurt." The formal gardens, orchards, and vineyards at Penn's "beloved manor," along with the main house and its outbuildings, reflect the calm, quiet mood which the great Quaker brought to seventeenth-century America. He purchased his lands from the Indians, for 350 fathoms of white wampum, a score each of blankets, guns, coats, shirts, and stockings, 40 axes, 40 pairs of scissors, 200 knives, and a handful of fishhooks; but Penn was not content with mere commercial settlement. In the spirit of Fox's wish, he confirmed the sale in a treaty of "purchase and amity," meeting the Indians at Shackamaxon in what is now Philadelphia and signing a compact which Voltaire called "the only treaty never sworn to, and never broken." A belt of wampum similar to that presented to Penn by Chief Tammany is owned by the Historical Society of Pennsylvania.

Another Quaker held in high esteem by the Indians was James Logan, who came with Penn on his second trip to America, to serve as his secretary. For half a century Logan represented the proprietary interests in Pennsylvania, carrying on the founder's policy of fair play with the Indians. In 1730 he completed construction of a country house at Germantown which is a fine example of the early Georgian style. A stately dwelling, three stories high, it combined Quaker plainness and taste with elegance, and its overall feeling of simplicity is characteristic of the scholarly, eminent man who built it.

Stenton and Pennsbury Manor are, of course, far more elaborate than the first dwellings built along the Delaware River. The Swedes had settled there in 1638, and were joined not long afterward by a new party headed by Johan Björnsson Printz, a man weighing 400 pounds who was immediately, and understandably, christened "Big Tub" by the Indians. Nothing but the foundation remains of the Printzhof, the old Swedish capitol at Tinicum Island (Essington), but nearby, on Darby Creek, there are still a few examples of that remarkable, durable Swedish contribution to the American frontier—the log cabin. Descendants of the first Tinicum Island settlers also built, in 1700, the red brick church known as Gloria Dei. In those days it was quite a way to the "clever town built by Quakers," but the church is now within the city limits of Philadelphia.

One of the most fascinating remnants of the Penn era was built in 1690 by Hans Milan, in Germantown. The original part of the long, ivy-covered stucco house stood beside what is said to have been an Indian trail, and a later house, erected across the way, was eventually joined to it. The Wyck House, as it is called, was never sold, but passed from one relative to another, preserved much as it was. It was ultimately given to the Germantown Historical Society.

A survivor of the short-lived Swedish colony on the Delaware, this Tinicum Island log cabin was built about 1650. It is probably the oldest structure of its kind in the United States.

LAURENCE LOWRY, REPRINTED FROM *Holiday*

Benjamin West's idealized painting above depicts William Penn's meeting with the Indian chiefs under the elm at Shackamaxon. At left center, Penn points to the charter parchment, while a blanket is held up for the approval of the sachem Tammany, the white-robed Indian standing at right. The photograph at left shows Pennsbury Manor, the reconstructed home of William Penn near Morrisville. The estate faces the Delaware River, on which Penn commuted to Philadelphia by barge in the days before the Main Line. The gravel pits of U.S. Steel's Fairless Works are in the background.

THE FOREST AND THE FORTS

CANADA

St. Lawrence River

C **A** **N** **A** **D** **A**

FORT FRONTENAC

Lake Champlain

CROWN POINT
(FORT ST. FREDERICK)

FORT TICONDEROGA

Lake George

Hudson R.

FORT WILLIAM HENRY

LAKE *ONTARIO*

FORT ONTARIO
(OSWEGO)

FORT STANWIX (ROME)

FORT GEORGE   FORT ANNE

FORT KLOCK   STONE ARABIA
JOHNSTOWN

Mohawk *R.*   FORT JOHNSON

Oswego R.

Oneida Lake

FORT NIAGARA
(YOUNGSTOWN)

FORT HERKIMER

FORT HENDRICK   FORT FREY
FORT PLAIN   SCHENECTADY

CHERRY VALLEY

SCHOHARIE   ALBANY

FORT ERIE

LAKE *ERIE*

N E W   Y O R K

Susquehanna River

Hudson River

FORT PRESQUE ISLE
(ERIE)

KINGSTON

FORT LE BOEUF
(WATERFORD)

French Creek

WYOMING   FORT PITTSTON
FORTY FORT
WILKES-BARRE

FORT VENANGO
(FRANKLIN)

Allegheny R.

FORT JENKINS (BERWICK)

P E N N S Y L V A N I A

Delaware River

NEW YORK

FORT AUGUSTA
(SUNBURY)

BETHLEHEM

Ohio R.

PITTSBURGH

FORT MCKEE

Juniata *River*

N E W

FORT PITT
(DUQUESNE)

BUSHY RUN
BATTLEFIELD ×

FORT LIGONIER   FORT SHIRLEY

FORT HARRIS
(HARRISBURG)

Susquehanna R.

TRENTON

BRADDOCK'S
ROAD

FORBES' ROAD

CARLISLE

LANCASTER

PHILADELPHIA

J E R S E Y

WHEELING

FORT LOUDON

Youghiogheny R.

FORT BEDFORD
(RAYSTOWN)

FORT CHAMBERS

YORK

FORT NECESSITY

Monongahela R.

FORT CUMBERLAND

FORT FREDERICK

D E L A W A R E

W E S T   V I R G I N I A

Potomac *River*

BALTIMORE

M A R Y L A N D

A T L A N T I C   O.

KEY:

■ EXISTING EARLY FORT

□ SITE OF EARLY FORT

The first white men edging westward from the settlements along the central coast found a forest that was simply beyond their imagination. Not in the memory of living men had there been anything quite like it. Nearly twenty centuries had elapsed since the Germanic peoples huddled together in settlements in the great woods, and Europeans had forgotten what a primeval forest was like. The deep impression it made is evident from the way men spoke of it. In their march through the wilderness, General Edward Braddock's men camped near a fearsome place known as the "Shades of Death." And there are stories of men walking through the giant sycamores, walnuts, and towering stands of pine and hardwood for days on end without catching a glimpse of the sun. In Pennsylvania's Cook State Forest Park, where some of the great virgin timber remains, one can get an idea of what it was like.

What was there had been there, virtually undisturbed since the last glacier retreated—majestic rivers, the "Endless Mountains," valleys where not even the red man had set foot, deer, buffalo, wolves, and elk, and lonely peaks where the panther screamed. Only the millions of birds who rose above the ancient leaf-banked forest could see its total immensity—the unbroken dark green mass that stretched from the Atlantic to the sea of grass far to the west.

But gradually into this hunting ground of the Shawnees, Delawares, and Mingoes the white man threaded his way, bringing with him those changers of nature, the ax and the plow. Along the tumbling blue ranges of the Alleghenies, isolated little forts and blockhouses sprang up in a protective arc, stretching southwesterly across central Pennsylvania to shield it from the Iroquois. At the Juniata River the line of outposts turned south, following the Conococheague. Beyond this, in 1758, there was only Fort Bedford at Raystown—pointing like an arrow at the heart of the Indian hunting grounds and New France. One hundred miles to the west lay Fort Duquesne, built by the French at the point of a "Y" where the Allegheny and Monongahela meet to form the Ohio.

In 1758 General John Forbes hacked a road across the mountains, captured Duquesne without firing a shot, and named the place "Pittsbourgh." To anyone visiting the tiny Fort Pitt blockhouse today, it seems inconceivable that its possession affected seriously the destinies of two great empires, yet Forbes' victory was one of the most significant of the French and Indian War.

Behind the four-foot walls and oak doors of the château at Fort Niagara, during the Revolution, the halls were hung with American scalps, for which the English paid the Indians eight dollars apiece. The old earthworks remain at Fort Ontario, a star-shaped redoubt built in 1759, and Fort Necessity has been carefully reconstructed. To the north, along the great corridor of the Mohawk, is the stone mansion named Fort Johnson and, twelve miles away, Johnson Hall with its protecting blockhouse. The Mohawk Valley has other forts—most of them built for peaceful purposes, but used as blockhouses out of necessity—like the farmhouse called Fort Klock, the Dutch Reformed churches at Schoharie and Stone Arabia, and Fort Herkimer church. Eastward, along the famous north-south route of war parties, are the ruins of Fort George. Only a few stones mark the site of Fort St. Frédéric, Fort Crown Point has the ruins of two original barracks, and Fort William Henry is restored. At the point where Lake George empties into Champlain, 100 feet above the water, is the stone guardian which has seen more American history than any such place in the country—Fort Ticonderoga.

ILLUSTRATIONS (FROM TOP): OLD FORT NIAGARA; FORT NECESSITY NATIONAL BATTLEFIELD SITE; KOSTI RUOHOMAA, BLACK STAR; A. AUBREY BODINE; PA. DEPT. OF HIGHWAYS; KOSTI RUOHOMAA, BLACK STAR.

Fort Niagara

The reconstructed stockade, Fort Necessity

Fort Klock

Ruins of Fort Frederick near Clearspring, Md.

Fort Pitt blockhouse, Pittsburgh

Fort Frey, Palatine Bridge, N.Y.

Sir William Johnson

The Mohawk Corridor

Of the men who lived in the Mohawk Valley 200 years ago, few are more fascinating from the standpoint of personality or their imprint on the region's history than the young man of 23 who arrived from Ireland in 1738 to manage his uncle's lands. In those days the 150-mile course of the Mohawk from Rome to Cohoes was marked with the paths of the powerful "People of the Long House." In one of those strange incidents of history which pop up again and again to alter the course of events, many of these people—the Six Nations of the Iroquois—had been alienated from the French in 1609 by Samuel de Champlain, who first used firearms against them.

The young man from Ireland was quick to take advantage of this inheritance. He made friends with the Indians, treated them with respect and kindness. He became a student of their language, customs, and habits. And they seemed to be impressed as much by his flowery language as by his fair trading and political adroitness. When the German girl who was his wife died, he bestowed his favors upon Molly Brant, sister of the Mohawk chief Joseph Brant. The "brown Lady Johnson," as she was called, not only gave him eight children but presided over his household with dignity while he went about such business as building churches

in the valley, sponsoring the translation and printing of an Indian prayer book, acting as Britain's Superintendent of Indian Affairs, conducting scientific experiments, and serving as an eminently successful general.

This was William Johnson, dubbed Warraghiyagey or "Chief Big Business" by the Indians and Sir William by His Majesty George II. One of the wealthiest men in the colonies, his influence with the Iroquois was such that he singlehandedly kept them on the side of the Crown during the French and Indian War.

One of the three homes built by Sir William in the valley is the gray stone, two-story building which became known as Fort Johnson after a palisade was built around it during the wars. The hip-roofed house, with paneling and hardware imported from London, was completed in 1749, and was the scene of many important Indian councils, with as many as a thousand Iroquois camped around it at one time.

Twelve miles away in Johnstown, partly hidden by trees, is the more luxurious home Johnson built in his later years. A stately Georgian Colonial frame house with wainscoted halls and rooms, it was situated on a royal grant of 80,000 acres. The house was flanked by two stone blockhouses, one of which still stands, just to the rear of the house.

Indians of the powerful Six Nations once gathered for councils at Johnson Hall, Sir William's large fortified house near Johnstown. At one such meeting in 1774 Johnson died after an impassioned harangue to the visiting Mohawks. As the photograph above indicates, only one of the blockhouses survives.

On a wooded bluff overlooking Nowadaga Creek is Indian Castle Church, site of the upper "castle" of the Mohawk Bear Clan between 1700 and 1775, and the place where Sir William Johnson built Fort Hendrick. It was here that Johnson met Molly Brant and had the simple clapboard church built for his Indian friends. After Johnson's death Molly returned to the castle, where she was to play an important part in the area's worst Revolutionary battle.

Even more than the French and Indian conflict, the Revolution turned the Mohawk Valley into a dark, bloody ground, torn by the fiercest kind of fighting between Tory, patriot, and Indian. Sir William's Tory son John, Joseph Brant, and Walter Butler led Indian attacks against such places as Stone Arabia, Wyoming Valley, and Cherry Valley, where 48 defenders were killed and more than 60 carried off as prisoners. But the major battle occurred at Oriskany.

As part of the three-pronged British attack designed to cut the colonies in half, Barry St. Leger was leading about 800 British regulars and 1,000 Iroquois east from Oswego to rendezvous at Albany with Burgoyne and Howe. Burgoyne was advancing south from Canada, and the plan called for Howe to march north from New York City to join them. Against St. Leger,

Nicholas Herkimer took off with 800 patriot militia of the valley to relieve the small garrison at Fort Stanwix. Hearing of this movement, Molly Brant sent a warning from the castle to her brother Joseph, and the British and Indians ambushed the Americans in a marshy ravine at Oriskany. In a bloody hand-to-hand battle which lasted six hours, Herkimer was mortally wounded and his men were severely mauled, but the action was halted by the threat of reinforcements under Benedict Arnold. This, with the loss of his Indian allies, forced St. Leger to return to Canada, and dealt a severe blow to Burgoyne's campaign.

Today a stone shaft overlooking the Mohawk marks the site of Oriskany battlefield, and you can see, between two low hills, the ravine where the ambush occurred. Near Little Falls is the interesting Herkimer home, where the hero of Oriskany is buried.

After the violence of revolution and Indian wars passed, the old valley became even more of a historic corridor with the digging of the Erie Canal, begun in 1817. The thick forests have vanished from the graceful, gently rising hills, and many changes have taken place; but somehow the fertile valley—with its battlegrounds, Indian castle sites, colonial houses, and towpaths—has never lost its air of history.

71

Rows of long-silent cannon protrude from the stonework battlements of restored Fort Ticonderoga.

Ticonderoga's British commander was trouserless when Ethan Allen surprised him in the fort's barracks.

Revolutionary Battlegrounds

It is easy to forget nowadays how important water transportation was in colonial times, but the classic reminder of how control of the water lanes could mean control of a continent is Fort Ticonderoga.

Between French and British, and later British and American settlements, the vast wilderness was penetrable only by means of narrow Indian trails, which meant that no army of the time could cross it readily. Strategists were quick to realize that the happy juxtaposition of Lake Champlain, Lake George, and the Hudson River provided a military highway. To the French, the route spelled conquest of the English settlements; to the British in Canada it offered a means of splitting the rebellious colonies in two. But the plan which seemed so easy was never once successful.

Between 1689, when the first invasion was launched, and 1814, when the last was attempted, every southward attack failed. Men under the easy spell of maps never seemed to realize that the route itself was behind their failures. Any advance up Lake Champlain had to be by the lake alone. And the lake precluded the use of skillful maneuvering or flank attacks, left little chance for surprise, and demanded a head-on collision between attacker and defender. No matter what any commander might wish, the focal point for that collision was almost inevitably the height of land between Lake George and Lake Champlain, commanded by Fort Ticonderoga.

This aerial view shows Fort Ticonderoga's strategic location between Lake George (background) and Lake Champlain.

The Iroquois' enmity for the French which William Johnson found so useful dated back to 1609, when Champlain met a band of Indians and defeated them near the fort's site. But not until 1755 did the architects of New France begin building the star-shaped stone building which they called Fort Carillon. For the next sixty years the great walls watched history being made along the Champlain shore. Here, in 1758, Montcalm and a relative handful of troops defeated 15,000 British and Colonials led by a fat, ineffectual man called "Aunt Nabby-Cromby"—General James Abercromby. A year later, with the French cause losing ground, Montcalm departed, leaving the near-empty fort to Jeffery Amherst, who rebuilt it and called it Ticonderoga. By the time of the Revolution the bastion had begun to disintegrate. Resembling a backwoods village more than a fort, it was manned by only fifty men, some women and children.

Before dawn on May 10, 1775, a flamboyant Ethan Allen and an ambitious Benedict Arnold crowded 83 men into two boats over on the eastern shore of the lake and landed half a mile below the fort. It was still dark, and the men huddled together against squalls of wind and rain. By the time they landed it was too late for the boats to bring over the rest of the group, so they advanced to the main entrance in the south wall, which at that time was almost in ruins. Overrunning the guard, they rushed inside, where Allen met an officer wearing a coat and waistcoat—his trousers in his hand. "Come out of there, you damned old rat!" shouted Ethan, who demanded the surrender of the fort (he wrote later) "in the name of the Great Jehovah and the Continental Congress." Although Allen was reputedly on poor terms with both parties, the British acquiesced, and by December of that year Henry Knox had dragged the fort's guns over the mountains for the siege of Boston.

In 1777 Gentleman Johnny Burgoyne's plan for conquering the rebels was approved in London, and he headed south to join St. Leger and Howe at Albany. The force which caused the Americans to abandon Ticonderoga must have presented quite a sight coming up the lake. There were Indians in war paint, the massed scarlet of British regulars, dark blue German uniforms, the green of the jägers, and the dragoons' light blue. Sunlight glinted on row after row of polished musket barrels, bayonets, shining brass, and regimental facings, and caught the cadenced flashing of thousands of wet paddles and oars.

Truly a conquering army, but after taking Ticonderoga Burgoyne's troops encountered one obstacle after another—not the least of which were their preposterous uniforms, which made wilderness marches nearly impossible. General Philip Schuyler put a thousand axmen to work destroying bridges, felling trees, and burning crops along the British route, and in three weeks Burgoyne was able to advance only 23 miles. A foraging expedition under Colonel Baum met disaster at Walloomsac, New York, near Bennington, where John Stark's militia and Seth Warner's Green Mountain Boys turned out in force. A pretty young girl named Jane McCrea was scalped by Burgoyne's Indians, inflaming the countryside with anger and sending hundreds of volunteers into the American forces. St. Leger was turned back after Oriskany, and finally Burgoyne received the crushing news that Howe was not coming to join him after all.

When Burgoyne arrived at Stillwater, south of Saratoga and about halfway between Fort Edward and Albany, there were 9,000 men—500 of them Daniel Morgan's riflemen—waiting for him. After an initial engagement, Burgoyne waited for reinforcements which never came, while the American ranks swelled to outnumber him two to one. Finally, on October 7, Burgoyne chose to advance.

Although Gates was technically in command of the Americans at Saratoga, it was the personal

DAVID E. SCHERMAN, REPRINTED FROM *Holiday*

Benedict Arnold was shot in the leg at Saratoga. This monument honors the only truly American part of him.

daring and leadership of Benedict Arnold, galloping onto the field to lead the attack, and of Daniel Morgan, rallying men again and again with his turkey call, which made possible the British defeat. In addition to its strategic significance, Saratoga was also the site of the war's most important single rifle shot. Arnold, who realized the importance of British General Fraser's personal leadership, assigned Tim Murphy, one of Morgan's Pennsylvania riflemen and an old Indian fighter, to dispose of him. And dispose of him Tim did, from a range of 300 yards—a shot which began the demoralization of the British troops, contributing to the long rifles' reputation as ". . . the most fatal widow and orphan makers in the world."

Finally, compelled to retreat to Saratoga, and completely surrounded, Burgoyne and his staff rode out to meet General Gates. "The fortune of war," he said, "has made me your prisoner." To this Gates replied, "I shall ever be ready to testify that it has not been through any fault of Your Excellency," and invited the party to dine with him. Because the victory at Saratoga led to the alliance with France, contemporaries recognized it as the turning point of the Revolution: "Rebellion which a twelvemonth ago was a contemptible pygmy, is now in appearance become a giant."

Following Burgoyne's defeat, Ticonderoga was occupied once more by Americans, but never again did it have much strategic importance. Finally abandoned, it fell into ruins until its restoration was undertaken in 1909. Because of the work done there, no fort of the Revolutionary period offers the visitor more rewards. The great brooding walls survey the magnificent sweep of Lake Champlain, and inside the original stone barracks are a wealth of uniforms, maps, guns, and other objects dating back to the days when the fort was a key to the continent.

Nearly two centuries afterward, the Revolution is so remote, so far distant as to dim the awareness of what really took place. A schoolchild learns that George Washington crossed the Delaware one snowy Christmas night and surprised some Hessians; and that sometime later he and his men had a terrible time at a place called Valley Forge. And because it was so long ago and because there is so little time to learn about it and so little space in the books for a real description of what happened, neither Washington nor the men who stuck it out with him ever quite come alive.

There were times when the flame of independence came so close to flickering out that it is a wonder we ever got it at all. Among the men who realized it at the time was a thin, bright-eyed Quaker who had elected to serve in Washington's army without pay. His name was Tom Paine, and he sat with the rem-

Crossing the Hudson with five thousand men, Cornwallis scaled the Jersey Palisades to rout the Americans at Fort Lee, and split Washington's army in two. Viewing the maneuver, Thomas Davies of the British artillery painted this watercolor.

nants of Continental forces in New Jersey one night in November of 1776, hunched over a drum, on which there was a piece of paper. He was a man who could write what he felt in a way that everybody could understand. General Charles Lee called him a "man with genius in his eye," and John Adams, who hated him, nevertheless admitted that he was "the first factor in bringing about the Revolution." Paine's pamphlet *Common Sense* had made a revolution out of rebellion and clarified the issues for which it was to be fought, which led Benjamin Franklin to observe that others could rule and many could fight, but "only Paine can write for us."

This is what he began to write, in the *Crisis*, that November night in 1776: "These are the times that try men's souls: The summer soldier and the sunshine patriot will, in this crisis, shrink from the service of his country; but he that stands it Now, deserves the love and thanks of man and woman. Tyranny, like hell, is not easily conquered; yet we have this consolation with us, that the harder the conflict, the more glorious the triumph."

Between July and December there had been nothing but disaster. At the time the Declaration of Independence was proclaimed in Philadelphia, General Howe was landing 32,000 trained, disciplined professional soldiers at Staten Island. He took 20,000 of them to Long Island and overran the Americans. Only Washington's planning, the skill of two amphibious regiments from Marblehead and Salem, and some God-given nasty weather saved the army from complete annihilation. In quick succession, Howe routed the colonials again at Kip's Bay—34th Street and the East River, in New York City, just down the street from the East Side Airlines Terminal—pushed them back through Harlem to White Plains, then captured Forts Lee and Washington on the Hudson in one of the great disasters of the war. Forced to retreat across the Jerseys, the broken remnants of the American army were in truly desperate straits and even Washington admitted, "If this fails, I think the game will be pretty well up."

At the time Tom Paine was writing the *Crisis*, Washington had less than 6,000 barefoot, exhausted men who had known nothing but defeat. Worse yet, this rabble had only two weeks more of life, for so many enlistments were due to expire December 31 that there would be no more than 1,400 of them left to face the greatest expeditionary force Great Britain had ever sent out from its shores. In this hopeless situation Washington came up with a plan born of "necessity, dire necessity," which he disclosed to his officers in the Merrick House on the west bank of the Delaware on Christmas Eve. It meant risking his entire army in one awful gamble, for once across the river, his retreat was cut off.

As dark fell on Christmas night the crossing began about nine miles above Trenton, at a place known as McKonkey's Ferry. At the old tavern which still stands on the Pennsylvania side, one of Washington's officers stopped long enough to make an entry in his diary: "Christmas, 6 P.M. . . . It is fearfully cold and raw and a snow-storm setting in. The wind is northeast and beats in the faces of the men. It will be a terrible night for the soldiers who have no shoes. Some of them have tied old rags around their feet, but I have not heard a man complain." It was one of the most daring movements in military history. On a bitter, pitch-dark night, in the middle of a driving blizzard, Washington's "flock of animated scarecrows" were ferried over the ice-choked river by Glover's intrepid Marbleheaders—the same men who rescued the defeated troops at Long Island—to surprise three regiments of professional soldiers.

It very nearly failed to come off. The crossing had been so difficult that the Americans were four hours behind Washington's schedule, and it was almost eight in the morning when they reached Trenton. Fortunately, the Hessians had celebrated Christmas in hearty fashion, and most of them were still in the barracks because their commander had failed to heed a warning message the night before. In the "great, informal battle royal" which followed the attack, both sides had to rely on artillery and bayonets since their muskets were too wet to fire, and in less than an hour it was over—a remarkable victory which would have satisfied a lesser man than Washington. Although his men's enlistments were due to run out in four days, and Howe was on the march, Washington took his prisoners to Pennsylvania and, in another fateful gamble, returned once more to the Jersey side.

Near Trenton, where Cornwallis confronted him on January 2, Washington again maneuvered brilliantly. Leaving a rear guard to keep his fires going, he marched around Cornwallis' left under cover of darkness, and surprised Mawhood just outside Princeton. Overpowered at first, the panicked Americans were rallied by Washington, who rode into the hottest fire within thirty paces of the British, and Mawhood's men finally fled down the road to Trenton. In Princeton, the Continentals forced the surrender of nearly 200 British in Nassau Hall, and the battle was over.

By this time, only a few days after they made the extraordinary crossing of the Delaware and took Trenton, the ragged Americans had been under arms for forty continuous hours in the dead of winter, with no time out for meals or any kind of rest. They had marched sixteen miles over terrible roads in total darkness, and then fought a battle. Realizing there was nothing left in them, Washington headed for winter quarters in the wooded, hilly section of Morristown.

These not inconsiderable victories had an effect totally beyond their military significance. They heartened the people of the colonies with hope of ultimate success, encouraged enlistments, and strengthened enormously Washington's reputation at home and abroad. As Christopher Ward says in *The War of the Revolution,* this feat "had been accomplished by an army of fewer than five thousand ragged, shoeless, ill fed, poorly equipped, often defeated amateur soldiers, mostly militia, operating against twice that number of veteran professionals, abundantly supplied with all martial equipment, and within a space of eleven days in the depth of winter."

For a fleeting moment, the crisis was past; but there would be many others in the six long years before the war ended. During that time, although they lost one battle after another, the Americans would demonstrate again and again the courage they had shown in this terrible December of 1776. Washington would learn only too well how many sunshine patriots there were, but somehow there was always a core of belief that never gave way. It was this weapon that Tom Paine knew so well, and it was this that the enemy lacked. The great idea that men were willing to die for was what made them, finally, unconquerable.

There are places in the Middle Atlantic region where the visitor is rewarded with a glimpse of surroundings little changed since the days when Continentals battled redcoats for their possession. One of them is the little town of Chadds Ford, with a population of about two hundred, which was the center of the Battle of the Brandywine in September, 1777. The creek that once ran deep enough to require a ferry is now a mere trickle, but the octagonal schoolhouse which changed hands eleven times in 45 minutes during the fierce engagement is little changed. In an incongruous way, this was a battle with religious associations. It took place within sight of the Birmingham Meetinghouse and the Kennett Meetinghouse; and the paper used in American cartridges came from the German "Brethren" at Ephrata, who placed the printed sheets of an edition of Fox's *Book of Martyrs* at the service of their country a few days before the fight.

After an evening full of Christmas spirits and carousing, most of the Hessian force was still asleep in Trenton's Old Barracks when Washington made his surprise attack.

From here Washington's ragged army was ferried across the ice-choked Delaware River. Once on the Jersey bank, they had to march nine miles before attacking Trenton.

Artist Edward Hicks painted this primitive version of Washington's Delaware crossing about 1834. He made two copies, one for each end of a covered bridge erected at the site. Without romanticizing the scene, he conveyed successfully the cold darkness and desperate drama of that bitter Christmas night of 1776. The determined Washington led his men across the river, while downstream two less resolute American commanders, deciding he would never make it, ordered their troops to turn back.

At Valley Forge, Washington's men were housed in crude log huts, like the snow-covered restoration at left.

The Ford Mansion was Washington's Morristown headquarters. At right, Baron von Steuben drills troops at Valley Forge.

Philadelphia and civilization have encroached on Germantown, but the Chew Mansion (or Cliveden) is still a little island of Revolutionary times right in the center of town. The handsome stone house is almost exactly as it was when it became the focus of the battle in October, 1777. In this home the British barricaded themselves and poured a continuous, deadly fire into the attacking Americans, and the marks of that fight are still visible on the exterior. In the same vicinity are Germantown Academy and the long, white Wyck house, both used as hospitals after the battle.

Near Freehold, New Jersey, the Old Tennent Church looks out across the three-mile stretch of Monmouth Battlefield and the graves of the men who fell near it so many years ago. Close by are Freehold Courthouse, St. Peter's Episcopal Church, and the Hankinson Mansion, all occupied by British or Americans at the time of the battle which brought fame and the name Molly Pitcher to Mrs. John Hays, and disgrace to General Charles Lee, who permitted the retreat.

It is fitting, however, that the real spirit of the Revolution survives best at two places which were not battlefields at all. The story of that war was one of survival and incredible courage, and at Morristown and Valley Forge these two qualities still hang on the cold winter air like thin notes from a Revolutionary bugle. Every summer thousands of Americans visit the old encampments, but anyone who goes there when the icy wind is out of the north will feel the image of gaunt, suffering men who endured untold agony for the sake of an ideal. What happened at Morristown and Valley Forge is no less poignant because of the conditions that made it—it is simply more incredible. A good deal of what the army went through was caused by the lack of manufacturing in the colonies—

woolens, for example, were almost unobtainable, regardless of price. But what was far worse, soldiers underwent privations because the country at large failed to support either the war or the pitiful little army that was waging it.

At Morristown, the Continental soldiers were "absolutely perishing for want of clothes." Sometimes two or three days without food, the men huddled in log huts and tents, where they "were actually covered . . . and buried like sheep under the snow." The first winter a smallpox epidemic ran through the camp; three years later the snow piled up twelve feet deep. On the old camp site the small redoubt and the log huts have been reconstructed, the parade ground on which the troops marched "over Frost and Snow, many without a Shoe, Stocking, or Blanket" is there, and so is the dignified old Ford Mansion, where the anguished Washington had his headquarters.

Similar monuments exist in the peaceful park at Valley Forge, the scene of horrible suffering during the winter of 1777-78. In addition to soldiers' huts, silent cannons, and the Grand Parade Grounds where von Steuben somehow made an army out of the "Ragged, Lousy, Naked" regiments, there are the houses where Washington, Knox, Lafayette, and Stirling stayed.

But the meaning of Valley Forge and Morristown is not in the buildings. It is to be found in the heart-stricken words of George Washington, writing: "To see men without clothes to cover their nakedness, without blankets to lie on, without shoes, for want of which their marches might be traced by the blood from their feet, and almost as often without provisions as with them . . . is proof of patience and obedience which in my opinion can scarce be paralleled."

79

Iron plow from the Farmers' Museum

K. PAZOVSKI, *Farm Quarterly*

Cooperstown

When the visitor arrives at the shore of Otsego Lake, the headwaters of the Susquehanna River, he is in the heart of Leatherstocking country. The round top of Council Rock, where the Indians once came to "make their treaties and bury their hatchets," is visible above the still surface of the lake, and the ghosts of Natty Bumppo and Chingachgook are not far away. This is the land where James Fenimore Cooper spent much of his childhood and most of his later years, absorbing the lore of Indian and pioneer and transforming them into the stories that have thrilled generations of American youth.

It is also a place where one may see a fascinating group of buildings housing some very diverse but authentic bits of Americana. There are the Farmers' Museum and the Village Crossroads, re-creating the life of an average settler on the early frontier. The museum's collection of tools and implements for home, farm, and shop, and its demonstrations of ancient crafts are as fine as anything to be seen. The Crossroads is actually a re-creation of a little New York settlement of the period 1800 to 1850, and it includes schoolhouse, country store, blacksmith shop, lawyer's office, tavern, and farmhouse among the many old buildings moved here from their former locations.

Fenimore House contains what is probably the most comprehensive collection of American folk art in existence, most of it nineteenth-century, with hundreds of objects from toys and trinkets to large figureheads on display. The museum's collection of wood carving is particularly impressive, as is the remarkable series of life masks done by Browere about 1825 —among them five of the first eight Presidents of the United States.

And few baseball fans need to be told that the National Baseball Hall of Fame and Museum is here at Cooperstown, where Abner Doubleday laid out what is claimed to be the first baseball diamond and played the game which grew out of One Old Cat, a favorite in colonial times.

COURTESY *Time*

Cooperstown's cigar store Indian once stood in front of a Kansas City shop. On the facing page is a typical 1820 kitchen, in the Lippitt Farm at the Village Crossroads. The shops and houses at right are also at Cooperstown's Village Crossroads, where the visitor may see a re-created New York village of pre-Civil War days.

NEW YORK STATE HISTORICAL ASSOCIATION

The unusual arcade through the center of New Castle's Old Town Hall originally led to the stalls of the town market.

The stuccoed tower and high, shingled steeple of Immanuel Episcopal Church rise above New Castle's elm-shaded Green.

Built in 1801, the elegant George Read House recalls a time when New Castle was an important Delaware River port.

New Castle and Winterthur

There is an air of tranquillity in the tree-lined streets of Delaware towns like Odessa or Smyrna or Dover which seems to say that nothing very momentous ever happened there. Each of these old-fashioned villages has its roots along the water front that brought it trade, and few communities in the country have changed so little in the past two hundred years. Walking up past New Castle's Packet Alley from the Delaware River, the visitor sees the cupolas of the town hall and the Georgian Colonial courthouse amid the great elms lining the broad open streets. Behind them is the Green laid out by Peter Stuyvesant, and close by are Immanuel Episcopal and Old Presbyterian—two ancient churches. The long, two-story brick building at the corner is the old Academy, planned in 1772 as a "public seminary of learning" and completed in 1811. Near the Green are two streets of houses built between 1675 and 1830 by landowners, merchants, and lawyers. Beautifully preserved, these homes are out-standing examples of a pure, simple architecture that dominated those years when New Castle was capital, court town, seaport, and market town. Architecturally, one of the finest is the George Read House, built in 1801 in late Georgian style. Superbly furnished, it is the high-water mark of the town's prosperity.

Demonstrating the close link between decorative arts and history, the Henry Francis du Pont Winterthur Museum near Wilmington is a great collection of Americana which has been brought together from other places. Formerly Mr. du Pont's home, the museum now contains about two hundred rooms, restored or in their original state, which are superb examples of American architecture, furniture, metalwork, textiles, ceramics, and paintings from the period beginning about 1640 and ending two hundred years later.

A tribute to those skillful craftsmen who were em-ployed by the young nation's merchants, clergy, and shipowners, the museum houses a fine collection of paintings by artists like Copley, Stuart, and Benjamin West; the silverwork of Paul Revere and some of the earlier Boston mintmasters; and a notable group of Duncan Phyfe furniture.

This graceful staircase was brought to Winterthur from the Montmorenci mansion in Warrenton, North Carolina.

Like other Winterthur rooms, the Walnut Room is a com-posite of different periods and places. The woodwork came from Belle Isle plantation in Virginia, and the trestle-foot folding bed is a mid-eighteenth-century New England piece.

Low Bridge

To an English visitor it appeared that "Old America seems to be breaking up and moving westward." By 1830 Ohio had more inhabitants than Massachusetts and Connecticut combined, and a hundred hamlets were growing into towns and cities, because of something called "Clinton's ditch." Also because of it, New York City changed almost overnight from a market town on the Hudson into the nation's leading port.

DeWitt Clinton was not the first American to think of a canal—George Washington planned what is still one of the country's most picturesque waterways, the lovely Chesapeake and Ohio Canal that runs along the north bank of the Potomac; William Penn dreamed of joining the Susquehanna with the Schuylkill and Delaware Rivers; and practical old Ben Franklin endorsed heartily this "quiet and always manageable" form of travel. But from the moment it was completed in 1825, the Erie Canal was one of those supremely happy combinations of the right thing at precisely the right time. For eight years and for 363 miles, laborers had dug with pickax and shovel, swearing, singing, brawling, and, it was said, drinking taverns into existence at the rate of one per mile of canal until they connected Albany with Buffalo. Almost at once, freight rates between Albany and the lake dropped from $100 to $9 a ton; emigrants by the thousands surged westward on packet boats; village outposts like Detroit and Cleveland became growing cities; and a vast communication system connected New York with the new western lands, the Mississippi, and New Orleans.

The old painting on this page makes canal travel look idyllic, but there was scant comfort aboard the boats. Fanny Kemble thought them preferable to a coach journey over abominable roads, but like everyone else she complained bitterly about the "bridges over the canal, which are so very low, that one is obliged to prostrate oneself on the deck of the boat, to avoid being scraped off it; and this humiliation occurs, upon an average, once every quarter of an hour."

Passengers might complain about the accommodations, but no one traveling the Erie failed to be impressed by the ingenuity which made it possible. The days have gone when fifty or sixty boats were lined up at a lock, waiting to go through, but even today the

vestiges of the canal in Lockport are quite a thing to see. In the center of town there are five of the original locks used to raise or lower the canal level sixty feet. And just west of the village of Amsterdam is Schoharie Creek Aqueduct, another remarkable monument to its builders. To carry the canal high above the river, thirteen great piers held up a wooden trunk containing the 41½-by-7-foot water section of the canal, and fourteen graceful 40-foot arches supported the towpath and braced the piers. Parts of the Erie have become the modern Barge Canal, but an observing eye will still locate some of the well-trodden towpaths, half-hidden by underbrush, that mark the old route.

The Erie, of course, was far from unique—the whole Middle Atlantic region seemed to go canal-crazy early in the nineteenth century. Evidences of many of these waterways still survive, like the Schuylkill, from Philadelphia to Pottsville; the Delaware and Hudson; the Lehigh, from Mauch Chunk to Easton; the Morris, a real engineering wonder from Jersey City to Phillipsburg; and most scenic of them all, the Chesapeake and Ohio. But for sheer inventiveness, none surpassed the Pennsylvania Canal, parts of which still wind peacefully through Pennsylvania farmlands.

Opened in 1834, the Pennsylvania was a combination of 118 miles of railroad and 283 miles of waterway. Starting from Philadelphia, passengers traveled ten hours by train to Columbia on the Susquehanna. There they transferred to a packet boat which was hauled 172 miles up the Susquehanna and Juniata rivers to Hollidaysburg, passing through 108 locks on the way. At Hollidaysburg the really spectacular part of the trip began. To cross the 2,500-foot crest of the Alleghenies, the boats were loaded onto flatcars and pulled—first by horses, later by steam engines—over a series of five levels and inclined planes up the mountain and then down the other side. At its most mechanized stage, this operation involved 33 power changes, and added to these hazards was the psychological one, described by Charles Dickens in 1842: "Occasionally the rails were laid upon the extreme verge of a giddy precipice; and looking from the carriage window, the traveler gazes sheer down, without a stone or scrap of fence between, into the mountain depths below. . . ." Many a passenger must have welcomed the sight of Johnstown, where he resumed the trip to Pittsburgh by canal.

Like many another, the Pennsylvania was a little too costly and a little too late. With the coming of the railroads, most canals fell into disuse and passed slowly from the American scene.

Westward-bound emigrants and their worldly goods crowded the roofs of Erie Canal barges like the one in this scene.

Mule-drawn tourist barges still navigate the C. & O. Canal.

An old drawing shows portage railway flatcars at the summit of the Alleghenies. Below, a crumbling arch remains of the canal aqueduct crossing the Mohawk at Little Falls.

Armchair table   **Printer's memorabilia**   **Benjamin Franklin**   **Fireplace stove**   **Electrical machine**

Ben Franklin's Philadelphia

When Benjamin Franklin walked up High Street in Philadelphia on a Sunday morning in October of 1723, he entered a busy city of some 10,000 people. William Penn in 1681 had instructed the city's builders to "Let every house be pitched in the middle of its plat . . . that so there may be ground on each side for gardens or orchards, or fields, that it may be a green countrie towne, that will never be burnt, and always be wholesome." But forty years later the population had increased, plots had been subdivided, and the narrow streets resembled picturesque Elfreth's Alley, which is the only one to survive nearly intact.

By packet from New York and the north, by horseback over rough trails from the south, by ship from Europe, new arrivals came to Philadelphia, making it the most important city in the colonies. There was no place in the New World like it: young men were studying French, light music was played in fashionable drawing rooms, and people thronged to fishing parties on the Schuylkill, and to dances. Just then, few of these activities were available to the young printer's apprentice; but not long after his arrival Benjamin Franklin began to exert on the city and on the whole country a profound intellectual influence.

So astoundingly diversified were Franklin's interests that it is almost impossible to list them. More than ever today, in an age of specialists, it is hard to imagine how he had time and energy to pursue his ever-widening range of activities. He invented bifocals and the lightning rod and the Franklin stove. He introduced Philadelphia palates to Scotch cabbage, their first kohlrabi, and Chinese rhubarb. He gave the city paved streets and street lamps—the first in America. In 1751 he persuaded Philadelphia's city fathers to replace the volunteer night watch with paid constables, although a uniformed police force was not

created for a hundred years. He organized the country's first fire department in 1736, and twelve years later the first insurance company—the "Hand-in-Hand," so called from its seal. He started the Library Company of Philadelphia in 1731; known as "Mr. Franklin's Library," it was the first circulating library in America. In 1751 he established the Pennsylvania Hospital and the Academy for the Education of Youth, which eventually became the University of Pennsylvania. One of his most important contributions was the formation, in 1727, of an informal club known as the Junto. From this small group the American Philosophical Society was formed in 1743—an organization which lists as members twelve Presidents, fifteen signers of the Declaration of Independence, and eighteen signers of the Constitution—whose collection of scientific books and papers, rare manuscripts, paintings, and other historical treasures is priceless today.

Meanwhile, Franklin prospered as publisher of the Pennsylvania *Gazette* and of his annual *Poor Richard's Almanack*. While he hoped to devote his time to the study of scientific matters, from 1754 until the end of his life he was drawn constantly into public affairs, in the service of his country. As a diplomat he knew Europe better than any other American, America better than any European. In diplomacy as in all his affairs, he was a man who perceived a need and sought its solution. When he died at the age of 84, people all over the world lamented the passing of the greatest American of his time. Perhaps the tribute he would have enjoyed most is the fact that his contributions to Philadelphia and to the nation he loved are as healthy and active today as they were in his own time.

Elfreth's Alley has changed so little in two centuries that Benjamin Franklin might recognize it if he were alive today.

Independence Hall

JEROME K. ANDERSEN, REPRINTED FROM *Holiday*, © 1955 BY THE CURTIS PUBLISHING CO.

For those Americans who want to recapture the spirit of their nation's beginnings, few places offer them more of it than the serene brick building on Chestnut Street, between Fifth and Sixth, in Philadelphia.

The small legislative Assembly which looked after the Province of Pennsylvania's affairs had no formal meeting place for many years; instead, it met in private houses, rented by the year. By 1729 the members decided the province needed something more permanent, and they agreed on a site on the outskirts of town. The uneven land was covered with whortleberry bushes, and across the street there was a fine peach orchard. Work on the new State House, supervised by carpenter Edmund Woolley, went slowly, and not until 1748 did the president and Council meet in the big room on the second floor. The doorkeeper and his family lived in the west wing, and now and again Indian delegations were lodged or entertained there.

In 1753 the bell tower was completed and the State House bell (which is, of course, the Liberty Bell) was hung. Ordered from London, it was a "bell of about two thousand pounds weight," and the Council stipulated that it should have cast around its crown the words from Leviticus: "Proclaim liberty throughout all the land unto all the inhabitants thereof." To everyone's disappointment the brand-new bell was cracked "by a stroke of the clapper without any other viollence as it was hung up to try the sound"; but two workmen named Pass and Stow recast it successfully, and up the steeple it went, early in 1753.

From that time on, the State House became the center of almost all Philadelphia's important happenings. The officers who survived Braddock's disaster in 1755 gave a memorable ball there after their return to civilization; settlers from the frontier came to plead with the Quaker-controlled Assembly for protection against Indian raids; and Germans from the "back settlements" sixty miles from Philadelphia drove a big Conestoga wagon up to the steps and unloaded the corpses of their scalped neighbors for the Assembly to see. It was the scene of mourning over passage of the Stamp Act, the scene of rejoicing over its repeal, the scene of town meetings to protest the tax on tea. Citizens filled the square at the news of Lexington and Concord, and a few weeks later John Hancock called the Second Continental Congress to order in the State House.

Independence was in the air during those months, and on June 7, 1776, Richard Henry Lee, delegate from Virginia, arose in the State House to propose "Certain resolutions respecting independency." It was

At night the square around Independence Hall is lighted by 56 gas lamps, one for each signer of the Declaration.

John Trumbull's painting shows the committeemen who wrote the Declaration presenting it to chairman John Hancock (seated). From left to right are Adams, Sherman, Livingston, Jefferson, and Franklin.

just a question of time now, and excitement rose with each passing day. A committee composed of Thomas Jefferson, John Adams, Benjamin Franklin, Roger Sherman, and Robert Livingston was appointed to "prepare a declaration to the effect of the . . . resolution," and on July 1 debate began. On July 2, Congress declared "these United Colonies . . . Free and Independent States," and gathered the next morning in the State House to hear the draft of the final and complete charter of freedom. As author Jefferson agonized, delegates edited his words and ideas, cut out passages of his text, and wrangled until evening; but on the morning of July 4 the Declaration of Independence was approved and signed by John Hancock and Secretary Charles Thompson.

For nine months during the Revolution, the British occupied Philadelphia, and they used the State House as a barracks and as a hospital after the battle of Germantown. When Congress finally was able to return, in June of 1778, New Hampshire delegate Josiah Bartlett reported that the building was in "a most filthy and sordid situation," with "the inside torn much to pieces." Three years later, the glorious news from Yorktown was announced at the State House, and in 1787 delegates began drifting into town for a convention which was supposed to draft a constitution.

For four months in the sweltering heat of a Philadelphia summer the debate went on, and when the Constitution was finally signed, Benjamin Franklin pointed to the chair which the visitor may still see there—the one with a gilded half-sun painted on the back—and said: "I have often and often in the course of Session, and the vicissitudes of my hopes and fears as to its issue, looked at that [sun] behind the President without being able to tell whether it was rising or setting: But now at length I have the happiness to know that it is a rising and not a setting Sun."

For a good many years after the Union came into being, the State House was neglected. Although Philadelphia was the temporary capital from 1790 until 1800, both House and Senate met in the building now known as Congress Hall, which witnessed Washington's second inauguration, his last message to Congress, and the inauguration of John Adams. As a matter of fact, the State House was almost torn down in 1816, but the city of Philadelphia fortunately bought the building and the square where it stands for $70,000. Even then, no one paid much attention to it until an aged Lafayette made a visit there in 1824. Then, suddenly, the public woke up to the fact that a great many important things had happened in the old brick structure. About this time, someone attached the name "Independence Hall" to it, and generations of Americans began paying their respects to the place that has heard more of the great voices of America than any other spot in the land.

89

Key to the view:
1. The Draw Bridge 7 John Witpain
2. Buds Building 8 Capt Anthony
3. Edw Shipen 9 George Painte
4. Ant Moris Brew Hous 10 Ios. Shipen
5. Capt Vineing 11 Wm Fisbourn S
6. Jonathan Dickinson 12 Thos Scales

WAYNE ANDREWS

Mount Pleasant, Benedict Arnold's house

WAYNE ANDREWS

The First Bank of the United States

Philadelphia's

At the time of the Revolution, Philadelphia was the second-largest English-speaking city in the world and, if we may believe the Duc de La Rochefoucauld, "one of the most beautiful." It was also, in the score of years before 1800, the gay, bustling center of America's cultural, political, intellectual, and economic life; a city which could point with pride to the remarkable Dr. Franklin and many other men of uncommon ability. There were the painting Peales; the naturalists John and William Bartram; Charles Brockden Brown; Philip Freneau, the "Poet of the Revolution"; David Rittenhouse; Dr. Benjamin Rush; Joseph Priestley; and fascinating French emigrés like the Duc de Talleyrand, La Rochefoucauld, and Chateaubriand.

The setting for eighteenth-century Philadelphia's social life may be seen today in Fairmount Park, where some of the city's historic houses have been moved to form a "Colonial Chain." There is a little two-story building known as the Letitia Street House, a rare specimen of an early urban dwelling, built about 1715, and furnished in Queen Anne style. The Georgian Colonial mansion Cedar Grove was built in 1721; Strawberry Mansion in 1798; Woodford in 1742; and all are furnished appropriately. Probably the masterpiece of this group is Mount Pleasant Mansion, a yellowish-gray stucco house which was begun in 1761 by a Scottish sea captain, and sold later to General Benedict Arnold and his beautiful wife, Peggy Ship-

Peter Cooper's 1720 view of Philadelphia is the oldest extant.

Colonial Chain

Christ Church, where patriots worshiped

THOMAS HOLLYMAN, REPRINTED FROM *Holiday*

pen. Bartram's Gardens, begun in 1731 by the naturalist, are among America's most important botanical exhibits, and inside the grounds is the stone house built by John Bartram in 1731.

Some other notable Philadelphia houses are the Samuel Powel House, home of the city's last pre-Revolution and first post-Revolution mayor; the red brick Wistar, or Shippen House; and the distinguished Morris House, built in 1786, which is set in its original garden. There is the lovely brick Christ Church where Washington, Robert Morris, Franklin, and so many other notables of the Revolution worshiped; and St. Peter's Episcopal Church is another fine example of colonial architecture. Carpenter's Hall, begun in 1770, was where the First Continental Congress assembled, and the First Bank of the United States is a tangible symbol of Alexander Hamilton's efforts to stabilize national finances. The American Philosophical Society and its priceless collections occupy the "neat, sufficient building" erected in 1787; and the cornerstone of the Pennsylvania Hospital—the first in America—reminds one that it was built in "MDCCLV, George the second happily reigning." Anyone interested in personal contact with American history will go also to Germantown, to see the Germantown Academy and the Historical Society, the Chew Mansion which was the focus of the 1777 battle, the Deshler-Morris House, and the handsome Upsala.

Cliveden, center of the Germantown fight

A few of the structures shown in this 1854 print of the du Pont Brandywine Works still stand. The mills were built with an open wall facing the river, to direct explosions away from town. Hopewell iron furnace, below, once consumed the equivalent of an acre of woodland every 24 hours. Among the pieces of early American glass at right are a creamer, bowl, and flask probably made by Stiegel.

Friends

Iron, Glass, and Powder Kegs

Years before men combined Lake Superior ore with Allegheny coking coal by means of the Great Lakes and created the heartland of heavy industry between Pittsburgh and Duluth, iron manufacturing had taken root along the eastern seaboard. The first attempt was made at Falling Creek, Virginia, in 1619, but this community was wiped out by unsympathetic Indians three years later. Saugus, Massachusetts, was the earliest successful works, and the industry soon spread down into Pennsylvania, New Jersey, and Maryland.

Most of the old forges and furnaces have all but disappeared into the landscape, but Hopewell Furnace in Pennsylvania survived long enough to make it worth reconstructing for future generations to see. Built in 1770 by Mark Bird near the site of his father's earlier forge, Hopewell prospered for nearly seventy years. Then coke-fired hot blast ovens began to replace the charcoal-burning furnaces, and in 1883 Hopewell was "blow'd out" for the last time.

Because Hopewell Village, isolated in the hills back of the Schuylkill River, became a ghost town, it remains today much as it was when the blast roared and flames lit up the sky for miles around. At the brink of a natural embankment is the stone furnace from which molten metal spilled into molds of scorched sand called sows and pigs. Across the road are the best-preserved buildings—the office and store, and the big house where Mark Bird and later ironmasters lived—and down the road, past the blacksmith shop, are four stone houses once inhabited by workmen.

Another man whose meteoric career began as an ironmaster was Henry William Stiegel. By 1764, when he built the first of the glass works which brought him lasting fame, his income from the iron industry enabled him to live in a style which earned him the title "Baron." Others, notably the South Jersey manufacturers, had preceded him in the making of fine glass, but to Stiegel belongs the distinction of producing superb lead glass—the first of its kind in America. Clear, amethyst, blue, and green, sometimes engraved or enameled, Stiegel glass possesses a beauty scarcely rivaled by other U.S. manufacturers.

With his debut as a glassmaker, the Baron had founded a little town called Manheim, in the rolling farmlands of Pennsylvania, and in 1770 he owned the entire community. His mansion, which still stands on Manheim's town square, was famed for miles around, and he donated the ground for Manheim's Lutheran church, in exchange for an annual rent of one red rose which the trustees still pay his heirs. But as colonial taxes rose higher and higher, Stiegel's customers dwindled, and after several years of splendor he was thrown into debtor's prison. After his release and until his death, he eked out a wretched living teaching in the church his fortune had built.

If industry was coming to the young country, nowhere was it more noticeable at the end of the eighteenth century than along the busy banks of the Brandywine. Ten years after the Revolution the Duc de La Rochefoucauld said Brandywine Creek turned nearly sixty mills in its course of seven or eight miles through Delaware. Actually, he underestimated the case. The Delaware *Gazette* in 1793 reported fifty mills grinding corn and wheat alone, and listed more than thirty of other types. Four of these were paper mills, which were largely responsible for the Duc's astonishment at another American phenomenon. "All these people busy themselves much with politics," he observed, "and from the landlord down to the house maid they all read two newspapers a day."

For the next fifty years, nearly every sort of mill product in America was made along the Brandywine, and just as its flour mills set the price of wheat for the country, the price of gunpowder came to be fixed by a concern which began life under the unwieldy name of Du Pont de Nemours, Père, Fils et Compagnie. Eleuthère Irénée du Pont made a personal survey of the competition, discovered that explosions and British manufacturers had put most American powder mills out of business, and bought a 95-acre tract along the river as the site of his operations. On a bluff above the winding stream he built a stone and stucco mansion which is still a du Pont home, and close at hand, the original office building, now used as a guest house. Below the residence there are still a few vine-covered walls, all that remain of the first mills which operated for more than a century. The curious construction of these buildings was intentional. Two sides and the rear wall were made of stone, and an open wall faced the river. Irénée du Pont knew enough about powder manufacturing to understand its hazards fully. If a nail got under the rollers, or if a bearing overheated, there was a flash and roar that rattled windows for miles around, and the insides of the mill were strewn all over the landscape. By placing an open wall toward the river, he directed the explosion that way, rather than toward the little community which lay behind the mills.

Dawn's Early Light

O say can you see ~~through~~ by the dawn's early light
what so proudly we hail'd at the twilight's last gleaming,
Whose broad stripes & bright stars through the perilous fight
O'er the ramparts we watch'd were so gallantly streaming?
And the rocket's red glare, the bomb bursting in air
Gave proof through the night that our flag was still there,
O say does that star spangled banner yet wave
O'er the land of the free & the home of the brave?

Francis Scott Key wrote "The Star-Spangled Banner" as a poem, on the back of a letter.

At 5:46 on the morning of September 13, 1814, the British fleet opened fire on Fort McHenry. Already 5,000 of Wellington's veterans had been ashore for 36 hours, striking toward Baltimore from the east in a combined land-sea attack. The navy was to reduce Fort McHenry by a massive bombardment, after which the British could take Baltimore as easily as they had taken Washington three weeks earlier.

For the rest of that day and all through the night, mortar shells and rockets poured down on the brick and sod fort. Inside the works, Colonel George Armistead had about a thousand men—and not one gun with enough range to reach the English fleet.

The War of 1812, which had begun with the eager cry "On to Canada!" had reached a critical stage. Abortive American attempts to invade their northern neighbor had died on the vine or been thrown back decisively. In the summer of 1814, the chief U.S. source of support—Napoleon—was exiled to Elba, and America's defenses were so pitiful that for five days in August 4,000 British regulars marched up the Patuxent River without firing a shot. In response to an urgent summons for 95,000 militia, less than 7,000 showed up at Bladensburg. Although they outnumbered the redcoats nearly two to one, most of the Americans panicked and ran when they had suffered 66 casualties, and the British pushed on to Washington that night, arriving in time for some of the officers to eat a White House dinner prepared for President and Mrs. Madison. During the days that followed, they diverted themselves by burning most of Washington's public buildings, including the Capitol and the White House, then proceeded leisurely back to their ships for the strike against Baltimore. En route, they stopped in Upper Marlboro, Maryland, and took captive "a medical practitioner called Beanes."

His close friend, a young Washington lawyer named Francis Scott Key, obtained permission from a har-

The fifteen-starred flag flying over the ramparts of Fort McHenry is a copy of the one Key saw "by dawn's early light."

assed Madison to obtain Dr. Beanes' release. Key took a packet boat from Baltimore under a flag of truce, and on September 6 met the British fleet preparing to attack the city. Admiral Cochrane agreed to release Beanes, but refused to let the Americans go until the movement against Baltimore had been executed.

From two miles out in the harbor, the anguished Key watched all day as the British shelled the helpless garrison. In the failing light of dusk, he could see nothing of the fort through the smoke and flames, but just as darkness closed around it, he caught sight of the flag. Half wild with anxiety, he paced the deck all night as the relentless bombardment continued. When the first light of dawn streaked the sky, Key strained for a glimpse of the fort. As the darkness lifted, he saw it—the flag still flew. And Francis Scott Key pulled a letter from his pocket and began to write on it some verses filled with the emotions of that night.

For nearly an hour more shells burst and smoke rolled over the fort, but at 7 A.M. on September 14 the attack ceased. Two hours later the fleet began to withdraw down the river, and Admiral Cochrane notified the land forces of his failure to destroy Fort McHenry. On September 15 the infantry re-embarked—some for Halifax, the rest for the West Indies, where the expedition against New Orleans was assembling.

In a hotel that night Key rewrote his verses, and a friend took the stirring words to a local print shop, where they were run off in handbill form. On September 20 the poem was published in the Baltimore *Patriot* under the title of "The Defense of Fort McHenry." One morning a few days later, an actor named Ferdinand Durang and some twenty companions well fortified with juleps sang it for the first time to a tune all of them knew well, a drinking song called "To Anacreon in Heaven."

In the years that followed, Key's song of an unconquerable flag came to be accepted popularly as the national anthem, but not until 1931 did Congress pass a bill recognizing "The Star-Spangled Banner" as the official song of the United States of America.

Harpers Ferry, at the junction of the Shenandoah and Potomac rivers (below), still looks much the way it did at the time of John Brown's raid in 1859. In the photograph at left, taken just before the raid, "Old Brown of Osawatamie" is wearing the beard he grew as a disguise. The brick enginehouse where he and his men were cornered by Robert E. Lee's marines stands today on the grounds of Storer College.

The Invasions of the North

The trail of the "middle-aged, middle-sized man, with hair and beard of amber color streaked with gray" began in Connecticut. It led out to Ohio and on to Kansas, where he was called "Old Brown of Osawatamie," north across the border to Canada and, in the summer of 1859, to the sleepy little town of Chambersburg, Pennsylvania. He said he was a prospector named Isaac Smith, so no one considered it strange when large boxes marked "Tools" were delivered to the weathered gray house at 225 King Street. Then he left town as quietly as he had come, taking his boxes with him to a little farm in Maryland, just across the Potomac from the long narrow hump of land known as Harpers Ferry. And on the night of October 16, 1859, while Harpers Ferry slept, the contents of the boxes became carbines, Isaac Smith became John Brown, and he and 22 followers marched over the bridge and seized the federal arsenal.

Robert Harper, 125 years before, had been so thrilled by the wild beauty of the place where the Shenandoah and Potomac rivers meet that he gave two squatters $65 for their cabin, canoe, and corn patch, paid Lord Fairfax sixty guineas for the land, and settled there He started a ferry service across the Potomac and gradually a little village grew up around it. The water power which eventually led Congress to establish an arsenal there was not always a blessing; the town suffered from floods, and for years men remembered the great Pumpkin Flood of 1753, so called because of the great numbers of pumpkins it washed downstream from the Indian fields.

Thomas Jefferson had seen Harpers Ferry as a place so lovely it was "worth a trip across the Atlantic." John Brown saw it as the natural entrance to the slave country, a stronghold in the southern mountains to which Negroes could flee. But it was not so easy as all that. By afternoon of October 17, companies of militia and bands of angry men from the Virginia hills converged on the town, blocking Brown's escape, and that night ninety marines arrived from Washington, led by Colonel Robert E. Lee and Lieutenant J. E. B. Stuart. Holed up in the square brick enginehouse which stands today on the grounds of Storer College, John Brown was wounded and ten of his men killed before he surrendered. Two of those men were his sons. And for John Brown it was all over but the hanging.

Harpers Ferry was destined to have little peace for the next five years, as the great struggle of which John Brown had been one wild symptom tore at the roots of American society. Just three years after Brown appeared there, the town played its part in the battle which, as much as any other, determined the war's final outcome.

The Army of the Potomac was reeling from the beating it took at the Second Battle of Bull Run, and Robert E. Lee decided to strike again quickly—this time in an invasion of the North. With supreme contempt for the abilities of General George B. McClellan, Lee had divided his army in two, sending part under Stonewall Jackson to take Harpers Ferry, while he and the rest worked their way north. As the fog lifted off the rivers on the morning of September 15, 1862, Jackson's men saw a white flag waving, and knew that Harpers Ferry, with 12,000 Union troops and 13,000 small arms, was theirs. Stonewall himself received the surrender—the "dingiest, worst-dressed and worst-mounted general that a warrior who cared for good looks and style would wish to surrender to"—and as he rode down into Harpers Ferry the boys in blue

Attacking from the hill in the background, Union troops crossed Burnside's Bridge at Antietam after heavy losses.

Divided We Fought, MACMILLAN

This pensive-looking young private from Georgia posed for his photograph shortly before he was killed at Malvern Hill.

were so curious to see this legendary figure that they lined the sides of the road, some of them uncovering as he passed them. Jackson returned their salute, and one of the Union lads said what many of them felt, that he didn't look like much, "but if we had him we wouldn't be in the fix we're in." To the unfortunate Federal troops and, indeed, to the victorious Confederates, it looked as if this might be it. Lee's great drive for the defenseless cities of the North was going according to plan. His army, tired as it was, had victory under its belts, and the element of surprise was all his.

All, that is, except for one small hitch. While McClellan and the Army of the Potomac were pursuing Lee, wondering where he was going and what he would do, a corporal in the 27th Indiana and one of his buddies, lounging in a field outside Frederick, found a bulky envelope in the grass. Corporal Mitchell opened it and pulled out a piece of paper wrapped around three cigars. The cigars alone would have satisfied any soldier, but the paper in which they were wrapped was something beyond the wildest dreams of generals. It contained Lee's Special Orders No. 191, which told in detail the whereabouts of every division of Lee's army, and his immediate plans. Probably never in American history was a commanding officer so favored by luck as McClellan was that day in 1862.

With this information, even as cautious a man as he

should have had no trouble finishing off Lee then and there. At this moment, Lee's army was in several different pieces, and McClellan was closer to them than the pieces were to each other. The only thing that was required to crush them separately was immediate action; but of this, George B. McClellan was incapable. Then, as always, he was obsessed with the notion that Lee outnumbered him, and when he decided to attack Lee's rear guard at South Mountain, it was done not quite vigorously or quickly enough. Actually, Lee had only 19,000 dead-tired men of Longstreet's and D. H. Hill's commands. Against him, McClellan had 70,000, and while these were not all combat troops, even if the rest of the Confederates did arrive in time from Harpers Ferry it would still be a two-to-one fight.

Yet Lee, in what was probably the boldest act of his military career, crossed Antietam Creek and turned to fight it out at Sharpsburg. This is as beautiful a spot today as it was then, and the little village that lies among rich farmlands between the creek and the wide-swinging Potomac River has changed hardly at all. Into this quiet, peaceful place the two armies moved that hot September 16, taking their places for the battle that would change American history. But time was beginning to run out for George McClellan and his opportunity. That morning Jackson's men—weary and sore of foot from a seventeen-mile night march from Harpers Ferry—had come up. Although Lee still had barely 25,000 men, McClellan thought he had 100,000—and decided to wait for Franklin's 18,000 troops to arrive.

Not until daybreak of September 17—nearly five days after Lee's lost order had been found—did McClellan launch his attack, and then, instead of making one big push, he did it piecemeal. Just about a mile north of what is now the National Cemetery there stood a Dunker church, a little white building backed by the West Wood on one side, and facing the East Wood across the Hagerstown pike. Between the wood lots was a cornfield, and just south of it a sunken road. Within these few thousand square yards, and within a little less than five hours, the bloodiest fighting of the whole war took place that morning. The battle exploded when Joe Hooker and his troops moved south along the Hagerstown road toward the cornfield, and Hooker remembered that soon "every stalk of corn . . . was cut as closely as could have been done with a knife, and the slain lay in rows precisely as they had stood in their ranks a few moments before." The Confederate line finally broke as the Union soldiers reached the fence at the end of the field, and the boys in blue ran toward the church, victory in sight. Suddenly, without warning, John Bell Hood's division boiled out from behind the church, and the Union charge changed to retreat. Back and forth across the forty-acre cornfield the conflict flamed, a hand-to-hand fight to the finish that ended with the Union troops at the Dunker church, but with Hooker's I Corps completely wrecked.

General Sumner, marching up to seal the victory, ran head-on into reinforcements Lee had sent up just in time, and at the end of fifteen minutes more than 2,000 Union soldiers were dead or wounded. After just four hours, 12,000 men were lying on the ground, killed or hurt, and when McClellan sent a courier to Sumner suggesting he renew the attack, Sumner's horror at the slaughter was so great that he cried out: "Go back, young man, and tell General McClellan I have no command." By this time Lee's battle line was a thin thread, held together by a few bits and pieces of outfits that just refused to give up, but when he got Sumner's message, McClellan decided not to throw Franklin's fresh troops into the attack.

The final stage of the furious battle began when the IX Corps crossed what has been called, ever since, Burnside's Bridge. Although the Antietam is so shallow a man can walk across it in most places, the Union commanders decided to storm the bridge—and storm it they did, at a horrible cost in lives before they got across. Burnside, who had 12,000 men in his command, inexplicably made his attack with only 3,000, but even so the 2,400 tired rebels were being pushed back slowly, just to the brink of Sharpsburg, when suddenly from out of nowhere Confederate General A. P. Hill came storming up at precisely the right time and place and drove back the blue line. Hill had made a terrible seventeen-mile forced march from Harpers Ferry, driving his exhausted men at the point of his sword, and although nearly half his division was left along the roadside, enough arrived to keep the war going for two and a half years more. It was just that close. While Lee had not a man left he could call a reserve, Burnside never used his extra troops, McClellan never sent in the 10,000 fresh men who could have put an end to the Army of Northern Virginia, and the Battle of Antietam was over.

The Union army lost fifteen per cent of its men on that unspeakable battlefield—the Confederates over one-fourth of theirs. Militarily, it was a standoff. What it accomplished, however, was to give Lincoln enough of a victory—a shaky, uncertain one, it is true—but enough for him to issue the Emancipation Proclamation. When Lee's gray columns turned back into Virginia, and when Lincoln announced that he would declare free all the slaves in territory still resisting the Union, it ended the threat of foreign intervention. The war would be fought out at home, to the terrible, bitter end, and the question of the Union and the

The expression of this youthful Northern infantryman seems less carefree than his Napoleonic stance and jaunty attire.

issue of slavery would be decided, right here.

Less than ten months after the Battle of Antietam the long gray lines were on their way north again, and ahead of them a rising tide of fear struck deep into the cities and countryside of Pennsylvania. Broadsides signed by Governor Curtin screamed, "The Enemy is Approaching!!" and local militia companies bustled into frenzied activity. Across the river from Pittsburgh, at the old Allegheny Diamond, a mass meeting was held on the evening of June 13, 1863, and within a few weeks 14,000 men—butchers, clerks, steelworkers, steamboat men and students—were building fortifications around the nervous city. They had good reason to be scared. Lee's lean, brown veterans were superb fighting men, and they were swinging north to an untouched land of milk and honey with the confidence born of having licked their more numerous opponents nearly every time they had met them. They were 70,000 strong, trained in combat, and about as fine an army as ever headed into action.

Within these same ten months the Army of the Potomac had fought the same four great battles—Second Bull Run, Antietam, Fredericksburg, and Chancellorsville—but they had fought each one under a different commander. The veterans were as good as anything Lee could throw against them, but the army was full of untrained regiments, and it had hardly been favored by topnotch generalship. They were pushing hard now, trying to keep up with Lee and stay between him and Washington, and on June 28 George Gordon Meade was roused from sleep by a War Department official and told that he was in command of the army. Just then that army was engaged in a race—a race to the finish that depended on how its legs held out—and there was no time for Meade to make changes or do anything at all except keep up; which meant that the battle they were heading for would be decided by the men in the ranks.

Up the thin strip of land between the Potomac River and the Chesapeake and Ohio Canal they marched, dead-tired men dropping out of the ranks by the dozens, up the dusty roads past Frederick, winding through the mountains past towns where cheering villagers and pretty girls came out to greet them with handouts of lemonade and pie, apple butter and fresh bread.

Lee's men had ranged from York in the east to Chambersburg in the west, but now they were beginning to concentrate east of the great barrier of South Mountain. Late in the afternoon on the last day of June, 1863, General John Buford and his division of troopers in skin-tight pants and big black boots rode into the town of Gettysburg to have a look around. Gettysburg then, as now, was the center of roads converging from all directions, and Buford figured that Lee could not be far away. The Army of the Potomac was on the march that bright moonlit night, but neither the men in the ranks nor the men who commanded them had any notion that a battle which would decide the destiny of the United States of America would begin on the morrow.

The monuments and statues that line the roads of Gettysburg today were put there toward the end of the last century by men trying to capture something of what happened at this place. They can be trying to the visitor who wants to hurry through, but no one in a hurry is likely to find much of what Gettysburg means. The best way to see the battlefield is to go there armed with some of the facts, and to walk from place to place, stopping every now and again to think about it all. To think, for example, that the battle was fought here by accident (not that it could have been avoided; it was going to happen somewhere), since neither Lee nor Meade had considered Gettysburg as a place to stand and fight.

The Confederates of A. P. Hill's corps were heading into town on that first day of July because they heard there were some shoes there, and as the light began to trickle over the hills into the fields and pastures along the Cashtown road, the dun-colored skirmishers of Harry Heth's division came striding over the western ridge, muskets at the ready. And when John Buford climbed up into the white bell tower of the Lutheran Theological Seminary on the ridge west of town to survey the situation, he saw them and knew that a fight was in the making—a big one. He had no support at the moment, but he was a man who liked to fight and he decided this was probably as good a place as any to do just that.

The first Federal infantry to come up was the Iron Brigade; and the 1,800 westerners with black slouch hats tilted over their eyes marched up the Emmitsburg road with flags waving and a fife-and-drum corps playing them into their last fight. They were the most famous outfit in the Army of the Potomac, and when the Confederates saw them they knew it wasn't going to be easy. Near the Seminary (and not far from the present Eisenhower farm) these "damned black-hat fellers," as the rebels called them, fought until they were hemmed in on three sides, and had to retreat. Along with the I Corps, they fought their way back through town and finally patched up a line on Cemetery Ridge. By that time, the I Corps had lost all but 2,400 men out of nearly 10,000, and the Iron Brigade lost 1,200 out of 1,800, which put an end to it as a fighting unit. On the night of July 1 there were only 5,000 Union troops occupying the line between Cemetery Ridge and Culp's Hill, and most of them were too worn out to notice a little sign which said that the town would fine anybody five dollars for discharging a firearm within the cemetery grounds.

On the second day boys who had never been in action before made up for it in a hurry. All over the field men traded their lives for the few minutes or hours the Army of the Potomac had to have if the war was not to end right then and there. The 1st Minnesota was one such outfit—262 men went into action and only 47 came out. Confederate James Longstreet smashed through the Peach Orchard at General Dan Sickles' extended line, and men fought and died for pieces of ground called Devil's Den and Little Round Top. Two lads from Gettysburg named Culp and Wentz who had gone south to join the Confederates came back for this battle—Culp to die on the hill where he was born, and Wentz to find himself with his battery in his father's back yard. General officers rode madly off for help, and outfits slated to go into line at one place were commandeered to plug a hole somewhere else. Over everything there was the ear-shattering roar of battle, the piercing screech of the Rebel yell, the unending crackle of small arms, and the screams of the wounded. As the great arc of flame and smoke surrounding the Federal position pulled inward, desperate men fought at close quarters, yelling at the top of their lungs and clubbing each other with anything

A Confederate cannon overlooks the town of Gettysburg from Oak Ridge. On the first day of fighting, outnumbered Union troops held out here against fierce assaults until a Rebel victory in the open fields below forced them to withdraw.

Near the Trostle Barn (above), the Union army corps commanded by General Sickles was shattered in the Peach Orchard fight. At left is one of the granite outcroppings of Devil's Den which sheltered Confederate snipers. From this position they picked off Union gunners on Little Round Top.

101

they could lay their hands on. All through the second uneasy night, men startled by a sound opened fire at it. The night was filled with moans and rending cries of the wounded; behind the lines field hospitals were hideous with blood and parts of bodies.

On the morning of the third day the Federal troops still held their position on the long ridge trailing off Cemetery Hill, and when they looked out across the valley they saw more guns staring at them than they had ever seen before. Until one o'clock in the afternoon the field was ominously silent, and then 130 guns opened in a roll of thunder that carried a storm of exploding hell to the Yankee line. The field around the little white house where Meade had his headquarters was the worst hit of all, and for what seemed like hours the terrible bombardment went on, blasting showers of awful debris into the air. Then, suddenly, the furious cannonade abated, and the signal station on Little Round Top wigwagged: Here they come.

The soldiers of the Army of the Potomac saw something across the mile-wide valley they would never see again—and never forget as long as they lived. It was a line of battle a mile and a half long—15,000 men shoulder to shoulder, marching forward with flags flying, musket barrels glinting in the sun, heading across that field as if they were on parade. The whole Union line opened on them, artillery blasting great holes in the ranks, but they kept on coming. Confederate General Lewis Armistead, holding his hat high on his sword, led the center right up into the Union line. There was a terrible hand-to-hand fight, every man on his own and the fate of a nation riding on what happened in those next few and dreadful minutes. Finally,

Paul Philippoteaux's epic painting of the battle of Gettysburg depicts the moment when Pickett's charge and the hopes of the South were broken along the stone walls of Cemetery Ridge. At center, Armistead's brigade has just penetrated the Union line

almost as suddenly as it had begun, the fighting sputtered out like a faulty fuse and the Confederates who did not surrender started back toward their own lines. When an officer rode up to tell George Meade that Lee's charge had been broken Meade raised his hand and thanked God.

The next day a wagon train seventeen miles long headed south, bearing what was left of Lee's supplies and his wounded, and along with this nightmare of pain and suffering went the hopes of the Confederacy for winning the war. Between them, the two armies had lost over 50,000 men.

It wasn't long before the governors of the Northern states decided to provide a proper cemetery for the men who fell at Gettysburg, and they planned to dedi-

cate the ground on November 19. They invited Edward Everett, the most illustrious orator of his day, to make the principal speech and, almost as an afterthought, the President of the United States to lend his presence. The night before the ceremony the President worked over a draft of his talk at David Wills' house in Gettysburg, and the next day he was part of the great procession marching out to the battlefield. It was a rare Indian summer day, but by the time the crowd had heard Everett drone on for two hours they were listless and ready to go home.

When his turn came to address the audience, the tall, gaunt man in the black frock coat spoke from two little sheets of paper he held in his hand. He talked for less than three minutes, and after it was all said and done he had the feeling that his remarks were unsuccessful, since few of the 20,000 people seemed to have heard or caught the meaning of his words.

only to be overwhelmed in a desperate crush of hand-to-hand fighting. The clump of rock oaks at right center was the "High-Water Mark" of the Confederate advance, if not of the Confederacy. In this single assault, Lee's army lost five thousand men.

This earthenware dish was fashioned by a Pennsylvania Dutch potter late in the eighteenth century. It was a love gift, the two doves uniting in a single, heart-shaped figure.

As they grow older, these smiling, quaintly dressed Amish boys will not pose for the camera so willingly, for photographs are considered by their religion as graven images.

A long funeral caravan of boxlike Amish buggies heads for the burying ground. With their aversion for new-fangled, "worldly" things, the Amish still hold out against cars.

DISH AND TROUGH: NATIONAL GALLERY OF ART, *Index of American Design*

The barnlike buildings at left, at Ephrata Cloister, housed Johann Conrad Beissel's Seventh Day Baptist monastic community. Above is a dough trough decorated with tulips.

Fast Clocks, Plain Food and "Fraktur"

Of all the people who found William Penn's colony a sanctuary, the "Pennsylvania Dutch" folk with their colorful customs and handiwork fastened themselves most firmly in the popular imagination. Frugal, hard-working, and God-fearing, these are people who still keep their clocks half an hour fast because it is frivolous to be late; who serve "plain food" in gargantuan quantities, loaded with butter; who eat *schwenkfelder* bread on Thanksgiving, *fasnachts* on Shrove Tuesday, and dandelion greens on Maundy Thursday to ward off fevers. They throw water from the baptismal bowl over a rosebush to ensure rosy cheeks for the newly baptized child, and feed ashes from Good Friday's fires to their pigs to keep them in good health.

Not Dutch at all (their ancestors came from Germany, and they referred to themselves as *Deutsche,* thus confusing generations of Anglo-Saxons), neither are they one homogeneous group. Each sect had its disagreements with the others, but one thing they did have in common—knowledge of the great German hymns and a background of the same devotional literature.

The settlements of Menno Simons' followers—the Mennonites—are much in evidence in Lancaster County, where the best-known sect—the Amish—still clings to the Pennsylvania Dutch language and the seventeenth-century culture of Swiss-German ancestors. The bearded, black-robed men and their plainly clothed wives are vigorously opposed to automobiles, telephones, and higher education.

Bethlehem has the finest examples of Moravian culture. Many of the buildings are old log structures, covered since with stucco or clapboard, but colorfully painted to relieve the severity of design.

There were the Dunkers, pacifists and antislavery people, who split up into several groups—among them the followers of Johann Conrad Beissel who founded a community called Ephrata Cloister. There are four main buildings, five cottages, and a few outbuildings still standing, the remains of this Christian communal colony. Beissel had written: "Asia has fallen and its lamp gone out. For Europe the sun hath set at bright midday. America shall see a lily blooming whose perfume shall spread to the heathen." Visiting the buildings, it is understandable that the bloom came off the lily for later generations. In the ascetic life of the cloister, there were two persons to a cell. Each cell was only four floor boards wide, with a small high window. Beds were narrow wooden ledges, too short for comfort, and pillows were wooden blocks eight inches long. Low narrow doors and passageways symbolized the straight and narrow path and required constant stooping, to remind the brothers and sisters to be humble.

The followers of George Rapp, founder of Harmony, were skilled craftsmen who enjoyed considerable prosperity. After selling Harmony, they migrated to Indiana, built up another successful colony, sold it to Robert Owen, and moved to Economy on the banks of the Ohio at Ambridge, to found their third and final home. The seventeen buildings which still stand are an impressive group, including the 35-room Great House of hand-made brick with large, well-furnished, high-ceilinged rooms. There is a three-story music hall with a beautiful Colonial doorway, a five-story granary with hand-timbered first floor, a store, post office, apothecary shop, tailor and shoe shop with a stone-vaulted wine cellar beneath it, a cabinet shop, community kitchen, and the community gardens with their grotto, a building of rough stone boulders and beautiful interior.

The most widely known contribution of the Pennsylvania Dutch, of course, has been the outpouring of their creative fancies: painted chests, decorated barns, colorful household articles, slipware and sgraffito pottery, *fraktur* (illuminated writing elaborated with decorations drawn in color), and *Taufscheine*—those lovely illustrated baptismal certificates. Almost never, in these original pieces of work, was the religion which played such a part in their daily lives forgotten. Flowers stood for Christ, the Flower of Life. Christ was also the rose and the lily. The heart stood for God's heart—the "heart" of man's nature. There were stars ("There shall come a star out of Jacob, and a sceptre shall rise out of Israel"), and the Sun of Righteousness.

Driving through the great farm country of Pennsylvania, seeing the fieldstone houses and barns with steep roofs, decorative signs, and outward-curving eaves, hardware shaped into hearts and lilies and peacocks, and the other evidences of their imaginative skill, it is plain to see that these good folk gave something of their own to the land, without which it would not be quite the same.

SURRATT.
BOOTH.
War Department, Washington, Ap
$100,000 REW
THE MURDER
Of our late beloved President, Abraham
IS STILL AT LAR
$50,000 REWAR
REWARD
JOHN H. SURRAT
TWO HUNDRED THOUSAND DOLLARS.
FORD'S THEATRE
Friday Evening April 14th, 1865
BENEFIT!
LAST NIGHT
OF MISS
LAURA KEENE
MR. JOHN DYOTT
AND
MR. HARRY HAWK.
TOM TAYLOR'S CELEBRATED ECCENTRIC COMEDY,
ONE THOUSAND NIGHTS,
OUR AMERICAN
COUSIN
BERLIN

Booth posed for this picture at the height of his acting career.

George Atzerodt went to murder Andrew Johnson; lost his nerve.

John Surratt fled to Europe; he was later tried but not convicted.

Caught with Booth in Virginia, feeble-minded David Herold was sentenced to hang.

Accused of helping Booth escape, stagehand Edward Spangler was imprisoned.

Ex-Confederate Lewis Payne knifed Secretary of State Seward.

Ford's Theatre

On Tenth Street in downtown Washington there are two old brick buildings which share a tragic memory. In one of these, Ford's Theatre, John Wilkes Booth assassinated Abraham Lincoln on the night of April 14, 1865; and although the theater was closed after Lincoln's death, the building remains as a museum. The mute fragments gathered here tell a nightmarish story of the plot carried out by the men on this page. There is the gun that killed Lincoln; Booth's spurred boot and the flag on which it caught as he jumped from Lincoln's box to the stage, causing him to break his leg; and the strange diary Booth kept during his flight. Across the street is the tailor Petersen's house, where the President was carried, mortally wounded. At the rear of the house is the close, dark room where he lay across a walnut bed which was pitifully small for his great frame. Here, on that rainy April morning, Secretary Stanton said, "Now he belongs to the ages."

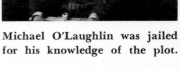

Michael O'Laughlin was jailed for his knowledge of the plot.

Among the mementos from Ford's Theatre shown are a Lincoln life mask; Booth's pistol, diary, dagger, hotel key, boot, and compass; Mary Lincoln's opera glass case; and the door to the presidential box with a peephole (lower right) bored by Booth only a few hours before he assassinated Lincoln.

Mrs. Surratt, who was hanged, ran the boarding house where the plotters met.

Capital of the Nation

Like a good many decisions which have been reached there since, the one that put the nation's capital on the bank of the Potomac River was the result of a political bargain. Since 1776 the government had been on the run. It had sat in Baltimore, Lancaster, York, Princeton, Annapolis, and Trenton, and when it moved from New York to Philadelphia in 1790, residents of New York predicted gloomily that their city would soon be deserted "and become a wilderness, peopled with wolves, its old inhabitants." The new site, chosen as a sop to the South, was hardly popular in the North. It was quite literally in the middle of nowhere, and most people described the location accurately as a fever-ridden swamp. Beyond Baltimore the road to Washington wandered through forests, and a driver picked the least dangerous-looking track to follow. Coming down from Philadelphia, Abigail Adams' hapless coachman lost his way completely, got off on the Frederick road, and spent more than two hours in the woods without finding so much as a path. Writing of the capital's beginnings, Henry Adams described what it looked like in 1800: ". . . the half-finished White House stood in a naked field overlooking the Potomac, with two awkward Department buildings near it, a single row of brick houses and a few isolated dwellings within sight, and nothing more; until across a swamp, a mile and a half away, the shapeless, unfinished Capitol was seen, two wings without a body, ambitious enough in design to make more grotesque the nature of its surroundings."

It was a long time before the capital began living up to the grandeur imagined for it by its planners. George Washington had appointed the engineer-architect Major Pierre L'Enfant to draw up plans for the city, but aside from L'Enfant and a few others, not many had the vision to see what the federal city might one day become. A number of landowners were persuaded to donate property (some, like the Scotsman David Burnes, on whose land the White House stands, held out for concrete evidence of gratitude), but when they heard the streets were to be as much as

The Jefferson Memorial in spring

160 feet wide they were horror stricken. Later, when a house was torn down because it stood in the path of what was to be New Jersey Avenue, the ambitious planner was fired.

Strange things sometimes happened after the L'Enfant scheme languished. When the Treasury building burned down for the third time, nobody could agree on a site for it. One day while President Andrew Jackson was out walking, someone asked him where he thought it should be. He stopped, drove his sword cane into the ground and replied firmly: "Right here!" And right there is where they put it, thereby interrupting the proposed sweep of Pennsylvania Avenue from the Capitol to the White House.

Fortunately, the L'Enfant plan was reactivated about the turn of the twentieth century, and little by little the city became what it is today—the one place in America that seems to sum up the aspirations of all its citizens. It is, too, the one place where Americans can see the men entrusted with their nation's future working against a background of the nation's past, and this makes it one of the most important and exciting cities in the land.

Yet Washington often gives visitors the impression that it is, underneath, a small town, probably because the people who live here are, after all, very much like those who are drawn to it as tourists. Few of those who come to see the great public buildings, monuments, and statues fail to be captivated as well by a city made more beautiful by trees, the sweeping Potomac, parks and gardens and flowering shrubs and a quiet old canal, long white bridges, the colorful atmosphere of foreign visitors, the openness of streets and broad avenues, and the towering, lovely cathedral on the heights overlooking the city.

Downstream and across the river is Alexandria, upriver is Georgetown—both thriving ports before the capital existed, now in their retirement exuding a kind of warm glow that comes from row after row of handsome old brick houses. On the Mall is the great shaft of the Washington Monument, reaching ever upward to honor the man who led the new nation into being, and due west of it, across the reflecting pool, is the beautiful white temple where Lincoln sits,

The floodlighted Capitol dome is made of a cast-iron shell painted white. It is capped by a bronze statue of Freedom.

caught forever in marble the way most Americans will always think of him. South, over the quiet surface of the Tidal Basin, the columns of Thomas Jefferson's memorial seem to rise out of the water, serene and shining in the sunlight; and to the north is the oldest public building in Washington, the white mansion where every President since John Adams has lived. Across Memorial Bridge, near the house where Robert E. Lee lived, is a simple and beautiful block of white marble, watched over by men in uniform, where a soldier known only to God sleeps eternally.

There are literally hundreds of places to visit in Washington, each one rewarding in its own way; but to millions of Americans the symbol of their country is the great-domed building at the end of Pennsylvania Avenue—the Capitol of the United States. This home of representative government faces east, away from the city of Washington, because it was L'Enfant's belief that it should look toward the rising sun. Jenkins Hill was chosen as the site for the Capitol in 1791, and two years later George Washington, wearing a Masonic apron embroidered for him by Madame de Lafayette, laid the cornerstone; but not until 1863 did the statue of Freedom finally stand on top of the completed dome. Inside the portico where the Chief Justice of the Supreme Court administers the oath of office to each President is the vast Rotunda canopied by the nine-million-pound dome. There is a cathedral-like atmosphere here that makes the visitor pause for a silent moment to look upward at the circling fresco far above the floor. Toward the House of Representatives is another vaulted chamber, a room lined now with silent statues where once the voices of men like Webster and Calhoun rang out, and beyond it is

the largest legislative forum in the world. In the north wing, across the length of the Capitol, is the Old Senate Chamber where the Louisiana Purchase was ratified, where Henry Clay brought the Missouri Compromise into being, and where men debated the issues of union and states' rights.

Democracy is the handiwork of people—people who make mistakes and people who have their moments of shining triumph—and democracy will offer them something better so long as a single voice is able to contribute to all that has been done before. Each day in the halls of the nation's Capitol the elected representatives of America have an opportunity to add to democracy's continuing tradition; and while the voices sometimes sound discordant and confused, the fact that they are raised at all is the best testimony to the American belief that the efficiency of one-man rule is not worth the cost of human suffering and the loss of individual dignity which accompany it.

Here in this city is the focal point of democracy in the United States—something Grover Cleveland realized when he became President in 1885. In a speech that described perfectly the meaning of Washington, D.C., he said that any man taking the oath of office "only assumes the solemn obligation which every patriotic citizen—on the farm, in the workshop, in the busy marts of trade, and everywhere—should share with him. The Constitution which prescribes his oath, my countrymen, is yours; the government you have chosen him to administer for a time is yours; the suffrage which executes the will of free men is yours; the laws and the entire scheme of our civil rule, from the town meeting to the state capitols and the national capitol, is yours."

Millions of visitors to the Lincoln Memorial have been moved by Daniel Chester French's magnificent statue of Abraham Lincoln.

Towering above the capital sky line, the shaft of the Washington Monument is a striking 555-foot-high obelisk of white masonry.

In Fraunces Tavern, oldest house in Manhattan, George Washington took leave of his officers in 1783.

This is the New York that Washington knew. Trinity Church is behind the rigging of the ship, the Battery to the right.

New York City:
Then and Now

In this city whose face is altered so constantly, where towering shafts of metal, glass, and concrete seem to rise almost overnight on the ashes of the old, it is a wonder that any historic landmarks remain. Those stubborn enough to survive are dwarfed now by the sheer walls around them, providing a striking contrast between ancient and modern, and reminding the visitor that twentieth-century New York does indeed have a past. At the very bottom of Manhattan Island, where once New Netherland thrived, nothing but street names recall the Dutch settlement bounded by the wall which gave the financial district its name. Fraunces Tavern, where George Washington bid farewell to his officers, dates from a later period but is the oldest house left in Manhattan. St. Paul's Chapel, built in 1764, is the oldest and one of the most beautiful churches in the city; and the Sub-Treasury Building stands on the site of Federal Hall, where Washington was inaugurated as the first President and where government under the Constitution began.

Out in the harbor is the great statue which has symbolized America and liberty to so many millions of people, and overlooking the East River is the modern headquarters of the United Nations, that organization on whose future so much may depend.

ide the United Nations building representatives of 132
ions work on problems of world affairs. The Secretariat
the skyscraper behind the domed General Assembly.

France presented the Statue of Liberty to the United States
in 1884. Erected in New York Harbor, it has been a symbol of freedom for millions who have come to America.

Appalachian Frontier

In George Caleb Bingham's idyllic painting, Daniel Boone leads a group of pioneers along the mountain trail known as Cumberland Gap. Originally discovered by buffalo, this passage was followed later by Indians and white men. The Indian threat was always present, and in some years as many as one hundred settlers were killed on the Wilderness Road.

Many settlers began the westward trek in sturdy Conestoga wagons, named for the Pennsylvania valley where they originated. The wagons were useless, however, on the Wilderness Road, which was not much more than a rough trail, so pioneers bound for the mountain frontier often transferred their belongings to pack trains or floated down the Ohio.

The Land Beyond the Mountains

A modern highway hugs the steep slopes of Cumberland Gap, crossing mountains still wild and heavily timbered.

Long before the first white man found his way into the wilderness beyond the Appalachian Mountains and brought back stories of the wondrous land that was there, the Indians knew it as a place almost mystically beautiful. The region between the Ohio and Tennessee rivers inspired a feeling of reverence, a belief that it was almost too good for man to inhabit. There is still splendid countryside in Kentucky, Tennessee, and West Virginia, as anyone who has been there knows, but it can hardly compare with the sight which greeted the first frontiersmen.

Sparkling clear rivers, teeming with fish, flowed through valleys surrounded by the boundless primeval forest. Buffalo and elk crisscrossed the land in vast numbers, trampling the earth into traces which formed roads for the Indians, and which, to this day, are followed by modern highways. Birds so numerous that they darkened the sun filled the forest's enormous roof, and vale and hillside were covered with an unimaginable profusion of wild flowers. Wherever the forest was broken, the ground was covered with a green, jointed cane which grew to a height of twelve feet; and in the woods there were sycamores, oaks, chestnuts, and tulip poplars from six to ten feet in diameter.

Strangely enough, this marvelous land was almost completely uninhabited when the first frontiersmen arrived. Until the Revolution there was almost continuous warfare between the Iroquois Indians of the north and the southern tribes, and no group from either faction could survive in the no man's land of Kentucky or Tennessee, which was known as the Middle Ground or the Dark and Bloody Ground. Hunters and war parties moved about in the region, especially on the famous Warriors' Path which ran from the Cherokee settlements south of Knoxville up through the Cumberland Gap, north across the Ohio River where it is joined by the Scioto, and from there through Shawnee country to Lake Erie, near the present city of Sandusky. As long as fifty years before the first white hunters moved in, a few intrepid traders had pushed into the deep woods in search of Indian commerce. But essentially, the long hunters—so called because of their two- and three-year absences—were the first whites to learn much about the mountains of Kentucky and Tennessee.

Their stories were something to kindle the imagination, and a young teamster on Braddock's ill-fated expedition of 1755 never forgot wilderness scout John Finley's description of the wonders of "Kentucke." That young man was Daniel Boone, whose life began in 1734 near Reading, Pennsylvania. In 1750 his family moved down into the Shenandoah Valley, then on to the Yadkin in North Carolina, whence Boone pushed off on his many exploration trips.

Daniel Boone did not discover the Cumberland Gap —his old friend John Finley showed him the pass through which thousands of settlers would cross the mountains—but more than any other man, it was Boone who led the way along the Wilderness Road. Like the name Cumberland Gap, the words Wilderness Road make it sound rather easy. Both were misnomers, and the Wilderness Road was at best a pack trail which climbed countless ridges, ran through almost impenetrable valleys, across rushing streams— and it was twenty years before it could be negotiated by anything on wheels. Yet in this period a human tidal wave of 100,000 restless, courageous people took themselves and their possessions on foot and on horseback over the mountains to Kentucky.

Like so many early trails, this one had been broken

by enormous herds of buffalo, traveling their ancestral routes from north to south each year. A long section of the Wilderness Road followed the "buffalo trace," which slanted across four modern states. Keeping away from lowlands or marshes where their vast weight would cause them to sink as the mastodons had in the Kentucky salt licks centuries earlier, the buffalo had discovered Cumberland Gap, at the point where Kentucky, Tennessee, and Virginia come together. After the hard climb up over the rocks, they paused to pant and blow at the top before thundering down the slopes into Kentucky. From Cumberland Gap their track went northwest, crossing the Ohio between New Albany and Louisville, slanting across Indiana and crossing the Wabash at Vincennes—the ancient route followed almost exactly by Abraham Lincoln's family. From here the trace went straight over Illinois flatlands through the waving turkey-foot grass of the wet prairies to the Mississippi River near St. Louis.

Boone had made two scouting expeditions for Colonel Richard Henderson, on the second of which Boone's son was tortured and killed by Indians. Then, in 1775, Colonel Henderson hired him to cut a path to Kentucky for the new Transylvania Company—a road which can be followed today with considerably more ease. Setting out from Long Island (now Kingsport, Tennessee), Boone and thirty men traveled north to Moccasin Gap, Virginia, then on to Natural Tunnel, where they turned left to "an important stopping place"—the site of the Duffield schoolhouse. Here they headed west along the route known today as 25 E to the Cumberland Gap. From the Gap, moving west and north along the buffalo trace to Rockcastle River and up Roundstone Creek, the men cut and fought their way through unexplored territory up to Big Hill, where they caught their first vista of the Kentucky plains. This was the end of the mountain wilderness, and they moved into gently rolling forest three miles

south of modern Richmond—fifteen miles from the place on the Kentucky River where Boone planned to build the first fort. In the night the Indians came, killing two of Boone's party, and the survivors had to wait twelve days before moving on to the place which became Boonesborough. Nothing but a monument marks the site of the fort at Boonesborough, but at Harrodsburg a fine reconstruction of another settlement Boone helped lay out shows clearly what these frontier communities were like.

There was another important segment of the thoroughfare which became known in its entirety as the Wilderness Road. Blazed by Ben Logan, this trail branched off from Boone's at an intersection in the thick brush known as Hazel Patch, eight miles north of today's London, Kentucky, and continued along the buffalo route (U.S. 150 today) from Mt. Vernon to the Falls of the Ohio (Louisville).

A man living in Philadelphia at the close of the eighteenth century had two choices of routes to the West. One, of course, led down into Virginia, and over the Wilderness Road. The other meant buying horses and a wagon to pack his family and belongings nearly 300 miles over the Pennsylvania mountains to the Monongahela, then building or buying a flat-bottomed boat for the equally hazardous trip down the Ohio. Whether he drifted downstream in a wallowing flatboat or walked across the mountains, the settler was spared almost no form of insecurity—Indian attacks; malaria, smallpox, or the strange milk sickness; the back-breaking toil of clearing the virgin wilderness; and the terrible loneliness.

Although the battle of Yorktown is generally considered the end of the Revolution, the fighting went on west of the mountains for thirteen more years, during which more Americans were killed than in all the major Revolutionary battles combined. The men and women and children who fought (and all of them did)

Westbound wagons gather at a Maryland inn. The Great Smokies wilderness, even today, retains a feeling of the primeval forest seen by the first white men to venture beyond the Appalachians.

On Blennerhassett Island in the Ohio River are the overgrown ruins of
the mansion where Aaron Burr laid his plans for a southwestern empire.

were utterly on their own, without support from the states they left behind or the country then in the making. Interminably besieged by French, English, Spanish, and the omnipresent Indians, they also had to govern themselves, work out their own laws, and survive. Not only did they manage to do so, but became, in the process, a new breed of American—as tough and durable a people as any the world has seen.

Everywhere in the new West, leaders sprang up—men of brilliance, ambition, eloquence—good men and bad. There was James Wilkinson, a scheming, influential man; John Sevier, "Nolichucky Jack," that ideal of frontiersmen who never fought an unsuccessful campaign; James Robertson, the courageous builder of the Cumberland settlement; George Rogers Clark, the outstanding hero of them all, who was

almost single-handedly responsible for the frontier's survival during the Revolution and who, aside from George Washington, probably contributed more to his nation's future than any Revolutionary soldier.

That there are no more early architectural survivals in this mountain frontier is explained by the fact that the buildings themselves were usually log cabins, subject to attack and the ravages of time. The most rewarding places to see date from a later period, like Henry Clay's Ashland, at Lexington, Kentucky, in the lush, rolling bluegrass country. Here, today, mile after mile of trim white fences line the borders of estates whose sole purpose is to produce the finest race horses in the world. And there is Belle Meade, the lovely old mansion in Nashville alongside the Natchez Trace, where the breeding of thoroughbred horses in the U.S.

120

began. But the construction of Belle Meade and the great bluegrass plantation homes did not begin until the families coming over the Wilderness Road found themselves with security and leisure time.

One way to glimpse America's first West is to see that great overland entry—the Wilderness Road, which runs for almost 700 miles across the Appalachian barrier, much of it along modern highways. There is Cumberland Gap, where Henry Clay is supposed to have stood, listening, as he said, "to the tread of the coming millions." About two miles south of Parkersburg, West Virginia, is the 507-acre Blennerhassett Island, where several ruined houses and some building stones hidden in the overgrowth of willow trees are all that remain of Harman Blennerhassett's magnificent estate. This was where Aaron Burr came after his duel with Alexander Hamilton, to plot with Blennerhassett an empire in the Southwest.

In Kentucky, near the town of Crab Orchard, a station on the Wilderness Road, is Walnut Flat, and the first brick house in Kentucky. It was built about 1783 by Colonel William Whitley, a steel-eyed, long-nosed Irishman who was one of the most fearless Indian fighters. At a time when the countryside swarmed with savages Whitley calmly decided to erect the finest house in the state—and the tall, two-and-a-half-story structure with his own initials set over the front door (his wife's are in the rear) is remarkably elegant inside. In addition to a ballroom there is a secret place where women and children could hide in the event of attack, a handsome paneled mantel, and a hall stairway on which an eagle's head with olive branch is carved on each step. In all his years as an Indian fighter Whitley was never taken prisoner or wounded (except when the tip of his nose was clipped off by a bullet). Then, at the age of 64, he enlisted as a private in the War of 1812, and fell in a furious battle with the great Shawnee chief, Tecumseh.

Throughout this area are other reminders of its most famous frontiersman, Daniel Boone. Near Elizabethton, Tennessee, is Sycamore Shoals Monument, a three-sided shaft of river rocks which marks the site where Boone negotiated a treaty with the Cherokees in 1775. Boone Creek and Boone Hill, near Jenkins, Kentucky, are traditional haunts of the explorer. At the present Blue Licks Battlefield State Park Boone was making salt in February, 1778, when he was captured by Indians. Taken to Et-Nah Woods near Chillicothe, Ohio, he was held captive and adopted by the Shawnees, but escaped to travel 160 miles to warn Boonesborough of an impending attack. A few years later, on August 19, 1782, "the last battle of the Revolution" was fought, at the Blue Licks, and peace finally came to this first American West.

Henry Clay's bedroom at his home, Ashland

James Polk's family home, Columbia, Tennessee

These log cabins are part of the reconstructed fort at Harrodsburg, the first permanent settlement in Kentucky.

Jackson's Hermitage

Once the way had been shown them by Daniel Boone and other frontiersmen, the unending stream of settlers poured into the new West—a great migration of poor, adventurous men, restless and land-hungry, cutting into the forest like a horde of beavers. Long before the frontier was settled these men, confronted by obstacles the like of which had seldom been faced, made a decision which was to affect for all time the future of America's opening frontier. Just over a month after shots were exchanged at Lexington and Concord, seventeen settlers gathered under a huge elm at Boonesborough and announced their right to govern themselves as they saw fit. Before them, English, French, and Spanish had moved into virgin territory, founding settlements; but never before had one of these colonies announced so boldly its independence or demonstrated so vociferously the belief that no man was superior to any other.

To the West, in particular, and slowly to the rest of the burgeoning nation, came the realization that one man—Andrew Jackson—somehow personified this new spirit, this new set of values. Born in 1767 in the Waxhaw settlements claimed by both North and South Carolina, he fought in the Revolutionary battle of Hanging Rock at the age of thirteen, and was slashed with a saber for refusing to clean a British officer's boots. During the War of 1812 he fought the Creek Indians, and in 1815, after the peace treaty had been signed, he won the greatest American victory of the war at New Orleans. Known as Old Hickory, he was swept into the presidency in 1828 as "the favorite of the people," the "last of the Revolutionary patriots," who had "slain the Indians and flogged the British."

Andrew Jackson grew up in the Carolinas, and after he became famous an old resident remembered him as "the most roaring, rollicking, game-cocking, card-playing fellow that ever lived in Salisbury"; but in Tennessee the long, thin shadow of the man is more tangible, even at this date. In Jonesboro, the state's oldest town, there is a gaunt, two-story log house sheathed in clapboards where Jackson boarded when he was first practicing law. Just outside of Kingsport

This portrait of Old Hickory shows the tall, lean frame which concealed energy, courage, and a fiery temper.

is the site of one of the hot-tempered General's many duels. And Greasy Cove Race Track, near Erwin, and Clover Bottom, where the highway crosses Stone's River outside Nashville, were two places where Jackson raced his horses.

And there is the Hermitage. This lovely old mansion is one of the few important historic houses furnished completely with original pieces, and because it is so little changed it reflects clearly the personality and times of Andrew Jackson and his family. In 1804, when Jackson bought the property, a cluster of log cabins stood on the grounds, and here Andrew and Rachel Jackson lived and entertained for fifteen years. By 1819 the Jacksons had outgrown the log-house style of living, and thanks to three good years of cotton prices, he was able to begin work on their new home. Jackson had just returned from the Seminole wars, so ill that he did not believe he could live long, but he showed a friend the site where he had determined to build—a level spot in a large flat field. When the

friend suggested another, higher location, Jackson replied: "No, Mrs. Jackson chose this spot, and she shall have her wish. I am going to build this house for *her*. I don't expect to live in it myself." But live in it he did, until his death in 1845—some seventeen years after Rachel Jackson had died.

In the beautiful garden are the tombs of Old Hickory and his wife, the smokehouse, carriage house, and a cabin which belonged to Alfred, Jackson's manservant. The Hermitage is the home of a man who grew beyond his frontier beginnings, yet never forgot their strength. One of the former President's neighbors told James Parton, the biographer, what kind of house this was: "Put down in your book," he said, "that the General was the prince of hospitality; not only because he entertained a great many people but because the poor, belated peddler was as welcome at the Hermitage as the President of the United States and made so much at his ease that he felt as though he had got home."

TENNESSEE CONSERVATION DEPARTMENT

Cotton profits made it possible for Jackson to build the Hermitage in 1819, replacing the log house in which he had lived previously. Although the Hermitage burned in 1834, it was rebuilt in his lifetime.

DAVID E. SCHERMAN, REPRINTED FROM *Holiday*

A Confederate cannon on Lookout Mountain, overlooking Chattanooga, surveys the Moccasin Bend of the Tennessee River. In 1863 Hooker's men struggled up the steep mountain to rout the Southerners in a spectacular "battle above the clouds."

The Battles for the West

When the lines of Federal troops crossed the Ohio River in 1861 and headed south, the slow strangulation of the Confederacy had begun. Somehow, whatever glamour the war possessed remained in the east, focusing on the Army of the Potomac and Robert E. Lee's Army of Northern Virginia; but the struggle which took place on the far side of the Allegheny Mountains was no less terrible or fierce; and because of what happened there, William Tecumseh Sherman and his tough westerners were finally able to sweep vengefully across the southern heartland, cutting it in two.

The long roll call of Civil War battles fought in

Tennessee—upwards of 300 engagements—began with Ulysses S. Grant's capture of Fort Henry on the Tennessee River and Fort Donelson on the Cumberland, and then exploded in the bloody struggle at Shiloh. This was a battle no one quite expected to happen here, a battle fought by 80,000 young men who hardly knew how to fire their guns, which ended only after nearly one-fourth of them had been shot. Today Shiloh is a national military park—acres of sleepy wooded hills and little fields, tied together with roads which take the visitor to all the important landmarks of the desperate engagement which neither side quite won. The little road from Pittsburg Landing leads past the cemetery and on to a church which stands on the site of the original frame building which gave Shiloh its name. Not far from the famous Peach Orchard is the Hornet's Nest, where several thousand backwoodsmen held out just long enough to save the entire Federal Army. In the park is a battle-scarred log cabin which stood in the midst of heavy fighting; and Bloody Pond, a shallow pool where wounded from both sides crawled to quench their thirst.

There are dozens of other battlefields to see in Tennessee—Murfreesboro, Franklin and Nashville—and Chickamauga, in Georgia, that tangled mountain wilderness south of Chattanooga where the Union armies took a fearful beating and "the pale river of death ran blood"; but none are more spectacularly visible or more interesting than Chattanooga.

The disorganized, demoralized Yankees who piled back into the town after the rout at Chickamauga in September, 1863, were in a box. To the east lay enemy territory, to the north were impassable mountains, to the south along Missionary Ridge was Bragg's Confederate army, and to the west the only road to safety was controlled by Rebels stationed on top of the great mass of Lookout Mountain. Today, standing alongside the Civil War cannon on this eminence, the visitor surveys the panorama that lay at the feet of the Confederates late in November, 1863. Everything about this fight was visible, and to the Southerners in their impregnable position, it must have seemed utterly impossible that Grant and the Union armies could fight their way out of the beleaguered town. Yet that is exactly what happened.

Off to the northeast, at the upper end of Missionary Ridge, Sherman hit the Confederate right, while Hooker surprisingly dislodged the Rebels above the clouds wreathing Lookout Mountain. But there things bogged down, and the Army of the Cumberland—the same men who were smoldering from the defeat at

From this point 20,000 fresh Union troops crossed the Tennessee River to support Grant's hard-pressed troops at Shiloh.

Chickamauga—were ordered to make a feint at the Confederate center on Missionary Ridge to ease things for the flanking movements. Thoroughly rankled by the implication that they were not good enough to carry one of the main attacks, these men, who had a score to settle with the Rebels, marched forward in a battle line two miles wide, flags fluttering in the wind, toward the great mountain wall held by the Confederates. They seized the first line of Southern trenches, looked up at the crest of the mountain, 500 feet above them, and, to the utter astonishment of the onlooking generals, began climbing. To the Confederates it must have seemed that men who would dare so much would stop at nothing, and as the irresistible line swept up toward them the Southern defense simply withered away. When the Army of the Cumberland reached the summit and saw the Rebels tumbling down the other side, incredible victory was in their hands, and from this moment on the Confederate cause itself would be all downhill, moving inexorably toward the little village of Appomattox Court House in southern Virginia.

JERRY COOKE, *Time*

Back-Country Folk

In the 1880's a well-armed group of Hatfields posed for a picture with the family patriarch, "Devil Anse," seated at center.

At Thacker Creek "Devil Anse" and five Hatfields were ambushed by 42 McCoys. They shot 17 of them, then escaped.

Before he died of natural causes at the age of 83, "Devil Anse" ordered this marble statue of himself carved in Italy.

Tucked away in isolated backwashes of the Appalachian Mountains are a few people whose origins go back to the first pioneers and frontiersmen to settle this region. In the mountain fastnesses are pure Anglo-Saxons who cling to phrases out of Chaucer and Elizabethan England, whose ancient ballads date from Tudor times. Inevitably, civilization has encroached on the manners and mores of these mountain folk; sons who have been off to the wars have returned dissatisfied with the old ways; but there remain, here and there, touches of Elizabethan speech, curious superstitions, and many of the old carols and ballads. It is a simple, primitive life, set against the backdrop of age-old blue mountains and quiet valleys, in little clearings carved out of virgin forest two centuries ago.

One of the best approximations of frontier conditions in America is preserved in the Great Smoky Mountains National Park, where many log cabins remain in surroundings of magnificent natural beauty. The log huts, barns, and implements at Cades Cove, an isolated, oval valley rimmed with mountains, and at the Pioneer Museum near Cherokee, North Carolina, are authentic remains of America's first West.

It is not so many years since these same mountain families were engaged in feuds which have become part of the nation's folklore. The Kentucky-West Virginia border carries the dark scars of the Hatfield-McCoy feud, a battle which began in the bitter strife of the Civil War and continued unabated for more than thirty years. Hatfields still farm the West Virginia side of the Big Sandy River as they did when "Devil Anse" Hatfield, a Confederate, killed Harmon McCoy, a Union soldier, in battle. The McCoys were landowners on the Kentucky bank of the Big Sandy, and when Devil Anse returned from the war, he quarreled with Randall McCoy over a stolen pig. When Anse's boy decided to marry Randall's daughter, Anse refused permission, and the young couple decided to live together anyway. From then on it was open war, erupting in cold-blooded murders, savage raids, and ambushes. Along the banks of Tug Fork, three McCoy boys were tied to the bushes and killed to avenge the knifing of Ellison Hatfield; and up Grapevine Creek is the spot where Lark McCoy and his cronies ambushed forty Hatfields, killing fourteen of them. A flat wooden bridge has replaced the protective drawbridge over Island Creek to Devil Anse's home, and the Hatfields and McCoys no longer live in dread of each other, but people still remember "the trouble" which hatred and fear brought to the mountains.

ELIOT ELISOFON, *Life*

W. EUGENE SMITH, *Life*

Like most mountaineers, the family who live in the rough board shanty above are devout, God-fearing people. Below, young girls stand waist-deep in water while a companion gets a baptismal ducking in a group immersion. Such ceremonies are usually followed by music and dancing. At left, an old man displays his battered banjo; below, another mountaineer plays on the jawbone of an ass.

BRADLEY SMITH

JOE CLARK

The Old South

The Mysteries of the Mounds

In discussing American history it is fairly common practice to begin with a fleeting reference to hardy Norse adventurers, recount the voyage of Christopher Columbus, mention some of the more remarkable Spanish explorations, and then settle down to business with the colonies at Jamestown and Plymouth. What is often forgotten is the fact that America has a fascinating prehistoric story of its own.

Humans had been in the New World for as much as 25,000 years before the white men came, and it is hard to realize that these people, and the enormous reach of land from sea to sea, enjoyed thousands of years of complete isolation; yet except for the handful of Norsemen who touched the coast of North America a few centuries before Columbus, there was no contact whatever. Within the great continent, no Indian tribe had any real knowledge of the land or its neighbors beyond a range of several hundred miles. Although there was a network of trails all over the country, long voyages of any sort had to be made by lake or river. There is nothing to indicate that Indian society discovered or made use of the wheel, and the only beast of burden (aside from the squaw) was the dog. Yet anyone who thinks of these natives simply as barbaric

A Master Farmer artisan fashioned this white-faced effigy in clay almost a thousand years ago. Such objects, often left with the dead in mound graves, had a religious significance.

savages must reckon, among other things, with their elaborate social structures, some of the finest modeling and carving ever to exist in North America, and genuine cultures which were well on their way toward true civilizations when the first white man appeared on the scene.

Down in central Georgia, on the bluffs overlooking the muddy, wandering Ocmulgee River, are the remains of a nomadic people who were here when giant ground sloths, three-toed horses, camels, and mammoths still roamed the continent. Of the six successive civilizations unearthed at Ocmulgee, the earliest may date back to 8000 B.C.; the most recent one came to an end fifteen years before George Washington was born.

Probably the first Indians to live at Ocmulgee were the almost unknown creatures of the Stone Age who are called Wandering Hunters because of their social pattern. These were descendants of men who crossed Bering Strait to America from Asia as the last of the great ice sheets retreated, and moved across the continent killing game with their distinctive grooved

JOHN E. THIERMAN

Boulders at Trackrock Gap, near Blairsville, Georgia, are etched with prehistoric symbols and animal-track carvings.

130

spears. It is estimated that these Indians lived in Georgia for as long as 5,000 years. After them came the Shellfish Eaters, attracted to the region by the mussel beds in the rivers and by the deer and bear. Remains of their pottery—made of clay mixed with moss fibers or grass—have been found at Ocmulgee, along with spear points and net sinkers. After they left the region—around 100 B.C.—the Early Farmers moved in, to stay for something like 900 years. Like their predecessors these Indians subsisted largely on game, but they also raised a few crops, probably beans and pumpkins, and found enough leisure time to make beautiful pottery which they decorated with elaborate designs. Then, in this inexorable procession of civilizations, the Early Farmers were pushed out by the invasion of the Master Farmers. These were highly skilled fellows; in addition to growing beans and pumpkins they raised corn and tobacco, and devoted their extra energies to the construction of temples, placed on large mounds of earth, and of circular earth lodges used for religious ceremonies and tribal government councils. A corn field once used by them has been perfectly preserved by a thick layer of red clay; and there are oval pits, surrounding a prehistoric village, which probably served as fortifications.

The Funeral Mound at Ocmulgee—a conical structure thirty feet high and over 250 feet long—was once a combined temple and burial place, formed of five different kinds of clay, each marking the summit of an earlier mound. From the ornaments, tools, clay pipes, and bowls of food found here, we know that the Master Farmers believed in an afterlife. And here, as in so many other mounds and stone graves found in the southeast and through the Mississippi Valley, one can see the striking similarity between their flat-topped mounds of earth, crowned with a wood and thatch temple, and the stone temple-topped pyramids of Central America.

The largest monument at Ocmulgee is the Great Temple Mound, also built by the Master Farmers, which was originally 40 feet high and 300 feet across at the base. It is pyramidal in shape, and was made sometime between A.D. 1350 and 1500 by the laborious process of carrying dirt and clay to the scene in baskets. At least four times during construction the project was "completed," a caplike layer of clay was laid on, and a ceremonial structure built on top. Then someone with a grander dream came along, and work began again.

Eventually, like all the others, the Master Farmers were driven out—this time by their old enemies the Early Farmers, who returned, acquiring from archaeologists the name Reconquerors. The Indians of this fifth civilization—ancestors of the Creeks and Cherokees—lived in small villages in the swamps, protected from attack by palisades of upright logs. They went on making pottery, they continued to build mounds. Then around 1690 white men built a trading post nearby, and the civilization of the Mound Builders, like that of so many other Indians in America, was about to be destroyed once and for all. Creek society, for example, degenerated sharply at this time. Once a group of independent farmers, they became hunters to reap the quick rewards of bartering deerskins for the copper bells, knives, guns, and rum so thoughtfully supplied by the traders. It was inevitable that they would finally take a stand against the white invaders, and this they did in 1715, when Emperor Brim of the Creeks decided to drive the English out of Carolina and then polish off the Spanish and the French. His "Yamassee War" lasted until 1717 when he was defeated; then the Creek nation moved west, and the mounds of Ocmulgee were deserted. Deserted, that is, by the living—but populated with silent remains which could tell in their own way the story of a people who had miraculously crossed and established their homes on this continent thousands of years before a European knew of its existence.

Temple mounds like this one at Ocmulgee not only served as burying places but were also civic and religious centers.

Spanish Florida

It was a time of fantastic dreams, of adventure and the lust for riches. Within a century the waters of the Atlantic, once peopled with demons and monsters and ending in an abyss, became a traveled highway over which Spanish treasure galleons hauled the plunder of a virgin continent intended to make the King of Spain master of all Europe. Columbus had shown the way, and the Castilians, toughened by eight centuries of struggle with the Moors, saw a golden vision that called for courage whose like the world had seldom seen. Off into the unknown they went, and there has never been a conquest like it. In one generation Spain acquired more territory than Rome overran in 500 years, and by the time Philip II ascended the thrones of Portugal and Spain in 1580, nearly ninety years after Columbus' first voyage, no other nation had yet planted a single permanent settlement in the New World.

The first Spanish colonies were nothing but headquarters for a gold hunt, and because no treasure was found on the seaboard of America no one settled there until 1565. Tales of a magic spring which brought eternal youth to the aged took Ponce de Leon to the balmy "island" of Florida in 1513, and although he failed to find the fountain he discovered the Bahama Channel which became the route of the treasure galleons. In 1521 he returned to colonize Florida but was attacked by Indians on the day he landed and received a fatal wound. Next to try was the red-bearded, one-eyed Pánfilo de Narváez, victim of one of the most harrowing expeditions on record. Narváez landed in 1528 at St. Clement's Point just north of Tampa Bay, and when he found a little gold ornament in a deserted Indian hut, set off at once on a frantic search for treasure. For three months Narváez and 300 men, weighted down with armor, staggered through the swampy, miasmic jungles, beset by Indians, reptiles, and insects, weakened by hunger and the terrible heat. Finally they ate their horses, managed somehow to put together five crude boats, and set sail—for where, no one quite knew. Two of the craft were captured and the men killed by Indians, Narváez was lost in a storm, but two other boats reached Texas. Unbelievably, Cabeza de Vaca and three companions kept alive for six years, to be found by a Spanish patrol in the deserts north of the Rio Grande.

In 1539 the iron-willed Hernando de Soto came through Florida on one leg of another frightful jour-ney. Starting with 620 knights and soldiers in armor, 223 horses, and hundreds of hogs on the hoof, he fought his way through the wilderness of Florida, Georgia, up into the Carolinas, Tennessee, Alabama, and after two years, to the bank of the Mississippi River.

In 1564 a group of French Protestants fleeing from persecution at home built Fort Caroline at the mouth of the St. John's River, near present Jacksonville. As the first European settlement north of Mexico, this was a real threat to Spain, and Don Pedro Menéndez de Avilés was sent to destroy the French. Arriving on St. Augustine's Day in 1565, he wiped out Fort Caroline by land attack and the French fleet in a naval battle, then sailed down the coast to establish a base at the Indian village of Seloy. There he fortified a barnlike Indian house, and this was the forerunner of the Castillo de San Marcos, seat of Spanish power in Florida.

San Augustín was formally established on September 8, 1565—the oldest permanent white settlement in the United States. The peninsular site selected by Don Pedro as a strategic point for defense was capital of a territory stretching north to Labrador and west to the Mississippi; but for years no one seemed to realize the importance of Spanish North America, and the tiny settlement of three or four hundred people struggled along with little attention from anyone. In 1586 Sir Francis Drake deemed it worthy of consideration and sacked and burned the town; but there was little further activity until 1672, when English settlement of Charles Town (South Carolina) goaded the Spanish into action. On the site of St. Augustine's old wooden fort they started building the castle that would protect Florida, and for the next 84 years Spaniards, slaves, and Indian laborers worked unceasingly on the great fortification. When, in 1702, Governor James Moore of South Carolina appeared with an army and occupied the town, the Spanish population simply moved into the castle and raised the drawbridge: the English cannon were useless against the thick coquina walls. After Moore's forces were repulsed, the Spaniards decided to build walls around their town, too, and these withstood attacks by Colonel William Palmer in 1728, James Oglethorpe in 1740, and others. Finally, with Spain's decline as a world power, Florida became part of the United States in 1821.

Along the narrow streets of St. Augustine there are still many reminders of its centuries under the Spanish flag—a thick-walled house which is probably the oldest in the country, an old Spanish inn, the Spanish treasury, and numerous others. But none of them can quite equal Castillo de San Marcos, symbol of all that Spain once held, and lost, in the New World.

These three buildings in St. Augustine are reminders of two centuries of Spanish rule in Florida. The vine-covered clapboard building above is a schoolhouse built in 1778. At right, the St. Augustine Cathedral, built in 1793-97, is the only church in Florida surviving from the Spanish period. Below, the coquina walls of Castillo de San Marcos overlook Matanzas Bay. Spaniards, slaves, and Indians worked for 84 years constructing the fort, which cost thirty million dollars. The King of Spain was prompted to remark that its "bastions must be made of solid silver," but it served the Spaniards well, withstanding a number of English assaults.

The Lost Colony

The Englishmen who landed at Roanoke in 1584 found fertile land and friendly natives.

The mystery of the settlement known as the Lost Colony is somehow heightened by the wonderful place names which mark that windswept coast of North Carolina. Starting south from the edge of the great Dismal Swamp and moving toward the "graveyard of the Atlantic," past the whistling swans of Currituck Sound, the visitor sees Kitty Hawk, Kill Devil Hill, Nags Head, Manteo, then Roanoke Island; and beyond lie Cape Hatteras, the treacherous Diamond Shoals, and Ocracoke. The beaches that shimmer with laughter and sunlight and dancing waves are accursed to the sailor with his long memory for tragedy: "If Tortugas let you pass, You beware of Hatteras." Here in the shifting sands are the skeletons of countless ships blown ashore in the wild fury of a howling gale; the hiding place of Blackbeard and other rascals who preyed on Atlantic shipping; and the spot where nearly 150 colonists—including the first English child born in the New World—disappeared, never to be seen again.

In 1578 Sir Humphrey Gilbert, a man with a little pointed beard and soulful eyes who wanted very badly to found an English empire in America, was granted a charter by Queen Elizabeth allowing him to discover and colonize "remote heathen and barbarous lands" not already owned by a Christian prince. After landing in Newfoundland, which he claimed for the Queen, Sir Humphrey sailed south, encountered "many stormes and perils," and on the way back to England was drowned.

His young half brother, Sir Walter Raleigh, a very good friend of the Virgin Queen, thus fell heir to Sir Humphrey's rights, and in 1584 dispatched two ships to explore the North American coast. On July 13 of that year the party landed in North Carolina, somewhere near Roanoke Island, and went into ecstasies over "the goodliest land under the cope of heaven." Captain Barlowe, one of the leaders, thought "in all the world the like abundance is not to be found," and described in detail the "most pleasant and fertile ground, replenished with goodly Cedars, and divers other sweete woods, full of Corrants, flaxe, and many other notable commodities." He also mentioned the "gentle, loving, and faithfull" Indians they had encountered.

On the heels of this expedition another, composed of 108 persons and including geographer Thomas Hariot and the artist John White, went to Roanoke to settle; but within a year's time they had antagonized the loving and faithful Indians to a point where it seemed prudent to accept a ride home offered them by Sir Francis Drake, who was passing by. Soon after their departure in June, 1586, Sir Richard Grenville, cousin to Sir Walter, arrived to find the settlement deserted; and being "unwilling to loose the possession of the country," he left fifteen men on Roanoke Island with provisions for two years.

The following summer some 150 "planters" sent out by Raleigh arrived at Roanoke, but the only trace of the fifteen men was one skeleton. Master Ralfe Lane's fort (a palisaded structure since reconstructed) had been razed, although the "sundry necessary and decent dwelling houses" around it were still standing. For some reason, despite orders to press on to Chesapeake Bay, the settlers stayed on Roanoke Island, and here on August 18 Governor John White's daughter Eleanor Dare gave birth to a child whom she named Virginia.

When trouble with the Indians flared up, Governor White decided to teach the natives a lesson by a sneak attack on the town of Dasamonquepeuc. The raid could not have been more unfortunate, for the hostile Roanoke Indians, sensing what was in the wind, had decamped, and the only people there were peace-loving Croatoans who were outraged at being subjected to fire and sword. With considerable difficulty the situation was patched up—at least the Croatoans pretended to forgive the white men—and in August Governor White sailed for England and provisions.

He had no end of trouble getting away from home, for 1588 was the year of the Spanish Armada, and there were no ships to be had. Not until August, 1590, did White return to Roanoke, and when he arrived it was to find the settlers vanished completely. Searching the island in sorrow, he did discover one clue—the word

A Roanoke colonist, John White, painted these watercolors, two of the earliest pictures of Indians by a European. The breechclouted native shown here was a Virginia chieftain. Below, White's sketch of the town of Secoton reveals a sedentary agrarian life unlike the popular stereotype of the nomadic, tepee-dwelling hunters of the Plains. Cornfields are seen, and in the foreground a ceremonial dance is in progress. The large hut at lower left was a tomb where bodies of kings were kept.

CROATOAN carved on a post of the fort. White had arranged for the settlers to use a distress sign or a Maltese cross if they were forced to leave, but there was no trace of such a mark. White decided to go to Croatoan Island (now called Ocracoke) to look for his family and the other colonists, but bad weather blew his ship south and he finally had to return to England. Lacking personal funds to finance another expedition, and unable to raise money elsewhere, White finally gave up, but his last recorded words were: "I would to God my wealth were answerable to my will." Sir Walter Raleigh also kept hoping to find some trace of the colonists, and in 1602 he sent out a search expedition. But nothing was discovered.

For generations men have sought to solve the mystery of Roanoke Island, but nothing further has ever been learned of the Lost Colony. It is likely that they were all killed by Indians, although some believe they mingled with the natives and that the so-called Croatoans of present-day Robeson County are their descendants. Others maintain that the Spaniards in Florida destroyed the colony, and there is evidence that Spanish officials in St. Augustine were planning just that. And finally, there is a possibility that the colonists, despairing of relief, sailed for England in a boat left them by White, and were lost at sea. Whatever the answer, men will always ponder what lay behind that one word, CROATOAN—all that remained of England's first real effort to establish a foothold in America.

Jamestown

Today Jamestown, Virginia, is a flat, wooded island nearly three miles long, separated from the mainland by a marshy inlet. There were many things about this place no one could have foreseen, 350 years ago, including the fact that it would one day be an island; but the men who landed there in May, 1607, thought it a fine anchorage, a place not overrun by Indians, and out of range of the Spanish—and decided to stay, making it the first permanent English settlement in America. Yet were it not for the mute evidence of ivy-covered church ruins, an ancient graveyard, and resto-rations of some of the first buildings, one might doubt its survival.

The first of many mistakes these colonists made was the site itself, surrounded by mosquito-infested swamps, with an unreliable water supply and unhealthy climate. Inside a triangular fort they built a church, storehouses, and some flimsy living quarters, and here trouble broke out almost immediately. There was mutiny, malaria, and the menace of Indians whom the colonists had treated unwisely. Then a real leader, Captain John Smith, turned up in their midst. Smith learned to speak Algonkian, bargained with the Indians for corn, and began to create organization out of chaos. Late in 1607, while out exploring, he was captured by Powhatan and saved, according to his story, by Pocahontas. When he returned to the colony the settlers were starving. A fire in January, 1608, destroyed nearly all their buildings, but Smith managed to get the colony through the winter. He begged the London sponsors to send carpenters, masons, and "diggers up of trees," but in September more gentlemen-settlers arrived. Miraculously, they survived yet another winter; then in August came 400 new, inexperienced settlers, with damaged supplies, fever, and plague. That autumn Smith was injured and sent back to England—probably because others coveted his position. His departure was followed by the "Starving Time," the terrible winter of 1609–10 which only sixty of the 500 colonists survived.

Lord Delaware had been appointed governor of the colony, and his advance agent was so appalled by what he saw at Jamestown that he decided to abandon the settlement. But Delaware determined to salvage the effort. Under his able rule Jamestown finally became a going concern, and the community began to spill out into the lovely James River Valley. Then in 1698 Jamestown burned, and it was decided to move the capital to Middle Plantation, or Williamsburg.

ELIOT ELISOFON, Life

Near the site of the first fort, an ivy-draped church tower is the last standing ruin of seventeenth-century Jamestown. Excavators have found delft tiles (top) which colonists used to adorn their homes. At right, John Smith's statue surveys the James River from the location of the first landing.

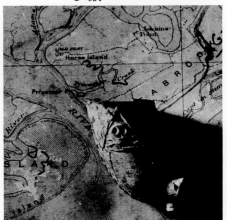

Pirate's pipe bowl, found at Charleston.

Skull and Crossbones Off the Carolinas

If there is any one place to seek out the haunts of pirates, it is that shoreline extending roughly 75 miles in either direction from Charleston, South Carolina, known as the Debatable Coast. So named because Spain, France, and England all claimed it, this picturesque mosaic of islands, inlets, marshes, and harbors once served as the ideal hiding place for seagoing cutthroats, murderers, and thieves.

It is not difficult to draw a parallel between pirates of the seventeenth century and racketeers of the twentieth. Both had a predatory outlook toward other people's property and a cheerful willingness to eliminate anyone who got in the way. Both enjoyed the protection of merchants and certain civic officials. Like latter-day rackets, piracy had its economic formula. The buccaneers disposed of their loot to favored merchants at bargain rates, far lower than those paid for goods legitimately landed. The merchants, in turn, put political and financial pressure on royal governors and their minions to look the other way.

The years 1550 to 1700 and 1714 to 1725 were the golden ages of international piracy, and as early as 1685 these outlaws swaggered through Charles Town, as it was then called. There were men like the satanic Edward Low, who once cut off and cooked a captured Rhode Islander's ears and forced his victim to eat them. There was "Gentleman Pirate" Stede Bonnet, a wealthy Barbados landowner who reputedly turned pirate to escape a nagging wife. One of the few known to have made captives walk the plank, he was captured in 1718 and hanged in Charles Town.

But the most fearsome scoundrel of all was the man who was born Edward Teach, or Thatch, in Bristol, England, and was known up and down the coast as Blackbeard. A contemporary explains that his sobriquet came "from that large quantity of hair, which, like a frightful meteor, covered his whole face, and frightened America more than any comet that has appeared in a long time." Blackbeard liked to tuck long hemp matches under his hat, then ignite them for the joy of the fire crackling against his hair. A privateer in Queen Anne's War, by 1716 he was an apprentice pirate to Benjamin Hornigold. When Hornigold took the King's Pardon, Blackbeard struck out on his own. With Stede Bonnet, he blockaded Charles Town in May, 1718, took five ships, and prevented anyone from entering or leaving the harbor until he had been paid off handsomely. Later he arrived in Bath, North Carolina, accepted a pardon from his friend Governor Charles Eden, married his fourteenth wife (a lass of sixteen), and set sail again, unreformed and unrepentant. Eventually some of the North Carolina merchants and planters whose businesses were being ruined by Teach made plans to do him in. Since their own governor was his friend, they appealed to Alexander Spotswood of Virginia—that rare creature, an honest royal governor. At his own expense, Spotswood fitted out two sloops commanded by Lieutenant Robert Maynard and Captain Ellis Brand, and on the evening of November 21, 1718, they slipped into Ocracoke Inlet, where Blackbeard tarred and caulked his ships. Blackbeard appears to have had warnings of the expedition, including one from South Carolina's secretary, but he pooh-poohed them as rumor and spent the night carousing. Brand's vessel was damaged in the attack next morning, and when Maynard closed, the pirates boarded his sloop. In the hand-to-hand combat Blackbeard, a walking arsenal, fought like a madman, and Maynard emptied his pistol twice into his seemingly indestructible body. Then, in the act of reaching for a pistol, the pirate fell to the deck, dead. His body bore 25 wounds, five from pistols, and Maynard's men finished the grisly business by cutting off his head, which they hung from the bowsprit on their return to Hampton Roads. That year the Carolinas were finally rid of the pirate trade.

At left, an old etching shows the satanic Blackbeard amusing himself by burning lighted matches under his hat. Below is the rotting hulk of one of the many ships wrecked on the treacherous shoals of Cape Hatteras, the "graveyard of the Atlantic". In colonial times the Hatteras coast was a notorious pirate haven. Ocracoke Inlet, shown above, was the place where Blackbeard tarred and caulked his boats; here the pirate was surprised and killed by Spotswood's men in 1718.

Colonial Williamsburg

A. AUBREY BODINE

At left is a street of restored colonial homes and shops. Ornate wrought-iron gates frame the Governor's Palace (center), and the formal gardens at right belong to the George Wythe House.

If the remnants of Blackbeard's crew had time for such thoughts before they were hanged in Williamsburg, they must have been impressed by the splendor of the colony's capital. This seat of royal authority was something to awe the most sophisticated colonial. Yet no one who saw it in 1718 would dream that the town would be practically deserted eighty years later, its buildings in a state of decay.

When Jamestown burned, many of its settlers removed to Middle Plantation, as the huddle of crude buildings near the College of William and Mary was called, and in 1699 Williamsburg became Virginia's capital. Alexander Spotswood, that energetic soul who had seen to Blackbeard's demise, was responsible for much of the town's growth. Arriving in 1710, he directed a good part of the construction program, including several college buildings and the present Bruton Parish Church. By the time the bedraggled pirates were herded into town, the magnificent brick Governor's Palace was almost complete; the general assembly was meeting in the building Christopher Wren designed for the college (the only one of his design in America, and the nation's oldest academic structure); and the octagonal public magazine was newly finished. Although Williamsburg's colonial population never exceeded 2,000, it was filled from the very beginning with planters and statesmen whose personal and political convictions were to shape American history. For 81 influential years it was the capital of the colony of Virginia, playing host to George Washington, Patrick

The Capitol where Patrick Henry defied George III has been reconstructed exactly as it looked upon completion in 1705.

Henry, George Wythe, Thomas Jefferson, George Mason, and many others. Here, on May 29, 1765, Patrick Henry rose in the House of Burgesses to condemn the Stamp Act, crying "Caesar had his Brutus; Charles the First his Cromwell; and George the Third ["Treason!" shouted the Speaker] *may profit by their example. If this* be treason, make the most of it." Henry apologized to the shocked House for his outburst, but the seed had been sown, and before long he, Jefferson, and other patriots were meeting at the Raleigh Tavern to develop inter-colonial committees of correspondence. Williamsburg was the scene of George Mason's Virginia Declaration of Rights; the May 15, 1776, Resolution for Independence which led directly to July 4; the framing of a Virginia constitution on which most other states patterned theirs; and Jefferson's famous Statute for Religious Freedom. Before and during the siege of Yorktown, Williamsburg was headquarters first for British, then for Continental and French forces. Both Washington and Rochambeau stayed in the handsome Wythe House, and American wounded were quartered in the Governor's Palace. Williamsburg had begun to decline when the capital was moved to Richmond in 1780 to escape the British. By 1795 its population was only half what it had been in 1779, and nine years later it was "very decayed."

Then, in 1926, John D. Rockefeller, Jr., came to Williamsburg at the invitation of Dr. W. A. R. Goodwin, rector of Bruton Parish Church, who had plans to restore the entire town. The result of their vision and generosity is the magnificent restoration which transports visitors back 200 years through time to see, in accurate detail, the once-great colonial capital.

141

A sketch from Benjamin Latrobe's journal shows Martha Washington serving tea at Mount Vernon.

George Washington's Virginia

Had it not been for a determined South Carolinian named Ann Pamela Cunningham, it is quite doubtful if George Washington's beautiful Mount Vernon would have survived to delight the millions of Americans who look to it as one of the nation's great shrines.

Washington had inherited the estate in 1754 and during his lifetime increased its acreage from 2,126 to something over 8,000. In his will he divided up the property, leaving the mansion and 4,000 acres to his nephew Bushrod Washington, but with the passing years Mount Vernon's owners found it impossible to maintain the disintegrating buildings and unproductive land on which they stood. One of them tried to interest the State of Virginia or the Federal Government in buying the property, and when neither expressed interest it began to look as if the estate would crumble into decay.

In 1853 Miss Cunningham stepped into the breach and penned her first appeal—a plea to the women of America to "guard and protect" this hallowed spot. When she retired from this work of love 21 years later, she could take pride in what she had bequeathed to her countrymen.

It is unfair to single out the work of the Mount Vernon Ladies' Association; yet it is worth reminding Americans, through this example, that the preservation of most of their treasured historic possessions has often been possible only when groups of private individuals have been willing to do something about it.

This 1793 map of the five farms comprising Mount Vernon was drawn from field notes by Washington, an accomplished surveyor. What he termed the "Mansion House Farm," where his countryseat still stands, is at bottom center on the map. As the photograph at right indicates, the view of the Potomac has changed so little since Washington's time that the family might survey the same peaceful scene from their tea table.

142

The manner in which Mount Vernon is maintained today would probably surprise and gratify its most illustrious owner. Washington was well aware of its possibilities: "No estate in United America is more pleasantly situated than this," he wrote. But in 1759 when he brought his bride Martha Custis there to live, the plantation was shabby and run-down, with endless repairs needed, indoors and out. It was a large and fairly typical Virginia plantation, and by the standards of the time Washington was a wealthy man; yet the apparent wealth of plantation society was sometimes deceiving—as noted by the Duc de La Rochefoucauld. "The Virginians are not generally rich," he said, "especially in net revenue. Thus one often finds a well-served table, covered with silver, in a room where for ten years half the window panes have been missing, and where they will be missed for ten years more. There are few houses in a passable state of repair, and of all parts of the establishment those best cared for are the stables."

Washington Irving, in his biography of Washington, hit on an apt description of plantation life. "A large Virginia estate," he said, "was a little empire. The mansion-house was the seat of government, with its numerous dependencies, such as kitchens, smoke-house, workshops and stables." At Mount Vernon, as at so many similar establishments of the time and place, the area immediately surrounding the manor house was designed as a gentleman's countryseat—an American copy of the English country estate, with meadows, sweeping views, rows of trees, and carefully tended gardens. Between house and river there was a sizable park, and those small areas which were under cultivation near the house were devoted mainly to testing new crops and improved methods of agriculture.

Economically speaking, Mount Vernon was far less profitable than one might expect. Partially this was due to the land itself, which failed to produce good tobacco, the cash crop on which so many relied. Various alternatives were tried—wheat, flax, hemp—and Washington attempted to make money out of his still or derive some profit from the Potomac's abundant shad and herring; but the odds were against him. The plantation system required close supervision to produce prosperity. In 1786 nearly ninety people were living in and about the main house, with 150 more

In Edward Savage's portrait, the Washingtons are pictured with their two wards, Martha's grandchildren by her first marriage. At the right is Mount Vernon, where Washington retired to enjoy "domestic ease under the shadow of my own vine, and my own fig tree . . . with the implements of husbandry, and Lambkins around me."

144

Martha's dressing table

Parlor card table

Washington's desk and chair

on its adjacent farms. All these people had to be clothed and fed, and nothing which could be produced on the estate was bought elsewhere. The managerial responsibilities in this self-contained community were enormous, but Washington was too much needed in public affairs for him to give them the time they required. From 1759 on he served in the Virginia House of Burgesses, and more and more played the part of counselor, executor, and private banker to his friends and neighbors. And when he wrote, several months after his retirement from the presidency, that he and his wife were sitting down to dinner alone for the first time in twenty years, it gives us an idea of the amount of entertaining involved in plantation life.

After he was commissioned commander in chief of the Continental Army in 1775, Washington was away from Mount Vernon for over eight years, except for brief visits en route to and from Yorktown in 1781. Inaugurated President in 1789, he visited his home only fifteen times during his eight years of office, and when he finally came home, only two and a half years of life remained to him.

Seeing Mount Vernon today, it is apparent that if plantation life had its drawbacks, it also had its charms. The beautiful parlors, the music room, the banquet hall, and the library were scenes of a life which was socially and intellectually stimulating. Nearby were the estates of Belvoir and Gunston Hall, whose owners, the Fairfaxes and George Mason, were frequent guests. Social position was the privilege of the highly gifted as much as the well born, and those whom the Duc de La Rochefoucauld calls "men of the first class" were certainly equal to any such group in history. Every plantation was attached to an Epis-

PRATT, *Ladies' Home Journal*

Prince Street in Alexandria has changed little since Washington's time. Its handsome homes are a reminder of the years when the town was a prosperous Potomac tobacco port.

copal parish, and nearly all Virginia gentlemen were closely associated with the established church. Philip Vickers Fithian, who tutored the Carter children at Nomini Hall, reported the "general custom on Sundays here with Gentlemen to invite one another to dine, after Church; and to consult about, determine their common business, either before or after Service—it is not the custom for Gentlemen to go into Church til Service is beginning, when they enter in a Body, in the same manner as they come out; I have known the Clerk to come out and call them in to prayers."

If the mansion at Mount Vernon reflects a leisurely life whose all-consuming topics of conversation were law and politics, the neat white outbuildings bespeak an era of handicrafts and the extent to which society depended upon the work of slaves. There is no activity today in the kitchen, smokehouse, or laundry yard, but these and the other service buildings make it possible to understand the problems of self-sufficiency at a time when nearly everything that was eaten or worn was produced within the borders of the plantation.

Standing on the white-columned piazza, the visitor surveys the same placid view George Washington looked out on two centuries ago. This home has more associations with the nation's beginnings than any other in the United States—a place whose tangible and emotional memories reveal the man beloved in his time and in our own. For George Washington, Mount Vernon was an island of peace in a world beset with troubles, and it remains a place where all Americans are privileged to experience the same feeling.

Washington drew plans for Pohick Church, located six miles from Mount Vernon. Construction was completed in 1774.

On Sundays the colonial planters gathered at churches like Bruton Parish in Williamsburg to worship and talk business.

Tidewater Golden Age

The half century preceding the Revolution was the Golden Age in Virginia. Third- and fourth-generation families, reaping the benefit of ancestral foresight and business acumen, lived on estates of thousands of acres. They were farmers, businessmen, and merchants; they collected great libraries, listened to music, danced and entertained endlessly. They held banquets, balls, and boat races; barbecues, musicales, and horse races. They hunted and went to church and were as insistent on their children's good manners as they were upon their education. But for all their success in the New World, for all their devotion to the colony, they still called England "home."

One of the most distinguished men of his time was William Byrd II, a handsome, dashing man known as the "Black Swan," who built his home "two miles above where the great ships ride" on the James River. This was Westover—one of the first houses on the grand scale in Virginia.

There was Gunston Hall, a simple, story-and-a-half Colonial house built on 5,000 acres along the Potomac near Alexandria by George Mason, fourth of his name and line in Virginia. A man who preferred to work behind the scenes, Mason framed Virginia's Declaration of Rights and most of its Constitution—two documents which profoundly influenced the Declaration of Independence and the Bill of Rights.

A gaunt shell of vast empty walls on the York River is all that remains of Mann Page's Rosewell, the estate which consumed most of his own and his wife's fortunes. The house had 23 rooms in its central portion and six in each wing, a wainscoting of carved mahogany, and a staircase which could accommodate eight persons walking abreast.

Of the surviving plantation houses among the best are Benjamin Harrison's Berkeley, near Charles City; William Byrd Harrison's Brandon, with its formal gardens of gigantic boxwood, yews, and cucumber trees;

This is the view from the front door of Stratford, Robert E. Lee's birthplace, which was begun about 1725 by an ancestor, Thomas Lee, an important colonial leader and native Virginian.

The great wealth of planter William Byrd II was reflected in the opulence of Westover. Built in the 1730's, this elegant Georgian mansion was one of the first of the great Virginia plantation homes.

One of the showpieces at Shirley is a handsome carved walnut staircase which climbs a square well three stories high. The Palladian Room of Gunston Hall (below) is an excellent example of a gracious colonial drawing room. The house reflects the taste of its builder, George Mason, a Virginia statesman and delegate to the Constitutional Convention.

Cotton, rice, tobacco, and indigo, the traditional money crops of the seaboard South, all depended on slave labor.

and Shirley, one of the largest Tidewater mansions. In Shirley's huge hall, which occupies more than a quarter of the main floor, is a "hanging stair" which seems to have no support on its way up a square well three stories high.

One spectacular house is Carter's Grove, set behind a row of giant tulip poplars overlooking the James River. It was begun for his daughter by "King" Carter, who owned more than 300,000 acres of land and 700 slaves, and completed by his grandson, Carter Burwell. The entrance to this beautiful estate lies between ancient cedars and locusts, and the rose-brick Georgian mansion is a perfect monument to a way of life which has gone from the scene forever.

Imported English artisans fashioned the graceful carved stairway and pine-paneled main hallway of Carter's Grove.

The grand proportions of Carter's Grove conformed to the refined but expensive tastes of planter Carter Burwell.

Low Country Aristocracy

All along the southern seaboard, wrote George Washington, "the lands are low, sandy, and unhealthy; [and] as I should not choose to be an inhabitant of them myself, I ought not to say anything that would induce others to be so. . . ." Obviously, there were those who disagreed with this view, and in the years before the Revolution Charleston was dominated by as exclusive and aristocratic a society as could be found in the colonies. Their remarkable wealth came from two easy-to-grow, easy-to-sell crops—rice and indigo. And if the owners of the great plantations had to spend several months in Charleston to escape the miasmic fumes and disease which resulted from the annual flooding of rice fields (Washington was right about the climate, it seemed), this served to make Charleston a glittering, civilized oasis on the barren southern coast line. English visitors thought the city the most agreeable in America, and by 1800, Henry Adams wrote, "Nowhere in the Union was intelligence, wealth, and education greater in proportion to numbers than in the little society of cotton and rice planters who ruled South Carolina."

Charleston today is full of eighteenth-century architecture, including some of the best English work of its time. Concessions were made to the climate, in galleries and in high basements which formed a full story on the ground level, and many houses were built flush with the sidewalk, turning their backs, as it were, to the street to insure the occupants' privacy. Beyond the colorful homes, the delicate grillwork, and the gardens of old Charleston are the outlying plantations, many of them carefully restored like Hampton, whose acreage along the Santee River has belonged to the Rutledge family since 1686.

Ironically enough, the guns they themselves set off in Charleston Harbor in 1861 began the end of this society and its counterparts in Savannah, Mobile, and elsewhere in the South. Yet in the homes that remain —some crumbled beyond repair, a few, like the handsome Wormsloe Plantation near Savannah, still in the possession of families whose forbears built them two centuries ago—one finds the echo of that other world, hanging in the air, unforgotten.

Wormsloe House (left) near Savannah stands on plantation land owned by the same family for two hundred years. At right is Charleston's Rainbow Row. These pastel-colored homes are typical of the city's beautifully preserved houses.

The World Turned Upside Down

At St. John's Church in Richmond, speaking before a revolutionary assembly in March, 1775, Patrick Henry made a plea for armed resistance to British misrule.

It was March, 1775, a month before men would die on Lexington Green, and a convention of Virginians was meeting at St. John's Episcopal Church in Richmond. In this serene clapboard building, Patrick Henry rose to make one of America's most impassioned pleas for freedom: "Is life so dear, or peace so sweet, as to be purchased at the price of chains and slavery? Forbid it, Almighty God! I know not what course others may take, but as for me, give me liberty, or give me death!"

At the time he spoke, the idea of revolt was confined to a small group. But as the tide of revolution swept across the land, it affected the relationships of all classes to each other and to their established institutions, so that revolution became, in many places, civil war. Nowhere was this more apparent, or the struggle more bitter, than in the South. Upcountry frontier was a very different world from Tidewater aristocracy. In the mountain communities, Germans, French Huguenots, Dutch, Scotch Highlanders, Scotch-Irish, English, Welsh, and Swiss pioneers began to ex-

press their differences through violent action.

In the back country one of the bitterest and most crucial battles of the war was fought at King's Mountain, where Southern patriots—many of them "overmountain" frontiersmen—shattered a Tory force whose leader, Major Patrick Ferguson, was the only non-American on either side.

There are few surviving landmarks of this all-but-forgotten war, largely because the war was one of quick thrusts, marches, maneuvers, and raids. When the able Nathanael Greene was given command of Continental forces in the South, his chief object was survival. He could do little more than harass Cornwallis' flanks, harry his outposts, and encourage the guerrilla operations of "Swamp Fox" Francis Marion, Andrew Pickens, and Thomas Sumter, the "Carolina Game Cock." Among the few victories was the one which Saratoga veteran Dan Morgan fashioned in a backwoods cattle pasture, called the Cowpens; but mostly it was a campaign described by Greene as "fight, get beat, rise and fight again." In no other battle could he claim victory

154

In the painting above, Francis Marion and his partisans cross the Pee Dee River in South Carolina during a guerrilla raid on the British. At right is a section of the reconstructed Grand French Battery at Yorktown. During the siege, heavy allied bombardment silenced most of the British batteries and eventually pounded Cornwallis' forces into submission.

—at Guilford Court House, Hobkirk's Hill, Ninety-Six, or Eutaw Springs—yet each achieved Greene's goal of inflicting such damage on the enemy that they would be compelled to retreat.

Although Greene's half-naked, ill-fed troops fought on for another year, the climax came elsewhere, suddenly, at the old tobacco port of Yorktown, Virginia. In 1781 the town consisted of about sixty houses, a few of which, like the Somerwell, Digges, Nelson, and Sessions houses, still stand. Near here are the restored British and American earthworks, and outside of town, near the battlefield, is the frame Moore House, where representatives of Washington and Cornwallis negotiated the final surrender. But the enduring memory of Yorktown is also to be found in the echoing words of Patrick Henry, and in the thrilling picture (next page) of British troops in new uniforms, marching out between lines of French and Americans. In one of those wonderful ironic touches, the British bands played them out to the tune of an old march called "The World Turned Upside Down."

Louis Van Blarenberghe based his painting of the British surrender at Yorktown on sketches made on the spot. Marchir out of their lines of defense, measured ranks of brilliantly redcoated English soldiers pass between rows of Frenchme

blue uniforms, and Americans, whose backs are toward the viewer. At upper left, some British are already stacking
r arms. Lord Cornwallis, however, did not march with his troops that day, excusing himself on account of illness.

Jefferson's Monticello

From the summit of the "little mountain" the long hills roll off toward the smoky haze of the Blue Ridge, little swatches of cultivated land patterning the earth where forests stood two centuries ago. When Thomas Jefferson came here in 1766 to clear the land and level his mountaintop he knew exactly what he wanted, and sixty years of his life were spent making it into an embodiment of his personal tastes and philosophy. Monticello became, after the death of his wife, his great love; the place where a man whose reputation was that of a warm, friendly man of the people could be what he was—remote, aloof, a democrat at a distance.

From the beginning Thomas Jefferson set his heart on a house unlike anything in America, and the beautiful symmetry of his mansion, capturing in soft warm brick the classic elegance he admired, was the forerunner of a new style in American architecture. The house is full of his inventions and innovations—a revolving chair which can be made into a chaise longue; a revolving tabletop to facilitate writing and record-keeping; a system of air shafts for ventilation; the first dumb-waiter; a porch-ceiling weather vane; the famous hall clock with cannon balls to mark off days of the week; a bed between study and bedroom which can be raised to make a passage through the suite.

These things and others reveal the scientist and inventor who inherited the mantle of Franklin. Here is the architect, farmer, author of the Declaration of Independence, President of the United States. Yet anyone willing to approach Monticello leisurely, and with care, will find also the personality and individuality of its remarkable owner. That story begins with a boy who dreamed of living on top of the mountain; it leads to college, where architectural books opened the path; to a law practice whose fees paid for clearing the land, planting gardens and trees. The big, sandy-haired man, "straight as a gun barrel," was as much the lord of the manor as any Hudson River patroon. He could have been merely that, but he chose not to limit outlook or intellect, and Monticello is the perfect reflection of his choice.

In New England, on July 4, 1826, John Adams lay dying, happy with the thought that "Thomas Jefferson survives." But Jefferson had died, too, a few hours earlier on that great fiftieth anniversary, leaving an epitaph for the little graveyard at Monticello which stated the three accomplishments of which he was proudest: "Author of the Declaration of American Independence, of the Statute of Virginia for Religious Freedom, and Father of the University of Virginia."

THOMAS JEFFERSON MEMORIAL FOUNDATION   ROBERT PHILLIPS, *Friends*   THOMAS JEFFERSON MEMORIAL FOUNDATION

Inside Monticello (left) are such Jeffersonian inventions as his pulley-lift bed, a quartet music stand, and a calendar clock.

James Madison   James Monroe   William Henry Harrison

The Virginia Dynasty

Virginia's great outpouring of political genius during the early years of the Republic was no accident. The Virginia planters were for the most part men who continued the conditions of life they had left behind in Europe; they kept in touch with that society, importing its literature and ideas along with the prevailing London fashions. They read the best books, sent their sons to Europe's universities, nurtured the traditions of scholarship, and gave themselves wholeheartedly to public life.

There were, of course, men of equal caliber in New England; but most of these gentlemen were absorbed in theological and philosophical studies. Unlike New England, with its democratic town meeting which made a political unit of each township, Virginia adopted the parish system. This system was forced upon it by the distances which existed between neighbors; and it meant, inevitably, government by a small group of men who were in the beginning representative, but who later filled any vacancies from within their own ranks and tended to become a closed corporation.

Virginia's parish system produced four of the young nation's first five Presidents—Washington, Jefferson, Madison, and Monroe—four men who served a total of 32 years in the country's first 36 years of life. Except for Jefferson, they were conservatives—men with a vision of an aristocratic republic governed by superior individuals. In founding the University of Virginia in the foothills of the Blue Ridge Mountains, Jefferson too sought to produce individuals of the same superior quality, but on a much broader base, and within the social atmosphere of a democracy.

After the first succession of Virginia Presidents ended with Monroe, America turned for a time to John Quincy Adams and then, having encountered on its frontiers conditions which no longer fitted the confines of conservative leadership, to Andrew Jackson, a man of the new West. To the nation's and to Virginia's credit, men of stature had been found in the Old Dominion when the struggling colonies needed them most; and the country would turn again to Virginia for William Henry Harrison, for John Tyler and Zachary Taylor, and, in the twentieth century, for Woodrow Wilson.

The homes of most of these Virginia Presidents survive today, reflecting gracefully the way of life of the men who occupied them. Washington's Mount Vernon and Jefferson's Monticello are perfect mirrors of their masters, and the same thing is true of Madison's Montpelier, in Orange County, and of James Monroe's two homes—Ash Lawn in Charlottesville, and Oak Hill at Leesburg.

The beautiful red brick Berkeley Plantation on the James River was the ancestral home of the Harrison family and it remains one of the great Tidewater mansions. Not far from it is Sherwood Forest, where John Tyler lived. In Staunton, the visitor may see the modest Manse where Woodrow Wilson was born.

John Tyler

Zachary Taylor

Woodrow Wilson

The colonnaded dormitory rows of the University of Virginia were designed by Jefferson along classical lines. As the University's architect and builder, the aging ex-President viewed its construction through a spyglass from Monticello.

From Bull Run to Appomattox

A "mass of throbbing nerves," Jefferson Davis had intense, somewhat Lincolnesque features.

Time was running out in the spring of 1861, one event piling on another with dismaying speed, rushing the nation to disaster. Even as a train carried Abraham Lincoln from Springfield, Illinois, toward Washington, an erect, tough-minded Jefferson Davis stood on the colonnaded portico of the Alabama capitol to take an oath of office, and a southern actress danced on the Stars and Stripes. Davis, the grandson of an illiterate Welsh peasant, was "ambitious as Lucifer," and his wife called him "a mere mass of throbbing nerves"; but neither of these traits was strong enough to make him want war, just then. A West Pointer, he knew what war meant, and he had a healthy respect for the North's industrial resources. Needless to say, a fight was the last thing Abraham Lincoln wanted, but when April came the guns in Charleston Harbor opened fire on a pentagon of stone called Fort Sumter, and it did not much matter what anyone wanted any more. The thing had happened.

There would be four long, terrible years of bloodshed on the North American continent—four years the nation could never forget—and it is a good thing for Americans to go, now and again, to see where this happened and try to understand it all. An enormous lot of fighting took place outside the state of Virginia, but partly because Richmond was for so long the goal of the Federal armies, and Robert E. Lee and Stonewall Jackson their principal opponents, this state has more associations with the Civil War than any other, in the popular mind. Here the real fighting began, here it ended, and here is where the Confederacy's greatest heroes were made.

A good place to begin an understanding of what the South was fighting for is down on Virginia's Northern Neck at a place called Stratford Hall, Lee's birth-

place. Lee was only three years old in 1810 when his father, "Light Horse" Harry Lee, Revolutionary hero and friend of Washington, and his mother Ann Carter Lee, daughter of the distinguished Carters of Shirley, packed the children and a few belongings into a coach and headed out the long drive. The Lees had fallen on hard, humiliating times and were forced to leave Stratford, the massive, H-shaped brick structure which is one of the finest Georgian mansions in America. The once-rich fields lay fallow, slaves had gone, the great house was on its way to neglect and ruin, and for the rest of his days Lee would long for what had been lost. There is a picture of Lee leaving another great, well-loved home—this one the columned Greek Revival house across the Potomac from Washington,

Severe fighting in both Bull Run battles centered around an old tavern called the Stone House, seen in a wartime photo.

162

A Union shell explodes in the rubble-clogged parade of Fort Sumter during the siege of Charleston in the fall of 1863.

where Lee had married the daughter of George Washington Parke Custis, adopted son of the first President. Arlington, when Lee saw it for the last time in April, 1861, had also grown shabby; the grounds were run-down and the fields only partially cultivated. Beautifully restored now, these two proud, lovely houses speak eloquently of family and position, explaining much of Lee the gentleman. For the rest of the gentleman-soldier combination, Virginia's battlegrounds hold the key.

War in earnest began 25 miles southwest of the nation's capital, near Manassas, an important railroad junction. Along the steep banks of Bull Run, the little stream that meanders through the gentle countryside, the North in particular discovered for the first time that nothing about this war would be easy. There are still two buildings at Manassas that survived two battles where about 25,000 Americans were shot—the Stone House, which was right in the center of action, and the Dogan House, a weather-beaten, one-room log hut. On top of a little rise is the famous equestrian statue of Thomas J. Jackson, looking out over the fields where he won his nickname for standing there "like a stone wall." The first battle began on the morning of July 21, 1861, when unlucky General Irvin McDowell, goaded by the public cry of "On to Richmond!" took 35,000 pathetically untrained boys in blue out to dislodge Beauregard's equally untrained Confederates. The felony was compounded by a near-army of Congressmen, sightseers, and correspondents who tagged along to see the fun begin. When McDowell's men began what was a fairly orderly retreat, Confederate artillery blocked a bridge across their escape route, and in the ensuing traffic jam the civilians panicked. Before long there was a full-scale rout, with soldiers and civilians turned into a helpless, completely disorganized mob that stumbled back to Washington for the next 24 hours.

A little over a year later, at the end of August, 1862, Union General Pope learned at Bull Run what it was to run afoul of what Robert E. Lee and Stonewall Jackson had planned for him. For a full day he mounted a furious attack against the entrenched Jackson, and somehow, next morning, he got the idea that Jackson was retreating. Not only was he totally in error on this score, but he was unaware that James Longstreet's veterans had come up to join Stonewall. Just as Pope was assaulting Jackson, Longstreet wheeled his gray line forward toward Bald Hill, rolling up the Union left flank as he drove along the Warrenton Pike. Second Manassas was another crushing defeat for the North, but the boys had come of age in a year's time. After this one the troops picked themselves up and were ready to fight again at Antietam, only seventeen days later.

Off to the west of Bull Run lies the lovely Shenandoah Valley, a fertile land where Dutch, Scotch-Irish, and Quakers began to settle in the 1730's, leaving their mark in prosperous little farms and a tradition of independent self-sufficiency. Once a gateway to the western frontier and a scene of George Washington's first military assignment, the valley in 1862 was the South's great "covered way" leading to the Yankee fortress. Confederates coming down the valley were headed for the heart of the Union; while Federals moving up the valley were going the wrong way, if they wanted to get to Richmond. The great valley was a strategic artery and an incomparable source of food and forage for southern armies, but above all it was Stonewall Jackson country.

Between the tiers of blue mountains the quiet Shenandoah winds through pleasant little towns, pastures, and woodland which the silent, dour Jackson made his own against all comers. Sucking a lemon, the harsh disciplinarian in the worn, mud-spattered uniform rode at the head of a gray column of men who would

163

At left, Stonewall Jackson reviews his weary but cheering troops. Although he drove them at a killing pace, his men were devoted to this dour, Cromwell-like man. They moved so swiftly that they were nicknamed "Stonewall's foot cavalry." In the Shenandoah Valley (below), Jackson's lightning-stroke attacks ran the Union forces ragged in the spring of 1862, securing the Confederacy's breadbasket until Sheridan devastated it two years later.

The American Wars, BY ROY MEREDITH
WORLD PUBLISHING CO.

Confederate artist Allen Redwood sketched this Rebel sharpshooter.

Protected by a stone wall, Confederates stood along the sunken road below Marye's Heights and slaughtered Federals advancing across the open fields of Fredericksburg. Burnside lost 12,653 men before he called off the assault.

march and fight like fools for him, giving the art of warfare a new concept of mobility. Beginning with Kernstown, the site of one of Jackson's few defeats, Stonewall's trail runs north to Winchester, oldest city in the valley, where earthworks remain from some of the battles fought here. It includes Harpers Ferry, winds down to Front Royal, Strasburg, and Cross Keys; and finally to the college town of Lexington, where Jackson taught at the Virginia Military Institute, and where he is buried.

For a concentrated dose of the Civil War as it was fought by the Army of the Potomac and the Army of Northern Virginia, few places can rival that wedge-shaped chunk of land bounded roughly by the Rapidan River in the north, the James in the south, and the foothills of the Blue Ridge Mountains to the west. Here Union armies pounded on the gates of Richmond, sometimes nearly destroying themselves in the process; and here the efforts of the southern states to establish themselves as an entity apart from the Union came to an end. From the standpoint of what can still be seen, the most rewarding section of this area is in and around Fredericksburg, Virginia.

The town itself goes back to the roots of America, to John Smith who visited there in 1608, to a group of early settlers who built a little fort on the Rappahannock River in 1671. Located at the foot of rolling hills at the head of tidewater and navigation on the Rappahannock, Fredericksburg was a trading center for rich cargoes of Virginia tobacco until the Civil War, when it found itself strategically located midway between Washington and Richmond, situated on major rail and road routes north and south.

In November, 1862, General Ambrose Burnside arrived on the north bank of the Rappahannock and surveyed a scene which has changed little since—a pleasant town of colonial houses and tree-shaded streets, just beyond which lay an open plain, three-quarters of a mile wide. On the far side of the plain is a long, low hill called Marye's Heights, running parallel with the course of the river. At its foot, behind a four-foot stone wall, is a road, and when the Federal attack began on the chill, foggy morning of December 13, 1862, that road was full of Confederate veterans, four to five ranks deep. Behind them on the hill was their artillery, which could crisscross the whole plain with fire, making this an almost perfect defensive position. All that day and long into the hours of darkness, wave after wave of Federal troops broke against Lee's position until the Confederates wondered why their fire "did not absolutely sweep them from the face of the earth." Never once did the Union troops falter, but not one man got within thirty yards of the fateful stone wall. And when it was over at last, the North had lost nearly 13,000 men.

That winter the two armies faced each other across the Rappahannock, and Joe Hooker, who had replaced Burnside, worked out a plan to outflank Lee

Civil War trenches still crisscross Virginia's Wilderness. Here the two armies slugged blindly through a jungle of second-growth timber in the battles of Chancellorsville and the Wilderness. The horror of both fights was compounded when the woods caught fire, incinerating hundreds of wounded.

dense brush and forest. All day Lee waited, not knowing if Hooker would assault his thin lines, or if Jackson would reach Hooker's right flank undetected. Then, at five fifteen in the afternoon, Jackson's men stormed out of the woods, red battle flags flying in the dusk, 28,000 men in a line more than a mile wide and three divisions deep. Against them there was nothing the Federals could do. In a matter of minutes a whole Union corps had collapsed, and the broken remnants of Hooker's right wing fell back on Chancellorsville in utter confusion. Next day the South resumed the attack, and the Union army was forced back to a position north of the town. Chancellorsville, however, was the costliest victory the Confederacy was to win; casualties were near 13,000, and Stonewall Jackson, surveying his position after dark, had been shot by his own men. A stone slab near the battlefield marks the place where his left arm was buried, and in the Chandler farmhouse south of Fredericksburg he died a week later. Lee, refusing to believe that he would not live, sent word that although "he has lost his left arm, I have lost my right"; but hours later Stonewall died, murmuring, "Let us cross over the river, and rest under the shade of the trees."

Twelve months after the southern victory at Chancellorsville, war returned to the deep, silent Wilderness. The tide had turned: Grant's victory at Vicksburg had opened up the Mississippi; Lee's defeat at Gettysburg had ended the threat of invasion; and the Union

and drive toward Richmond. It was a good plan, and it might possibly have worked. Hooker divided his army into two groups, sending Sedgwick and 40,000 men to cross the river below Fredericksburg while Hooker and 80,000 men moved to the west around Lee's left flank. Not for two days did Lee discover the movement, but when he did he acted with characteristic initiative, setting in motion the last and most daring of all the Lee-Jackson maneuvers—one which brought dramatic victory out of apparent defeat. Hooker had reached Chancellorsville when he felt Lee's resistance for the first time, and he decided to set up a defensive position there and await attack. Chancellorsville was in that dismal dense tangle of second-growth forest, nearly fifteen miles square, called the Wilderness.

On the night of May 1, Lee and Jackson sat on a cracker box discussing their situation and working out a plan which, for sheer audacity, has scarcely been equaled. Although they had only 45,000 troops to nearly twice that many for Hooker, they split their forces to launch a surprise attack. Lee, with less than 20,000 men, was to hold off Hooker, while Jackson, on the morning of the second, took off through the

As the Confederates evacuated Richmond, valuable supplies were put to the torch. In the confusion, however, the flames spread and most of the southern capital was burned. When the Union army entered the city which it had fought so long to capture, the place was in ruins; nowhere was there "sound of life, but the stillness of a catacomb." These gutted buildings were photographed by Mathew Brady after the surrender.

Sherman, Sheridan, and Grant (left to right) were the three Union generals who contributed most to the Confederate defeat.

triumph at Chattanooga had put the western armies in position to cross Georgia to the sea, cutting the South in half. Ulysses S. Grant, now the general in chief of all Union armies, assumed personal direction of the campaign against Lee, to "hammer continuously against the armed force of the enemy and his resources, until by mere attrition, if in no other way, there should be nothing left to him. . . ."

Grant had no intention of fighting again in the tangled woods near Chancellorsville, but Lee was a man devilishly clever at making his enemies fight exactly when and where they chose not to. Lee struck, and for two horrible days thousands of men fought and died in the flaming underbrush. A high wind whipped

brush fires into a blazing inferno, and the entire area seemed to be aflame. When the fighting played itself out on the morning of May 8, both armies were just about where they had been at the start; but unlike Chancellorsville, when Union troops had withdrawn to the north to lick their wounds, they now headed south. This time there would be no turning back.

The next day the two armies hit each other again at Spotsylvania Court House. For ten days the savage hand-to-hand struggle went on, culminating in the Bloody Angle, a hideous, writhing death struggle that was the most terrible 24 hours of the war. Two weeks after Grant crossed the Rapidan he had lost 33,000 men—an average of 2,000 casualties every 24 hours.

Further south, in the Petersburg National Military Park, well-preserved remains of Union and Confederate earthworks and trenches speak of those ten months the two armies spent here, facing each other. Petersburg was an important supply depot for the Richmond area, and the point where five railway lines, vital to the Confederacy, converged. Between June, 1864, and April of the next year, the Union forces assaulted or jabbed at the southern defenders, at one point tunneling nearly 600 feet underground to blow up a huge section of the Confederate lines, forming a great crater which the visitor may still see today. Here also are the sites of batteries, the remains of earthen forts and embankments built as the Federal noose slowly tightened around the city's defenses. As the southern plight became more and more desperate, Lee, almost completely encircled, pulled out of the city his men had defended so bravely, and headed west along the north bank of the Appomattox River, hoping to join General Johnston in North Carolina.

The little crossroads village of Appomattox Courthouse is about 22 miles east of Lynchburg in rolling farm country near the headwaters of the Appomattox River. In 1863 a newcomer named Wilmer McLean had come to town and bought a modest red-brick house in the middle of a locust grove. McLean was fed up with the war; he had owned a farm in northern Virginia which bordered a stream called Bull Run,

Brady took this photo of Lee one week after Appomattox.

and when his property was overrun with soldiers in the war's first battle, he sold out. Now, by a queer twist of fate, the same armies he had tried to avoid were returning to his very door. Lee's ragged troops, near starvation and outnumbered four to one, just could not go any farther. Phil Sheridan had cut off their escape path, and Grant was moving up with the main forces. Shortly after sending a letter to Grant proposing a meeting, Lee and an aide were riding toward Appomattox Court House, when they met Wilmer McLean. The farmer offered his house as a meeting place, they accepted, and the war had come full circle—from Bull Run to a modest parlor in Appomattox. In the simple brick house the two great soldiers—personifying the two opposing civilizations and philosophies—met and decided on surrender terms. After it was over, Lee stood on the porch steps for a moment, absently striking his hands together as he looked off to the hillside where his army was camped, and then mounted his horse Traveller to face his worst ordeal—breaking the news to what was left of his great army, and bidding them farewell. Across the nation church bells were pealing. It was Palm Sunday.

At Harrison's Landing near Brandon on the river James, the Union Army entrenched after the 1862 Seven Days' Battle.

The old tavern shown at right was there when Lee and Grant met on Palm Sunday, 1865, at Appomattox Court House.

ALFRED EISENSTAEDT, *Life*

Near this pylon on Kill Devil Hill, the Wrights made man's first powered heavier-than-air flight.

Birth of an Age

From Appomattox Courthouse to the barren dunes of Kitty Hawk, North Carolina, is a far cry; but an old civilization yielded to a new one just as completely on these sand hills as it had in Wilmer McLean's parlor. In 1900 the postmistress of the isolated village of Kitty Hawk received a letter from two Dayton, Ohio, bicycle mechanics named Wright, inquiring about the area's topography. Orville and Wilbur Wright wanted to make some "scientific kite-flying experiments," and U.S. Weather Bureau reports of steady winds in the area had prompted their inquiry.

Six hundred feet from a triangular pylon honoring the Wright brothers, a granite boulder marks the spot where, on December 17, 1903, a contraption of bicycle chains, wood, cloth, and wire left the ground in man's first powered flight. Only three newspapers covered that event, and even five years later, when a reporter telegraphed the Cleveland *Leader* that he had seen a Wright machine leave the ground, his editor wired back angrily: "Cut out the wildcat stuff. We can't handle it."

As Wilbur Wright watches, his brother Orville pilots their contraption in the 120-foot flight which opened the Air Age.

170

Intricate ironwork balconies frame the view from many Vieux Carré houses. At the end of Orleans Street is St. Louis Cathedral, built when Spain ruled the city.

The City of Three Nations

St. Louis Cathedral on the Place d'Armes is on the site of a church built here by Bienville.

One hundred and seven miles by water from the mouth of the Mississippi, in a majestic bend of the river, is a city which owes its character to three nations and the great waterway which gave it birth. In 1718 Sieur de Bienville, the French explorer, founded New Orleans as a trading center for New France. Levees were built, a town laid out in a rectangle of narrow streets, and thanks to John Law's grandiose real estate project, the settlement prospered. The first hastily-built houses of cypress slabs were replaced by low-roofed, story-and-a-half brick structures, many combining shop and residence like those in European towns. Two of these old buildings can be seen in New Orleans today—the Ursuline Convent, begun in 1727, and a private dwelling called Madame John's Legacy, built about the same time.

In 1763, eighty-one years after La Salle took possession of the Mississippi Valley, New Orleans—along

The eagle and motto on this charming 1803 painting of New Orleans reflect the possessive, confident American attitude toward the city immediately after the Louisiana Purchase.

with all Louisiana territory west of the river—was ceded to Spain. The Spanish flag flew over the Place d'Armes for forty years, a period which produced not only the stuccoed brick Cabildo with its massive arches and wrought-iron balconies, but a marriage of French and Spanish cultures—the blend known as Creole. In the midst of lush tropical wilderness, eighteenth-century New Orleans was elegant, with operas and lavish balls, Creole aristocracy and emigrés from the French Revolution—and it was brutal. Frontiersmen, soldiers, and slaves mixed with pirates and smugglers, with explosive results.

Then came 1803 and Thomas Jefferson's Louisiana Purchase, adding New Orleans, along with the vast, fabulous lands west to the Rockies, to the United States. Disdaining their new rulers, the Creoles withdrew into the Vieux Carré, whose narrow streets and picturesque French and Spanish buildings with patios and intricate wrought-iron balconies, are among America's most interesting architectural sights. Upstream, the Americans began building a new, distinctly different section of the city, the Garden District.

Despite its unwelcome reception, U.S. rule ushered in a period of remarkable prosperity and growth that lasted until the Civil War. Nowhere was it reflected so well as in the Garden District, where Greek Revival mansions and handsome gardens were created on the foundations of New Orleans' burgeoning riches. Gateway to a huge, bountiful interior, the city was the outlet for Illinois lead, Kentucky tobacco, furs from the upper Missouri, grain and meat from midwest farms, cotton and sugar from neighboring plantations. And when the *New Orleans,* first steamboat on western waters, arrived from Pittsburgh in 1812, the city's greatest era began.

The West's natural resources were visible along miles of New Orleans docks, and in 1815, just six miles south of the city, Andrew Jackson and 5,000 tough westerners demonstrated the quality of the area's human resources. Jackson assembled a motley crew of Kentucky and Tennessee militia, the New Orleans garrison, and Jean Lafitte and his pirate crew, and awaited the assault of the British expeditionary force led by Sir Edward Pakenham, brother-in-law of the Duke of Wellington. In the fields known today as Chalmette National Historical Park, Jackson lost 71 men while inflicting 2,000 casualties on a British army which outnumbered him two to one. Not long afterward, a popular song told, in true riverman style, how they threw up entrenchments, and—

> *Behind it stood our little force—*
> *None wished it to be greater;*
> *For ev'ry man was half a horse,*
> *And half an alligator.*

Cajun Country

West of New Orleans, fringing the Gulf of Mexico, is a region crisscrossed by endless stretches of swampland and watered by innumerable streams or bayous. It is a place of haunting, moss-draped beauty, a luxuriant maze of water and swamp where turtles and alligators sun themselves on logs, birds of every description flutter among the entangled cypress, magnolia, and live oaks, and winding roads follow the meandering bayous past slumbering, white-columned plantation houses at the end of tree-lined avenues.

This is Cajun country—home of descendants of the refugees from Nova Scotia, which was the first permanent French colony in Canada. After 1755, when the British seized their lands and turned them out, more than four thousand Acadians came to Louisiana to settle, and since that time, physically isolated and set

In the village of St. Martinville on Bayou Teche is the statue of Emmeline Labiche, supposedly the Evangeline of Longfellow's poem. According to the Acadian version of the legend, she went mad after finding her lover married.

BRADLEY SMITH

The tradition is that this white house belonged to Louis Arceneaux, the faithless lover of Emmeline. Now it is a museum near St. Martinville. At right, young Acadians prepare a shrimp boat for the annual blessing of the bayou fleet.

apart from the main currents of American life, they have clung to their old ways, remaining one of the least assimilated peoples in the United States. Speaking an ancient French dialect which few outsiders can follow, mixing little with the modern world, they earn a living by fishing, boating, trapping, and by selling hand-woven baskets and cloth. In a region of few roads, they live on simple wooden houseboats, dependent on the waterways and the pirogue—a slender, graceful canoe hollowed out of a single cypress log—for transportation.

A New England poet who never visited Louisiana preserved for American folklore the legend of the Acadians—the tragic story of Evangeline making the long trek from Nova Scotia to Louisiana in search of her sweetheart. According to legend, Longfellow's poem was based on the story of Emmeline Labiche, whose statue now stands in the St. Martinville churchyard, near the old Acadian cottage which belonged to her lover. St. Martinville, on Bayou Teche, enjoyed a brief period of glamour and prosperity when refugees from the French Revolution made it "a pretty little village . . . full of barons, marquises, counts and countesses," but in the middle of the nineteenth century a yellow fever epidemic, the Civil War, and the diversion of trade from bayou to railroad combined to bring about its decline as the "little Paris."

The Bayou Teche and Bayou LaFourche regions are as lovely as any in Louisiana, and the people with the musical names who live along the waterways have preserved their old customs and a simplicity of life which suits the serenity of their surroundings.

In single file, Admiral Porter's fleet ran the gantlet of Vicksburg's guns after midnight of April 16, 1863. Two weeks later, below the Confederate citadel, Porter ferried Grant's army across the river.

Citadel of the Mississippi

The visitor who goes to Vicksburg today, expecting to see a town which was, during the Civil War, one of the South's most vital strategic positions, is in for something of a surprise. For the Mississippi River, which once flowed past the town on the high bluff, making it a citadel whose master commanded the river and its valley, is no longer there. In 1876 the Mississippi, whose crossing and control had been for so long objects of Ulysses S. Grant's undivided attention, broke through a narrow tongue of land north of Vicksburg, made a new channel for itself, and left the town high and dry. Although Vicksburg is fronted once again by water, now it is the Yazoo River, whose flow was diverted into the old riverbed early in the present century.

In 1862 the Confederate stronghold at Vicksburg was the key to control of the Mississippi Valley. Its powerful batteries commanded a five-mile stretch of river, giving the South access to troops and supplies from the west, and prohibiting the uninterrupted passage of Union shipments from the north to New Orleans. As Grant commented after the war, "Vicksburg was the only channel . . . connecting the part of the Confederacy divided by the Mississippi. So long as it was held by the enemy, the free navigation of the river was prevented." Vicksburg's strategic location defied easy capture: from the north it was protected by the soggy land of the Yazoo delta, stretching northward for 175 miles; to the south, well-fortified bluffs barred

invasion; across the river the land was marshy and treacherous. The only access to the city was from the rear, over the high, dry land to the east. From this direction, after a number of other attacks met disaster, General Grant finally approached in what was probably his most brilliant campaign.

Early in 1863, Grant had taken personal command of the Army of the Tennessee and stationed himself at Milliken's Bend, on the Louisiana side of the river. Throughout the winter months he made several movements in the marshy lands around Vicksburg. In one attempt he had his men begin a canal across a peninsula opposite the city. Twice he tried without success to cut his way through the alluvial swampland north and west of Vicksburg and secure a foothold on the east bank, out of range of the city's batteries. Each of these operations failed, but they kept Grant's men occupied during the winter, and served to confuse General John Pemberton, the Confederate commander at Vicksburg.

By spring the rainy season had passed and the waters had subsided; but there was criticism of Grant in the North, from politicians demanding either a speedy victory or his removal. Lincoln defended his general with the classic remark: "I can't spare the man—he fights." And Grant embarked on the daring plan he had conceived.

Moving his men down the west bank of the river through Louisiana, Grant waited for Admiral David

D. Porter to run the gantlet of Vicksburg's guns, join him south of the city, and ferry the army across. After midnight on April 16, 1863, Porter's vessels, piled high with bales of cotton and hay for added protection, got under way. As row after row of Confederate batteries cut loose, the fleet steamed past the city in single file, so close that those aboard could hear the clatter of falling bricks on the streets. Somehow, they made it without the loss of a single man, and two weeks later Grant captured Port Gibson on the east bank of the Mississippi. To keep Confederate General Joe Johnston from joining Pemberton at Vicksburg, Grant purposely cut himself off from his supplies, marched east, and in quick succession, won the battles of Raymond, Jackson, Champion's Hill, and Big Black River—a seventeen-day campaign which was one of the most successful of the entire war.

Turning now to Vicksburg, Grant took a position along a series of ridges which circled the city for nearly fifteen miles. And what the visitor sees today in the Vicksburg National Military Park is the elaborate system of offensive and defensive positions with which Vicksburg was ringed during the forty-seven-day siege. Opposing the Union approaches are Confederate lines of defense—redoubts and trench lines extending in an arc to the north, east, and south, strengthened by a system of parallel ridges about seven miles long. In the city, on a terraced square overlooking the business district, is the Greek Revival Court House from whose tower Union troops finally hauled down the Stars and Bars on July 4, 1863, a building which contains one of the largest collections of Confederate relics in the South. And in the park itself are the statues, the stately monuments to the brave men who died here, and the redoubts where this crucial battle was fought.

That July 4, 1863, the nation's eyes were focused on Lee's retreat from Gettysburg; but Vicksburg was the Confederacy's point of no return. As a result, Lincoln said, "The father of waters rolls unvexed to the sea," and one month later the first Union merchant steamboat safely completed the thousand-mile passage from St. Louis to New Orleans.

In 1876 the Mississippi River (rear) changed course, and today the Yazoo River flows past Vicksburg, at upper left.

JERRY COOKE, COURTESY *Time*

Before the steamboat, Mississippi cargoes traveled by raft and flatboat, piloted by colorful rivermen such as these.

River Plantations

In the 1840's what seemed like an endless procession of boats was moving up and down the Mississippi. There were flatboats and keelboats, operated by tall, big-boned pioneers—the "most rip-roaring of all sons of perdition"—who brawled, bragged, and sang their way into one of the most colorful chapters of American folklore. Across the water came the haunting note of a boatman's horn, or snatches of songs like "Some rows up, but we rows down; All the way to Shawnee town; Pull away—pull away!" When the riverman went ashore after the long passage, it was to "out-run, out-hop, out-jump . . . and lick any man in the country," for the men and the stories they told were as big and unruly as the river which was their world. The steamboat had come, too—the "floating palace" that belched steam and smoke and gave every boy along the river a vehicle for his dreams.

What a man could see from one of these boats when he came within 200 miles of New Orleans was one of the great spectacles of the American scene. Within sight of each other, on both sides of the river and along the bayous, were the magnificent plantation houses—tall, pillared white residences built by the wealth derived from cotton and sugar. Cultivated fields of tassel-topped sugar cane and long, low rows of grayish-white cotton balls came down to the levee's

edge, and all around was the lush foliage of the semi-tropics—clumps of live oak and cypress hung with Spanish moss, huge flowering bushes of camellias and magnolias, hedges of roses, and the sharp-pointed palmettos and Spanish dagger.

Although cotton had been planted in Louisiana in 1718 and sugar cane as early as 1700, not until the last decade of the eighteenth century were the potentials of these two crops fully realized, with the invention of the cotton gin and the development of sugar refining on a commercial scale. The mild climate and fertile soil were well suited to both crops, there was plenty of slave labor, and the Mississippi and its complex network of waterways provided economical transportation to New Orleans, where vessels from all over the world were tied up two and three deep along the miles of water front.

The years between 1820 and the Civil War were the opulent ones for the river plantations, and nothing reflects that fact better than the houses themselves. In general, plantation architecture was of two kinds: the early houses built by French and Spanish before the Louisiana Purchase of 1803; and the later, American adaptation of Greek Revival style, which dominated the years from 1820 to the war.

French planters of the late eighteenth century built

FRED RAGSDALE, FPG

A fine Greek Revival mansion in Natchez is D'Evereux, which has classic columns, hipped roof and a belvedere from which the fields were inspected.

Greenwood's beautiful proportions are reflected in an artificial lake dug by its first owner so that he could enjoy the sight of his mansion twice.

homes well suited to the hot, damp climate, following a tradition already established in the West Indies estates. The main floor stood well above the ground, supported by pillars eight or nine feet high to provide protection against floods and heat. Ground-floor walls, columns, and floor were made of plastered brick, while the upper story was of cypress, held together with clay and Spanish moss. A *galerie* encircled the house, and slender wooden columns supported a steep hipped roof. Inside, the house was simply laid out—two or three rooms wide, and one or two deep—all of the rooms opening out onto the *galerie* through shuttered French doors. Seldom was there a central hall, since access to the rooms could be achieved from the broad porch. Darby, on Bayou Teche, and the Keller Plantation in St. Charles Parish, are good examples of the French style, as is Parlange, built in 1750 by the Marquis Vincent de Ternant of Dansville-sur-Meuse. Another is Ormond, built before 1790, which is quite reminiscent of the West Indies plantation homes. This house, whose owner disappeared mysteriously in 1798, has been restored recently, and is one of the most striking examples of a plantation house snatched from the edge of ruin.

When Americans moved into this region in great numbers after the Louisiana Purchase, they brought with them the new, popular Greek Revival style, and soon adapted it into one of the most original architectural forms of the nineteenth century. This was what is known as Louisiana Classic, a completely indigenous house which was usually square, with a tremendous hipped roof and a great attic for insula-

In a seashell spiral, this unusual staircase climbs a Gothic turret of Afton Villa, near Bains, Louisiana.

A tunnel of live oaks 300 yards long leads from the Mississippi River to Oak Alley. Thought to have been planted by a French pioneer about 1690, they were fully grown when the house was built in 1832.

Behind the river plantation houses were formal gardens, like these at Evergreen. Farther back were the slave quarters (right) and fields. The decorative white structure seen here is a Greek Revival privy.

tion against the sun's heat. Below were two floors of large, high-ceilinged rooms which opened onto both a central hall and a deep gallery which circled the house. The gallery shaded the rooms from all but the early morning and late afternoon sun, and there was a maximum of cross-ventilation.

Most of the Classic plantations were laid out along a similar pattern. The main house faced the Mississippi, which was the route to the outside world and its markets, and between house and landing there was frequently an *allée* of magnificent trees, like the one at Oak Alley, shown on page 235. On either side of the house, in front, were *garçonnières* for guests. To the rear were the gardens, flanked by *pigeonniers,* or dovecotes; then the carriage houses, the long rows of

slave quarters, and the cotton gin or sugar mill.

Although the basic building materials came from the surrounding area, the embellishments were from Europe: silver hinges, hand-painted Dresden door-knobs, French tile for the roofs, and ceilings and panels decorated by European artists. As the scale of life expanded, houses became bigger and grander. Belle Grove, which was destroyed by fire in 1952, had 75 rooms and could accommodate fifty guests at a time. One of the best-preserved plantation homes is Houmas, which was once a 12,000-acre estate worked by 550 slaves. An English visitor reported that the view from Houmas was "one of the most striking of its kind in the world," and went on to say that "If an English horticulturist could see six thousand acres of the finest land in one field, unbroken by hedge and sprouting sugar cane, as level as a billiard table, he would surely doubt his sense." Here, a visitor's morning bath of tepid Mississippi water was cooled with ice, and three mint juleps before breakfast was the limit.

Not all the plantation homes are Louisiana Classic, of course. There are houses in Natchez, and elsewhere in Mississippi, like ruined Windsor near Port Gibson, which are almost pure Greek Revival. On the east bank of the river, between New Orleans and Baton Rouge, is San Francisco, the apogee of a style called "steamboat Gothic"; and Afton Villa, near St. Francisville, above Baton Rouge, is a curious Gothic type.

Fifty miles from New Orleans is Evergreen, one of the most beautifully designed plantations in Louisiana, and near St. Francisville is Greenwood, often considered the finest remaining example of a large plantation house. Built in 1830, Greenwood once had 12,000 acres, including a deer enclosure and a private race track; and inside the house are central hallways twenty feet wide and seventy feet long.

Social and economic changes brought about by the Civil War killed the prosperous plantation era, and gradually many of the great mansions went, too—some lost in the shifting river's course, some abandoned to slow decay. Some of those remaining have been opened to the public, and while a few are in ruins, enough have been preserved so that one may still see what is left of America's last great non-urban culture.

Nothing but stark columns remain of the once-lovely Windsor Plantation, built in 1861 near Port Gibson, Mississippi.

Fifty miles north of New Orleans, Evergreen was built in the 1830's at the height of the classic revival. Beautifully designed, the handsome house has 18-inch walls and floors and timbers of cypress. Behind the restored house are the plantation's 25,000 acres.

Midstream in the "monstrous big" Mississippi is Turtle Island, where Tom Sawyer and Huck Finn played. Mark Twain grew up in Hannibal, Missouri, in the house below at right. Next to it is a replica of the "thirty yards of board fence nine feet high," which Tom Sawyer's Aunt Polly wanted whitewashed. Here Tom learned that "in order to make a . . . boy covet a thing, it is only necessary to make the thing difficult to attain." At left, he tests his discovery.

Mark Twain's Mississippi

It was not much more than a hundred years ago—a short time, as history goes, but a time almost beyond recall, in American tempo—that Mark Twain experienced the thrill of boyhood in small-town America. Beyond Hannibal, Missouri, were sunlit prairies and cool dark woods; at its doorstep was the life-giving river; and in its dusty, unhurried streets boys went barefoot, dreaming of the day when each and every one would be a steamboat captain. "Once a day a cheap and gaudy packet arrived upward from St.

One of the last packet boats on the Mississippi River, the *Gordon C. Greene* turns downstream toward New Orleans.

Louis, and another downstream from Keokuk. Before these events, the day was glorious with expectancy; after them, the day was a dead and empty thing. "I can picture," Twain wrote, "the white town drowsing in the sunshine of a summer's morning; the streets empty, or pretty nearly so; one or two clerks sitting in front of the Water Street stores, with their splint-bottomed chairs tilted back against the walls . . . a sow and a litter of pigs loafing along the sidewalk. . . . Presently a film of dark smoke appears above one of those remote 'points'; instantly a Negro drayman, famous for his quick eye and prodigious voice, lifts up the cry, 'S-t-e-a-m-boat a-comin'!' and the scene changes! . . . Every house and store pours out a human contribution, and all in a twinkling the dead town is alive and moving. . . . Ten minutes later the steamer is under way . . . After ten more minutes the town is dead again, and the town drunkard asleep by the skids once more."

Hannibal's story is the story of dozens of other river towns that grew and dwindled and grew again, dependent on the winding river's whims. Yet the town still retains much of what Twain knew there. The river between it and St. Louis has altered but little since Huck Finn floated downstream. Around a bend north of town is Turtle Island, and south is Jackson Island, where Tom Sawyer and Huck used to swim, and decided to become pirates. At its northern edge is Holliday Hill—"Cardiff Hill" to Tom—which still yields, as it did to Twain, "the most extensive view up and down the river, and wide over the wooded expanses of Illinois." On the south is the higher point of Lover's Leap, and the cave where Injun Joe died.

The house where Mark Twain lived is a plain, two-story frame house built by his father in 1844, typical of the unpretentious pre-Civil War homes along the Mississippi. To one side of it stands a replica of the famous "thirty yards of board fence nine feet high," which Tom's Aunt Polly told him to whitewash. Nearby is a modest frame structure where the Hawkins family lived in Twain's youth, home of the Becky Thatcher who was Laura Hawkins in real life. A tablet marks the site of the house where Tom Blankenship, Huck's prototype, lived with his father and older brother. Where Hannibal has changed, so has America; but it is possible to recapture here some of the long, long dreams of youth which were Tom Sawyer's and every boy's, not so very long ago.

IKE VERN, REPRINTED FROM *Holiday;* © 1949 BY THE CURTIS PUBLISHING CO.

Lakes and Prairie

Heartland of a Nation

Of the many thousands of visitors to this region of lakes and prairies, none had a more lasting effect on its geography and history than the huge, inanimate ice sheets which paid their final call about 25,000 years ago. Out of the north the inexorable glaciers moved across Canada, gouging off the tops of hills, mixing topsoil with pulverized rocks and minerals, scooping out the basins of the Great Lakes from old river beds, and finally depositing the whole rich mixture over the land as far south as the Missouri and Ohio rivers. Not only did the glaciers determine the size and drainage of the Great Lakes and change the direction of the Missouri River, but they created an agricultural heartland which is one of the richest farming areas in the world.

In a very real sense, this central prairie land became the crossroads of America, marked by the paths of nearly all the diverse peoples who have made a nation's history. Here are the curious monuments left by prehistoric Indians, the hunting grounds of the red men encountered by the first settlers, the outposts and water routes of French *coureurs de bois*. In Alexandria, Minnesota, is the mysterious Kensington Runestone, discovered by a farmer in 1898. The subject of heated controversy ever since, the stone is inscribed with runic characters which, if genuine, would indicate the presence of a band of Vikings in the area as early as 1362.

Into this heartland came the first waves of settlers from the eastern seaboard, most of them Anglo-Saxon or Scotch-Irish in origin. Later the Germans arrived, followed by Irish, by people from the Mediterranean's shores, by Russians, Poles, and Balkan and Baltic immigrants. And they were followed in turn by the great influx of Scandinavians who selected the northlands of Michigan, Minnesota, and Wisconsin that resembled so closely their homelands.

At first there were only individuals moving in, then came little communities, each group adding its unique patch to this quilt of American life. Colonies of Frenchmen established Gallipolis in Ohio and pockets of settlement in Illinois and Iowa; Amish, Mennonites, Mormons, and other religious sects built communal societies which still dot the region; southerners imported Jefferson's Greek Revival ideas to towns like Gambier and Mount Vernon, Ohio; Swiss came to Indiana; Dutch to Michigan; Cornishmen and Germans to Wisconsin; and New Englanders deposited their architecture and village greens almost intact in places like Canfield, Norwalk, Milan, Copley, and

Chicago was located on the French portage from Lake Michigan to the Mississippi. In 1803 the U.S. constructed Fort Dearborn here.

Voyageurs and trappers bought supplies at Grand Portage on Lake Superior, Minnesota's first white settlement.

Traces of ancient Indian copper mines may be seen at Isle Royale, Michigan. Shown above is a reconstruction of Fort Recovery in Ohio, on the site of the fort Anthony Wayne erected here in 1793.

Sault Ste. Marie was a French outpost until 1762. The British built the first locks here about 1797.

Galena, Illinois, never lived up to the promise it seemed to have in 1856. At right is the mysterious Kensington Runestone, center of a controversy since its discovery by a farmer in 1898.

A magazine and foundations of French Fort de Chartres are in Illinois.

New London. These Ohio towns were part of the Western Reserve, claimed by Connecticut, and even today they retain the atmosphere of New England villages, complete with a traditional "common" and white-steepled church nearby.

Gradually the cities began to grow, in a manner no one could have predicted. There is Galena, in Illinois, whose future was bright with promise a century ago, which today has less than half its 1856 population and remains an almost perfect prototype of the mid-nineteenth-century Middle Western town. Or there is Chicago, a sleepy village on the banks of the Chicago River in 1833, today the second city in the nation, and possibly as representative of modern America as any metropolitan area in the land.

For almost the first two hundred years of life in America, the only way to create a farm was the hard way—by the back-breaking toil of clearing the forest. In the early nineteenth century, frontier farmers had reached the western edge of the wooded Appalachian Plateau. Before them, in what is now western Ohio and the state of Illinois, lay the eastern pocket of the prairie where they could see for the first time the horizon and the full sweep of sky. Because they had never known farmland where trees did not grow, they settled for a time, stubbornly, in the forest at the edge of the grass. Perhaps a generation passed before any of them moved onto the tempting open land, and not until 1833, when the first steel plow was made, could they do much with the deep, thickly-matted sod. Then, very quickly, this region came into its own as a marvelously productive area.

The chain of inland fresh-water seas, together with the Ohio and Mississippi and their tributaries, were the lines of communication and of trade in the early years. The marketable foodstuffs went south, over the Mississippi's natural highway. Then the Erie Canal and the National Road put this region into contact with the thickly-populated East, and by the time of the Civil War all the movement seemed to be an east-west flow. That was the route of the wagon trains and the railroads, and when whole mountains of iron ore were discovered in Minnesota, and the Sault Ste. Marie canal opened, this whole sector became a nexus of an overpowering change in American life, as well as a connecting link between the cities of the East and the beckoning West.

For the man who had his back to the Appalachian Mountains and his face toward the Mississippi River, the vastness of the prairie made other continents seem unreal, or relatively unimportant. Throughout its history, the land of lakes and prairie has had a sense of security, in the heart of its natural riches, which has given it a character all its own.

195

Objects like these, found in prehistoric burial mounds in Ohio, Indiana, and Illinois, indicate the skilled craftsmanship of the ancient peoples who made them. The most famous example of their handiwork is the Adena pipe, made in the form of a man's figure.

Prehistoric Mound Builders

During the same period when nomads on the other side of the world were exploring and settling the Nile Valley, when the first farmers in lower Mesopotamia were inventing the wheel, wandering people were filtering into the eastern half of America. For several thousand years these descendants of Asiatic migrants lived along the river banks, subsisting on shellfish, small game, roots, and nuts, and left behind, for the speculation of archaeologists and anthropologists, shell heaps, village sites, and stone implements.

About the beginning of the Christian era a more advanced people appeared in the Ohio Valley, called the Adena Indians. The present state of Ohio was a center of their activity, and even today there are more than 5,000 mounds, fortifications, and village ruins within its borders, the evidence of several ancient civilizations. Still others may be seen in Wisconsin and in Illinois, at the famous Cahokia and Dickson Mound sites. These Adena people, known for their construction of funeral mounds like the huge one near Miamisburg, Ohio, buried ornaments of hammered copper, mica, beads, woven fabrics, and carvings with their dead. The most famous example of their handiwork is the Adena pipe. They also made the first grit-tempered pottery, built large ceremonial earthworks, and constructed circular homes and community halls.

They were followed by the most advanced prehistoric society in Ohio, the Hopewell people, who roamed as far east as New York and west to Kansas. Remains of this civilization were found first at the Hopewell site near Chillicothe, but the most remarkable earthworks are Seip Mound State Park, near Bainbridge, and the Mound City Group near Chillicothe. Over twenty burial mounds stand in the thirteen-acre Mound City area—enough to provide considerable information about the habits of these people. The site of each mound was probably occupied first by a wooden structure, where the last rites for honored Hopewell dead were conducted. It is believed that these structures were later burned, perhaps with the idea of purification, or to allow the spirit of the dead person to escape, and then, after offerings were left, the site was covered by a mound. Since the only tools available to the Hopewells were sticks, or hoes of shell or bone, this must have been a formidable task.

Skilled craftsmen in wood, stone, copper, and bone, the Hopewell people were also skilled pottery makers, and conducted an extensive "foreign" trade. In one Hopewell site excavations revealed copper from the Lake Superior region, obsidian from the Rocky Mountains, ocean shells from the Gulf of Mexico, and mica from the southern Alleghenies.

In addition to the many burial mounds still existing in Ohio, there are fortifications built by the Hopewell Indians. One of the best examples of these is at Fort Ancient, near Wilmington, where some 100 acres enclosed by earthworks are situated on a bluff that rises high above the Little Miami River. At Glenford near Somerset, there is a rocky plateau once circled by a stone wall seven to ten feet high, and over a mile long. At intervals along the ruined parapet causeways were cut from the sandstone of the plateau, and a moat protected what was a vulnerable section of the fort. Another mound-builders' fort is at Fort Hill State Park, near the site of a prehistoric village.

After the decline of the Hopewell people, the next important group to appear was the Late Woodland civilization, Indians who occupied the Ohio Valley perhaps four hundred years before the white man arrived, and who may have been related to the Shawnees. Various centers of their activity may be seen today near Lebanon, Cincinnati, and in Ross and Scioto counties.

Most mysterious of all the remains left by these Indians are the so-called effigy mounds, constructed in the shape of a bird, beast, or serpent. A number of these effigy mounds exist in Wisconsin, but the largest and finest in the country is Ohio's Great Serpent Mound. This is an embankment of earth near Fort Hall and Hillsboro, nearly a quarter of a mile long, which represents a gigantic serpent in the act of uncoiling. The greater part of the snake's body is extended in seven deep curves, and partly within the monster's open jaws is an oval wall of earth resembling an egg. The average width of the serpent is about twenty feet, and its height along tail and body is four or five feet. No man-made objects have been found in Serpent Mound itself, and although some scientists believe that it is the burial place of priests or medicine men, one can only guess at its purpose.

Whatever secret the mounds may hold, their meaning for the Indians was eloquently suggested by a man who may never have seen one. Speaking at the signing of a treaty with the white men in 1855, Chief Seattle said: "Every part of this soil is sacred. . . . Every hillside, every valley, every plain and grove, has been hallowed by some sad or happy event in days long vanished. Even the rocks, which seem to be dumb and dead as they swelter in the sun . . . thrill with the memories of stirring events connected with the lives of my people. . . . When your children's children think themselves alone in the field, the store, the shop, upon the highway, or in the silence of the pathless woods, they will not be alone. . . . At night when the streets of your cities and villages are silent and you think them deserted, they will throng with the returning hosts that once filled them and still love this beautiful land. The white man will never be alone."

Ohio's remarkable Great Serpent Mound may be seen best from the air, as in this photograph. Nearly a quarter of a mile long, the uncoiling serpent holds what seems to be an egg in his jaws (upper right).

La Salle

Père Marquette

Empire in the Wilderness

In 1534 Jacques Cartier made the first of his three trips to the New World in search of a passage to the Orient. Although he discovered the rock of Quebec, gave a name to Mont Real, and prowled into the interior, he found neither passage nor gold, and France paid scant attention to his discoveries. The royal point of view toward ventures of this kind was expressed by the Duc de Sully, who observed: "Far-off possessions are not suited to the temperament or to the genius of Frenchmen, who to my great regret have neither the perseverance nor the foresight for such enterprises, but who ordinarily apply their vigor, minds, and courage to things which are immediately before their hand and constantly before their eyes."

But the Duc reckoned without such men as Samuel de Champlain, who gave France a footing in the St. Lawrence Valley which would last for 150 years. From this base the *voyageurs* and *coureurs de bois* set out on their explorations into the wilderness, and side by side with them went missionaries—mostly Jesuits,

and a few Récollet fathers. Sharing the Indians' lodges, hopefully teaching the children, and stoically eating the lichen *tripe de roche,* these adventurous missionaries frequently suffered unspeakable tortures and death with quiet courage.

Best known of the French "Blackrobes" was Père Jacques Marquette, who arrived in Quebec in 1666, studied Indian languages, and was sent to the mission at Sault Ste. Marie—a place once described by Henry Clay as "the remotest settlement in the United States, if not in the moon." In 1672 he was joined by the young French explorer Louis Joliet, and the next May they and five companions set off in canoes to find the "great river" about which the Indians told them.

From St. Ignace on the Straits of Mackinac they went to Green Bay, traveled southwest to Portage, where a marker commemorates their passage into the Wisconsin River, and a month later they had gone down the Mississippi as far as the mouth of the Arkansas. Learning from Indians that the river flowed into the Gulf of Mexico, they decided to return, and headed up the Illinois River. Passing Buffalo Rock, near the present site of Père Marquette State Park, they stopped at Starved Rock, the principal Illinois Indian village. Now a state park, this was the site of a mission founded by Marquette two years later, and the base of La Salle's operations in 1683.

After leaving the Illinois River, they paddled up the Des Plaines, portaged across a swampy tract in the southwest section of present-day Chicago, then headed down the South Branch and the Chicago River into Lake Michigan. In four months they had traveled more than 2,500 miles and established a trade route between the Great Lakes and the Mississippi (the Fox-Wisconsin waterway) which for 150 years would be the main artery of travel in the old Northwest.

Today, except for place names throughout the area, almost all tangible evidence of such heroic men as Marquette, Joliet, La Salle, Tonti, Du Lhut, and others has vanished, like France's New World empire.

An Illinois Indian village was at Starved Rock, above, when Marquette and Joliet visited here in 1673. The British took Fort Michilimackinac from France in 1761, later built the fort shown below.

An old map shows Cartier landing in Canada where he claimed the St. Lawrence area for France in 1534. North is at the bottom of the map.

From the Revolution through the War of 1812, the Northwest Territory was almost constantly in the throes of Indian warfare led by such chiefs as (left to right) Logan, a Mingo; Little Turtle, a Miami; and the Shawnee Tecumseh.

The Old Northwest

It was late in 1776, and Kentuckians, crowded into isolated little forts like Boonesborough and Harrodsburg, could sense the mounting pressure of Indian attacks. Warfare had been a habit in this region since the first red inhabitants fought each other for its possession, but in 1776 the outcome of skirmishes in the wilderness was being watched across the seas, in the capitals of Europe. In fact, the increased tempo of attacks on the colonial frontier had been planned in London to gain control of the Northwest Territory, and they were organized by Lieutenant Governor Henry Hamilton, "The Hair Buyer," in Detroit.

Fortunately for the Americans, there was one man who seemed to know what to do, and after telling Governor Patrick Henry and the Virginia Assembly "if a country is not worth protecting, it is not worth claiming," he had persuaded them to contribute 500 pounds of powder for Kentucky's defense. In 1778 George Rogers Clark was 26 years old, and he was as determined as the British to take control of the Northwest. He collected 175 men, and on a late spring day they set out to conquer the Illinois territory. They went first to Fort Massac (where you can see a reconstructed portion of the old French fort), camped the next night at Indian Point, the forested bluff near Vienna, Illinois, and after a six-day march arrived at Kaskaskia, which they took on July 4, 1778. By August, Clark had captured Cahokia and Vincennes, and began making plans to take Detroit.

Governor Hamilton, outraged to hear of Vincennes' fall, headed an expedition to recapture the fort, and arrived there in December of 1778. The town was held

This is the way Detroit looked in 1796, at the time the British surrendered the outpost to the U.S. Long after the Revolution the British here abetted Indian attacks on American frontier settlements.

by only twenty men under Captain Leonard Helm, who could do little but surrender to Hamilton's 700 whites and Indians. Hamilton knew there were only 80 Americans at Kaskaskia and half that many at Cahokia, but for some reason he decided to settle down for the winter at Vincennes.

Two hundred miles away, in Kaskaskia, George Rogers Clark heard of Hamilton's victory at Vincennes, and knowing he could not defend his own position, decided to divide his tiny force, recruit some French, and attack the enemy. Few campaigns in history, on which so much depended, have been conducted with more resourcefulness or daring, and even Hamilton, contemplating Clark's campaign in his cell at Williamsburg some time later, wrote that it was a military feat "unequalled perhaps in History."

Across plains, forests, and swollen, icy rivers Clark and his 170 men marched. One of Clark's men wrote: "Set off to cross . . . Horse-Show Plain, all covered with water breast high. Here we expected some of our brave men must certainly perish, having froze in the night, and so long fasting. Having no other resource but wading this . . . lake of water, we plunged into it with courage, Col. Clark being first." By the time they crossed the Wabash, west of Vincennes, they had been eighteen days on the march, and without food for the last two. At dusk Clark had twenty American flags attached to poles, spaced them at wide intervals along his line of march, and started his handful of men off on a zigzag course toward the town. The defenders at Vincennes, believing they were attacked by twenty companies, held out through the night but gave up by morning, and formally surrendered to Clark the next day, February 25, 1779. It was the first significant

General Rufus Putnam's house at Marietta, Ohio, formed a part of Campus Martius, the colony's fortified stockade.

The Northwest Territory Land Office, built in 1788, is located near the Campus Martius Museum at Marietta.

William Henry Harrison occupied an office in the old Territorial Capitol at Vincennes (left). His home, Grouseland, appears in the background. At right is a restoration of Elihu Stout's print shop.

201

At Fallen Timbers, Little Turtle's Indians were concealed within a two-mile treefall; but Wayne's well-drilled infantry flushed them out with a bayonet charge, and his cavalry routed them.

American victory in the old Northwest.

George Rogers Clark was thirty years old when his western campaign ended, and for 36 years more he lived, deep in debt, his claims and services ignored by his country, watching civilization bear down like a steamroller on the forests and plains he had loved and conquered. Late in life the state of Virginia sent the sick old man a sword engraved with words of honor, but Clark said, "Damn the sword! I had enough of that—a purse well filled would have done me more service!" Not until 1936 was the handsome monument to one of the West's outstanding heroes dedicated in Vincennes, Indiana's oldest town. Inside the columned building on the site of his victory are the ironic words Clark wrote to Patrick Henry: "Great things have been effected by a few men well conducted—our cause is just—our country will be grateful."

Vincennes is, in fact, one of the few places in this region where it is still possible to see some of the historic buildings of the Northwest Territory. Here is the Territorial Capitol, a frame building which was from 1800 to 1813 the seat of government of an area which now includes Indiana, Illinois, Michigan, Wisconsin, and the part of Minnesota which is east of the Mississippi. The first occupant of the governor's office was William Henry Harrison, who defeated Tecumseh at Tippecanoe in 1811. His stately home, known as Grouseland, or the White House of the West, is near the old Territorial Capitol, and is well worth visiting.

At Marietta, Ohio, a few buildings date back to the first organized settlement in the territory under the Northwest Ordinance of 1787. General Rufus Putnam's house, which was part of the fortification called Campus Martius, is enclosed in a wing of the Campus Martius Museum. Nearby is the Northwest Territory Land Office, built in 1788, and the oldest surviving building in the state.

Today if you follow Route 127 north from Cincinnati you will be retracing the approximate road taken by General Anthony Wayne in 1793 and 1794, on his way to and from the crucial battle of Fallen Timbers. It passes the sites of Forts Hamilton, St. Clair, Jefferson, and Greenville, where the Treaty of 1795 was signed with the Indians. To the west of the road is a reconstruction of Fort Recovery, where Little Turtle defeated General Arthur St. Clair in 1791 and attacked Wayne's men in 1794. A few earthworks of Fort Defiance remain in the city of Defiance, Ohio, and there are remains of Fort Miamis, in Maumee. Near here a monument marks the site of Wayne's victory at Fallen Timbers in the Maumee Valley.

But mostly what remains here are the memories of a time when this was part of America's first West, occupied by a handful of courageous men and women, who saw in it a land of promise, and who were willing to fight, and fight again, and frequently die for it.

In 1792 U.S. control of the Northwest depended on Anthony Wayne.

George Rogers Clark and his "Long Knives" captured Vincennes in 1779.

William Henry Harrison, later President, was the victor at Tippecanoe.

A rare contemporary painting shows Wayne and his officers negotiating with Indians near Fort Greenville. The long-winded proceedings lasted for two months in the summer of 1795, but resulted in U.S. control of the Northwest Territory.

War on the Lakes

Although we are often inclined to think of the War of 1812 as one which was fought to preserve freedom of the seas, it is entirely possible that it would never have happened at all had it not been for the bumptious Americans in frontier settlements who coveted land along their northern boundary still held by Indians and the British. Urged on by "war hawks" like Henry Clay, John Sevier, and John C. Calhoun, Congress declared war on June 18, 1812.

Nearly all the land battles in that war were disastrous from the American point of view, and only when General William Hull surrendered Detroit to the British did it occur to the government that control of the Great Lakes was going to be important. During the spring and summer of 1813, 28-year-old Oliver Hazard Perry, stationed at Erie, Pennsylvania, hastily built and equipped ten ships with supplies hauled over the Alleghenies to Pittsburgh and poled up the French River. The largest vessels were the sister-brigs *Lawrence* and *Niagara,* 480 tons each.

Until August of 1813, British Commander R. H. Barclay blockaded Perry's little fleet in Erie Harbor and then, for a reason which has never been clear, he sailed away. On August 4, Barclay returned to discover that Perry had got his vessels over the harbor bar and was out on the lake.

Put-in-Bay in the Bass Islands was Perry's base of operations, and from here, at sunrise on September 10 he sighted Barclay and sailed out to meet him. By 10 A.M. the *Lawrence* was cleared for action and flying a battle flag which carried the words of the dying Captain James Lawrence: "Don't Give Up the Ship." Less than two hours later the *Detroit,* Barclay's flagship, opened on her, and after two hours of fighting,

Oliver Hazard Perry and his twelve-year-old brother, a midshipman, were rowed from the flagship *Lawrence* to the undamaged *Niagara* under heavy enemy fire.

The painting above shows British and Americans burying their dead after the Battle of Lake Erie in 1813. Years later the bodies of three men from each side were buried beneath the floor of the rotunda of the Perry Monument (below), which stands near the site of the important 1813 victory at Put-in-Bay.

every gun was out of action and most of the crew dead or wounded. By 2:30 that afternoon the ships on both sides were in such dreadful condition that it looked as though the battle would go to the first one who could produce an undamaged ship.

Fortunately for the Americans, the *Niagara* was behind and was almost untouched. As she neared the scene, Perry climbed into an open boat and rowed over to her. By this time the *Lawrence* had struck her colors, but the British were unable to take possession because of the *Niagara's* approach. Fifteen minutes later the battle was over; Perry reboarded the *Lawrence,* received Barclay's surrender on her deck, and sat down to write his famous message to General William Henry Harrison: "We have met the enemy, and they are ours."

His victory not only had an electric effect on the nation's morale, but it changed the entire complexion of the war. It meant the end of the British occupation of Detroit; it shook the British-Indian alliance; and it opened the road to Canada for Harrison, who defeated the British and Indians at the Battle of the Thames in October.

Today a massive pink granite column stands at Put-in-Bay in South Bass Island, Ohio, looking out over the waters where Perry's great victory took place. The *Lawrence* and the *Niagara* were scuttled after the Battle of Lake Erie, but in 1913 the *Niagara* was raised, and in 1931 she was moved to Pennsylvania State Park on Presque Isle peninsula, where the historic vessel has been restored.

About 1860 A. F. Phillips painted New Salem's first mill (center) as it looked in the 1830's.

Land of Lincoln

The baby who was born on Sunday morning, February 12, was named Abraham, after the grandfather who had been killed by Indians only 23 years earlier. One window shed light on the dirt floor of the log cabin, and a twig-and-clay chimney carried the smoke out of a room that looked like all the others on the Kentucky frontier. It was 1809, and the child who began life here would, from the beginning, draw his ideals and his strength from a land that was still rough and new, and almost always difficult.

To follow the early years of Abraham Lincoln one begins in Hodgenville, Kentucky, at a spring and a giant white oak which mark the site of Thomas Lincoln's Sinking Spring Farm. This is a national park now, and a cabin like the one in which the child was born is enclosed within a columned marble building. Ten miles to the northeast, in a region of rolling, wooded farmland, a similar cabin stands on the site of Knob Creek Farm, where the Lincoln family moved in 1811. Near this place of "high hills and deep gorges," not far from the old Cumberland Pike, Lincoln first attended school, trudging four miles to learn reading, writing, and ciphering.

This life-size painting, probably done during the Lincoln-Douglas debates, was used as a Republican campaign poster.

Near Lincoln's Kentucky birthplace is the reconstructed Knob Creek cabin, with split-rail fence such as Lincoln built.

Utopias on the Prairie

It is interesting to consider how many early American communities were founded by people seeking a haven for religious and intellectual principles. All through the eastern and central states are remains of distinctive settlements which grew from the labors of religious or utopian societies. Each added something unique to the landscape, and each reflects the character of its founders.

There is the village of Zoar, Ohio, a tidy place of low rambling cottages and picket fences, founded in 1817 by Joseph Bimeler and a group of German Separatists. Like some other groups, the Zoarites thought that the best way to preserve their unity and beliefs, while conquering the frontier, was to form a society where all members shared in the ownership, labor, and fruits of the community. Here the visitor may still see well-preserved homes, the old hotel, village store, and the beautiful two-and-a-half-acre garden which follows the Bible's directions for the New Jerusalem. The Number One House, once a business office and quarters for the aged and infirm, is now a museum of the Zoarites' handiwork; and on a hill overlooking the town is the lovely Meeting House they built.

In Iowa are the seven villages of the Amana Society, led to America in 1843 by Christian Metz. Many of the old shops, homes, and mills are still in use, as are the plain churches with bare floors and whitewashed walls; and descendants of the first colonists live along the quiet streets of the towns. Oldest of the communities, the town of Amana is also the most reminiscent of a German village.

On the banks of the Wabash is New Harmony, Indiana, with its memories of two utopian colonies. The first, called Harmonie, was settled by Father George Rapp and his German followers whom he kept working in the fields, without pay, from sunrise to sunset, blowing a horn at them if they relaxed. In 1825 Rapp and his flock sold their community to Robert Owen and headed east, to found Economy, Pennsylvania. Although it lasted only three years, Owen's colony established the first U.S. kindergarten, a scientific laboratory, and other educational innovations. Today one may still see in this quiet town the Rappites' stone granary; Gabriel's Rock where the angel supposedly spoke to Father Rapp; a men's dormitory; and Father Rapp's mansion. There is also a fine restoration of an intricate maze Rapp designed, a hedge labyrinth through which his followers wandered in the only amusement permitted them.

Father Rapp blew this horn at slackers in the fields. At right is the restored hedge labyrinth at New Harmony. In the center, a stone tower symbolizes the heaven which Rappites would gain after a tortuous journey through life.

THE OHIO HISTORICAL SOCIETY

At Zoar older children minded the babies, since women were expected to work in the fields. For a while celibacy was enforced, because childbearing interfered with work.

212

The Iowa villages founded by the Amana Society retain many of the original buildings, and descendants
of Christian Metz s followers live in old communities.

One of the few buildings in New Harmony which date
from the Owenite era is the odd structure built by Robert Owen's son to house an experimental laboratory.

213

The Great Plains

Early Life on the Great Plains

South from the town of Wall, South Dakota, the broad, flat prairie begins to rise in a long ground swell of bluffs. Before the traveler has gone much farther, these bluffs break up suddenly into a scarred, arid land of fantastic shapes and colors, a maze of sandstone spires, gargoyles, and pinnacles. This is the region the Indians called "mako sica"—the Badlands.

To see the Badlands National Monument is to see the early history of the earth, for embedded in the accumulated layers of sandstone are fossils dating back to the Age of Reptiles, almost sixty million years ago. In that time much of North America lay under the waters of a huge sea whose shores were flat, swampy jungle. Over the land lumbered giant reptiles—creatures like the brontosaurus, a long-necked vegetarian with a fifteen-ton body and a two-ounce brain; tyrannosaurus rex, the monster with a kangaroo-like body, a huge head, and vicious, grinning jaws; giant crocodiles; and the rhinoceros-like triceratops. Eventually, all these creatures perished, and their bones were covered with layer upon layer of sediment which the flooding streams deposited on the marshy plains. Then, about twenty million years later, in the Oligocene Period, the Badlands region exploded in a series of upheavals at the same time the Rocky Mountains were being formed, and volcanic matter hurled into the air settled like an ashen blanket over the area. This layer covered and preserved the remains of many of the first mammals—mastodons, the tiny three-toed horse, and others—but as the centuries passed the Badlands slowly eroded, its silt washed down gullies into the White River, while spring rains and melting snows cross-sectioned the brittle sandstone to expose the ancient fossils. Some of the best museum collections in America have come from the Badlands area, the Black Hills, and the shale outcroppings near Bismarck, North Dakota, and in this region itself there is a fine paleontological exhibit at the Museum of the School of Mines and Technology in Rapid City, South Dakota.

Although the northern Plains have none of the spectacular ruins of the Southwest, men have lived on the Plains ever since the first Asiatics wandered down from Alaska, about twelve thousand years ago. Coming at the end of the final glacial age, they arrived in time to kill the last animal giants—the mammoths, mastodons, and huge bison. Nomadic Stone Age hunters, these earliest plainsmen lived in caves or tent villages like the one found at Old Signal Butte, near Scotts Bluff, Nebraska. There, on a windswept plateau, they watched for the appearance of deer and buffalo herds, and went after them with their stone-pointed spears.

Not until well into the Christian era did the Indians begin to lead a sedentary, year-round life on the plains. Between A.D. 500 and 1300, groups from the southeast moved into the river valleys, bringing with them pottery and a knowledge of agriculture. Some of these farmers were mound builders, whose strange relics have been found in eastern South Dakota, while others constructed earth lodges of the kind white men imitated hundreds of years later. When Pierre de La Vérendrye claimed the Dakota region for France in 1738, a few of these agricultural settlements still flourished, and he was amazed by one Mandan village, where he found hundreds of acres of tilled fields and a palisaded fort so well constructed that it was practically impregnable. In this village he counted 130 "cabins," in streets so uniform that "often our Frenchmen would lose their way in going about." What he called "cabins" were actually igloo-shaped structures made of earth, measuring from forty to ninety feet in diameter at the base, and supported by heavy cottonwood pillars.

Several good examples of the Mandan lodges may be seen today at Fort Abraham Lincoln State Park in North Dakota, where part of a village site has been restored. This community stood in an unusually well-protected spot, between the Heart River on one side and a deep coulee on the other, with its exposed sides protected by deep moats. Depressions in the earth show that the settlement contained 68 lodges, and the visitor may see four restored homes and a large ceremonial lodge, as well as crude tools and furnishings which have been found here. The Mandans, the Arikaras, and other Plains farmers measured their wealth in terms of how much food they had, and while they were relatively prosperous, by the time the first white adventurers made contact with them, their culture was beginning to lose its vigor, for it was rapidly being replaced by a freer way of life.

This new culture, paradoxically, was fostered by the coming of the white man at the same time that it was being hindered by his presence. Whole populations of Indians had been set in motion in the east, and although the tribes closest to the white man had lost their homes, they had acquired firearms, which

In 1832 George Catlin painted the Bull Dance of the Mandans, a form of buffalo worship which took place in a clearing between the distinctive earth-covered lodges. Several examples of Mandan huts may be seen at Fort Abraham Lincoln State Park in North Dakota. The picture at right shows a long view of the fantastically eroded Badlands.

enabled them to dislodge the western Indians from *their* lands. The Chippewas, for example, had pushed into Minnesota, driving the Dakotas, or Sioux tribes, out of the forests into the plains. Here, except for one great discovery, their way of life would have conformed to that of the Stone Age hunter thousands of years earlier. This discovery was the horse.

The Spanish in the Southwest had horses, and although they did everything to prevent Indians from acquiring them, the animals multiplied, ran wild, moved north through California and Texas, and at some stage discovered the magnificent grazing grass on the plains. The Dakotas saw horses for the first time in 1722, and for a time they ate the "mystery dogs," as they were called. Then they learned to ride them, and before long all the great fighting tribes were mounted—Sioux and Blackfeet, Cheyennes, Arapahos and Crows, Kiowas, Comanches, and Piegans. Cornfields were abandoned, and instead of farming, they followed the buffalo. On horseback they could attack the herds directly; with bows and arrows they could kill the animals easily, and relatively safely; and soon the buffalo supplied the Plains Indian's every need. His chief source of food was the meat; his tepees, clothing, and shoes were made from the hides; hoes and axes came from the shoulder blades; thread and bowstring from the sinews; his fuel from the chips. The free, nomadic existence which resulted could last only so long as the great herds of buffalo survived, and by 1880 the white man had killed them off, and with them the whole fabric of Plains Indian life.

ARNOLD NEWMAN

Horses, captured from herds brought to America by the Spanish, completely revolutionized Plains Indian life and warfare. Alfred Jacob Miller's painting (right) captures a moment of battle between two tribes. Above is a reconstruction of the way Crow Indians lived a hundred years ago.

GILCREASE INSTITUTE OF AMERICAN HISTORY AND ART, TULSA; ELIOT ELISOFON, COURTESY *Life*

Jumping-off Places

Jim Baker, famous trapper and scout, lived in the mountains until he died at eighty. He had six wives, all Indians.

In an age when a person can travel across the continent in a matter of hours it is difficult to conceive that, not much more than a century and a half ago, there was only a handful of white men in the vast area beyond the Mississippi River. For a brief interlude of time those who had gone there—the wild, unrestrained breed known as the mountain men—probably achieved the most complete freedom known to recorded history.

Between 1820 and the 1840's, when the beaver was finally trapped out, men like Jed Smith, Jim Bridger, Kit Carson, Thomas Fitzpatrick, and Bill Williams ("Old Solitaire") lived completely on their own in an infinity of open spaces. Taking with them a few of civilization's implements—a rifle, knife, traps, powder, lead, and awl—they disappeared completely from the view of established society to roam the rivers and find the trails which are highways and railroads today, ranging through the trackless unknown from Kansas to California, and from Oregon to the New Mexico deserts. Once a year, in the summer, they traveled to the lusty trappers' rendezvous in the mountains to meet a caravan from St. Louis and exchange their pelts for a brief, glorious binge and some baubles for an Indian woman; but the rest of the time they were content simply to hunt beaver, to go where no other men had been, and to face the constant dangers of the enormous, unbroken wilderness. The Louisiana Purchase in 1803 made this land available for settlement; the expedition of Lewis and Clark opened men's eyes to what it held; and after the first trickle of movement, an unending stream of humanity began surging into the West.

The jumping-off places were back in Missouri, and the first of them was a town which Pierre Laclede had founded as a trading post in the winter of 1763-64, just below the junction of the Missouri and Mississippi Rivers. Located at the foot of a bluff on a bench of land high enough to provide protection from all but the worst spring floods, St. Louis commanded the principal water route to the fur-rich West. In 1817 the first steamboat docked at St. Louis, and within a short time hundreds of boats were stopping there each year, providing access to the town of Independence, where the Oregon and Santa Fe trails began, and to the commerce of the East.

Few of the old St. Louis buildings survived the disastrous fire of 1849 which swept through most of the waterfront area, destroying many of the original houses, stores, and warehouses; but in the Jefferson National Expansion Memorial three early structures are preserved. One is Old Rock House, a two-story limestone building erected by a fur trader in 1818, which became a warehouse for John Jacob Astor's fur company and then a sailmaker's loft where wagon covers, tents and tarpaulins were made for the streams of emigrants. Another is the Old Courthouse, a domed, Greek Revival building begun in 1839. Here Thomas Hart Benton advocated a transcontinental railroad, Henry Clay sold real estate, U. S. Grant freed his only slave, and Dred Scott sued for his freedom.

By 1842 St. Louis had changed from French provincial town to American river city. Colorful, noisy, its levees were crowded with Mexicans, Kentucky woodsmen, Germans, Indians, French, mountain men, and Negro stevedores. Up the Missouri in the rich, black bottomland were plantations worked by slaves. Beyond St. Charles the settlements thinned out into the "land beyond the Sabbath," where squatters eked out a living. Three hundred and sixty miles, or about fifteen days west of St. Louis, a traveler could see, in the early 1840's, signs of the great westward movement. Parties of emigrants, in tents and wagons, camped in open spots along the river, en route to the common rendezvous at Independence.

At that time Independence was the big town on the Missouri frontier, the busiest town in America west of St. Louis. Francis Parkman, arriving there in 1846, found himself "at the farthest outskirts of the great forest that once spread from the western plains to the shore of the Atlantic." Looking westward, he could see only "the green, ocean-like expanse of prairie, stretching swell beyond swell to the horizon." A pioneer woman wrote, "It matters not how far you have come, this is the point to which they all refer to, for the question is never, when did you leave home? but, when did you leave the Missouri River?"

Each spring brought more people to the tent camps outside of town and to Smallwood Noland's inn (accommodations for 400 people, if they did not object to two or more in a bed), and a new town, Westport, grew up to take the overflow. Nearby was an old American Fur Company trading post which also became a town, known as "Kansas." It had a better landing place than Independence, and when the older town was hit by a cholera epidemic in 1849, Kansas became the favorite jumping-off point. Soon it grew so large that it absorbed Westport and became Kansas City—big, booming and, when the Civil War had gone and the railroad had come, ready to handle a fresh army of emigrants.

VIEW OF ST. LOUIS.

This charming view of St. Louis was done about 1840-46, when the town was a gateway to the vast West.

221

Landmarks
of the
Trek West

Wagon trains rumbled past Jackson County Courthouse in Independence.

Each spring, from 1842 until the late 1880's, long lines of prairie schooners, horses, cattle, and oxen lumbered out of Missouri's towns on the first lap of a five-month, 2,000-mile westward trek. Each party elected a leader, but the expedition's safety usually depended on the hired guides, many of them ex-mountain men who had turned to this new profession when their beaver empire began to decline. Wilson Price Hunt blazed a trail in 1811, but the route mapped by Robert Stuart in 1812–1813 is the one that came to be known as the Oregon Trail. It began in the grassy swells of Kansas prairie erroneously named the "Great American Desert."

As the parties set out in 1849, spirits were high, the road was easy, and people even enjoyed the novelty of wagon travel. Not far west of Independence, the forests thinned out, and suddenly the emigrants were confronted with a grand sweep of grasslands, running away to the west as far as the eye could see. From here, one stream after another had to be crossed—the Blue River of Missouri, Indian Creek, Bull Creek, the Wakarusa River, Kansas River, and the Big and Little Blue Rivers of Kansas. Where the stream beds were too deep to be forded, there were aggravating waits for a turn at the ferry. Often impatient emigrants calked their wagon beds, stripped off the wheels, and rowed across.

Frequent prairie squalls, with high winds and hail, made the low places soft, and to avoid them the wagons traveled along the swells. Besides, it was safer to stay on high ground in Indian country, for down in the wooded hollows Pawnees would pounce on stragglers. Sometimes during dry spells the Pawnees started grass fires to reduce the animals' ground fodder; often they attacked lone stray wagons; and in the middle of the night they would ride down on a wagon train, whooping and hollering, and frightening off the horses before the emigrants knew what had happened. Because of this, the emigrant companies joined their wagons together at night, forming a hollow circle which served both as fort and corral.

By the time they reached Alcove Springs, near present-day Marysville, Kansas, on the Big Blue River, they began noticing an increasing number of graves along the way. Nearby, the route from St. Joseph joined the Oregon Trail, traffic became heavier, and as the emigrants headed north into sandy, grass-covered hills, they knew they were approaching the valley of the Platte River and the dry, wind-swept "Coast of Nebraska." At the Platte, where nothing but earthworks remain today, was Fort Kearny, one of civilization's few outposts along the trail. From Kearny, the emigrants followed the broad valley to the forks of the Platte, encountering huge buffalo herds which often shook the earth as they roared past. Along the Platte's south branch it was nearly sixty miles to the famous "California" crossing near Brule, Nebraska, where they double-teamed across the quicksand bottom, and then turned north toward the Platte's upper fork. Soon the land broke up into the wooded dell of Ash Hollow, across from present-day Lewellen, Nebraska, and the wagons sloughed through hub-deep sand before heading up the North Platte, where one may still see wagon ruts cut by thousands of wheels.

Through a strange country of fantastically-shaped buttes the trail ran, past Court House and Jail Rocks near Bridgeport; Chimney Rock near Bayard; and Scotts Bluff. From the crest of Mitchell Pass today's visitor will see the Laramie Mountains, far in the distance, which were the emigrants' first view of the Rockies. This was the last of the Great Plains, and from here on the going was infinitely harder.

CHRISTIAN STUDIO

DOWNEY'S MIDWEST STUDIO

Near Scotts Bluff, Nebraska, ruts made by thousands of wagons may still be seen. This was one of the natural landmarks on the Oregon Trail.

One of the easiest landmarks to sight was Chimney Rock in Nebraska, visible to pioneers for days before their slow-moving wagons arrived there.

The drawing of Cathedral Rock was done in 1849 by W. H. Tappen, who accompanied the U.S. Mounted Riflemen garrisoning posts along the Oregon Trail.

STATE HISTORICAL SOCIETY OF WISCONSIN

Stephen F. Austin and Sam Houston, both from Virginia, were rivals in independent Texas.

The first capitol of the Republic of Texas was Byars' smith shop at Washington-on-the-Brazos, where the 1836 declaration of independence was approved.

Independent Texas

When Stephen Austin brought the first few American settlers to Mexican Texas in 1822, he had no intention of making trouble with the country to the south. In the little colony of San Felipe on the Brazos River, he made every effort to be a loyal Mexican citizen, advising his people to do likewise. Looking at the wide, well-watered and unsettled Texas plains, Austin had a vision of expansion and prosperity as big as the country itself. To most Americans, the Plains were the "Great American Desert"—something to get across as quickly as possible—but Austin's followers were the first to see them as something entirely different: a place to settle.

At the same time that Austin was writing friends in the United States, describing Mexico as "the most liberal and munificent government on earth to emigrants," bad blood was developing between the American colonists and their Mexican rulers. The two peoples had little in common—there were differences in religion, language, and customs which were made no less difficult by a Texan attitude of Anglo-Saxon superiority. And the Mexicans, only briefly removed from three centuries of autocratic Spanish rule, resented the American introduction of slavery into Texas—an institution which had unpleasant connotations for them.

During John Quincy Adams' administration the United States made some efforts to buy Texas, and these overtures were pressed with renewed vigor under Andrew Jackson. Time and again, Mexico refused;

The Alamo chapel is all that remains of a larger establishment which 180 Texans defended to the death in 1836.

yet there was always the underlying fear that the U.S. might try to gain by force what it had been unable to purchase, and in the event of such a move, the Mexican government would have few allies among the settlers. By 1830 there were 30,000 Americans in Texas, or nine-tenths of the population. Their log-cabin settlements were scattered across the rich coastal prairies from Nacogdoches on the Louisiana border down to the Guadalupe River, and beyond. The result of Mexico's fears was the law of 1830 which forbade further American immigration into Texas. When this statute failed to curb the movement into the territory, Austin found himself in the middle, on the one hand trying to placate the Mexican government, on the other trying to restrain his followers.

While friction between the two peoples was mounting, General Lopez de Santa Anna staged a successful revolution in Mexico and set up a dictatorship. In September 1835, after a group of Texans seized a Mexican customs station, Santa Anna sent his brother-in-law General Perfecto de Cos with a force of 500 men to San Antonio. By this time Austin realized that negotiation was impossible, and wrote that "War is our only resource." Late in September, armed men began gathering to resist the Mexicans.

After taking the arsenal at Goliad, the Texans laid siege to Cos in San Antonio, and on December 5, 1835, they attacked. House by house they fought their way into the town, and by the night of the eighth, the Mexicans were surrounded in a partially ruined mission known as the Alamo. With all hope gone, Cos raised a white flag in the morning, and by the end of 1835 there were no more Mexicans troops in Texas.

Meantime, the moderate Austin was defeated as governor, and a more radical group of Texans launched an expedition to capture Matamoros on the Rio Grande. At the end of January two columns started south, one moving down the coast, while the other—a group of Americans who were sick of garrison duty at San Antonio—planned to approach Matamoros from inland. This group left behind them less than a hundred men to protect the town, and although the commanding officer wrote to San Felipe, begging for help, few reinforcements arrived. Among those who did come were the legendary Jim Bowie, with nineteen men; Colonel William B. Travis, with 25; and the frontiersman Davy Crockett, who brought twelve Tennesseeans with him.

General Sam Houston, who commanded all the Texas forces, had ordered Bowie and his men to blow up the San Antonio fortifications and retreat eastward, but the idea of retreat was an insult to the men in the town. Meantime, Santa Anna was moving north. On February 23, a lookout spotted the vanguard of the Mexican cavalry, and the 180 Texans holed up in the Alamo. Located east of the San Antonio River, on the outskirts of town, the Alamo had not been used as a mission since 1793, but as a military depot and storehouse. All that is left of the Alamo today is a roofless chapel, but in 1836 there was also a great walled plaza connected to a convent with a large patio, some stone rooms used as a jail, and a corral. The whole establishment sprawled over two and a half acres, and its walls were a quarter of a mile in length. With a maximum of 180 men, the defenders had less than fifteen per cent of the number needed for an adequate defense of the various buildings.

Biding his time, Santa Anna built earthworks on all sides of the old mission, harassed the defenders with light artillery, and put out a cavalry screen to prevent their escape. On February 24 Travis wrote "To the people of Texas and all Americans in the world," saying, "I am determined to sustain myself as long as possible and die like a soldier who never forgets what is due to his own honor and that of his country. VICTORY or DEATH."

No reinforcements came to the Alamo defenders, while Santa Anna had collected 5,000 men. On March 6, he decided to attack. At 4 A.M. four columns, totaling 2,500 men, were sent off to attack the old mission from all sides. Armed with axes, iron bars, and scaling ladders, they moved forward only to be sent reeling back by heavy cannon and rifle fire from the Alamo. As they reformed for another assault, a band across the river played "Degüello," the word and tune that meant "throat-cutting," which, when played in battle, signified that no quarter would be given.

A somewhat fanciful painting depicts the Alamo's fall. In the

In the second attack the Mexicans pressed so close to the walls that the Texan artillery was no longer effective. The Mexicans forced a breach in the north wall, another in the south one, and poured in on the defenders, who fell back to the convent and the roofless church for a desperate last stand. Now the Texans' own cannon were turned on them and, retreating from room to room, those who were left were forced into the chapel, where they were wiped out in a final hand-to-hand combat. When the battle was over, Santa Anna had the corpses of the Texans dragged out onto the open ground in front of the mission and cremated. Not one of the defenders had survived. Yet Santa Anna's victory had cost him dear, for it is estimated that more than 1,600 of his troops were casualties in the one-hour fight.

While the Alamo was still under siege, a group of men had gathered at the town of Washington, on the Brazos, and there, in a little shed, issued a declaration of independence on March 2, 1836. Sam Houston, lately returned from the Indian country, was re-elected commander in chief, and it was his job to create some order out of the chaos resulting from news of the Alamo. "The Raven," as the Cherokees had named him, was a remarkable man—tall and husky, an eloquent speaker who had served two terms in Congress and one as governor of Tennessee—who believed firmly that Texas would be far more useful to the United States than to Mexico.

roofless chapel (left center) the Texans made their last stand.

As he pulled together his disorganized forces in that muddy spring of 1836, his strategy was to move eastward, staying inland where the going was easier, and putting plenty of distance between the Mexicans and the straggling, ill-disciplined men he was trying to shape into an army. Progress through the rain and mud and across swollen rivers was painfully slow, and terrified bands of refugees constantly obstructed the army's "runaway scrape." Houston managed to escape across the Colorado River, just ahead of the Mexicans, and on March 31 he called a halt in a river bottom by the Brazos where he began molding an army.

All the Texan forces to the south had been defeated, and Santa Anna, assuming Houston to be fleeing for the U.S. border, headed for Lynch's Ferry on the San Jacinto River, north of Galveston Bay. Discovering this, Houston quick-marched to the ferry, arriving three hours ahead of the Mexicans. There, along Buffalo Bayou, a stream which emptied into the San Jacinto River, he formed his men in the moss-draped oak woods and waited. In front of them the thick prairie grass extended for nearly a mile of plain over which Santa Anna had to pass to reach the ferry. Early in the afternoon of April 20 the Mexican battle formations came in sight, but in the face of the accurate Texan rifle fire, they retired. Santa Anna selected a position on a low, tree-covered hill and declared a day of rest—he doubted if the Texans had the nerve to attack.

At four-thirty in the afternoon of April 21, the Mexican pickets saw cavalry and infantry moving toward them through the tall prairie grass in perfect battle order. Surprised and confused, and in no mood to fight, they fell in behind a flimsy line of breastworks and opened fire on the Texans, who kept on coming without bothering to shoot back. Soon the Texans broke into a run, and at point-blank range opened fire with a yell: "Remember the Alamo!" Swarming over the breastworks, they swung their rifles like clubs, slaughtering the disorganized Mexicans. Those of Santa Anna's men who retreated down the reverse side of the hill found they were hemmed in by water; those who headed for the bridge at Vince's Creek found that it had been burned by "Deaf" Smith, a Texas scout. Out of a force of 1,300, only forty Mexicans escaped, and Santa Anna, who fled when the shooting started, was found next day crouching in some tall grass, disguised as a cavalryman.

In September of that year Sam Houston triumphed over Stephen Austin to become the first president of the Republic of Texas, and for ten erratic years the new government survived. At last, a majority of the American people came to favor annexation of the area, and on December 29, 1845, President Polk signed the act making Texas a part of the United States.

Today only a few of Texas' earliest buildings remain, like the Eggleston House in Gonzales, and the handsome Fanthorp Stagecoach Inn at Anderson. There is a reproduction of Stephen Austin's log cabin at San Felipe, near an old well built by the first colonists, and one may see, of course, the battlefield of San Jacinto, and the museum in the state park there. In addition to the famous remains of the Alamo, one can get an idea of what San Antonio looked like in 1836 by visiting the restored settlement of La Villita, with its old, high-walled houses of rock and adobe.

Off the beaten track, in Independence, are some fine examples of houses built during the Republic period. The Anson Jones House, home of the last President of Texas, was originally in Independence, but this frame structure with hand-hewn timbers and wide center hall has been moved to Washington-on-the-Brazos State Park.

Two other interesting towns are Fredericksburg and New Braunfels, which German immigrants settled in the 1840's. Fredericksburg's *Vereinskirche,* a combination fort, school, and meeting house, is one of the buildings well worth seeing, as are the stone houses with fancy iron lacework in these towns. In Huntsville, one may see the simple frame house in which Sam Houston spent his last years, and the curious building, patterned after a Mississippi River steamboat, where he died.

The Open Range

From the Canadian border to Mexico there stretches a huge swath of land which rises almost imperceptibly as it fades off to the west. This last American frontier, the Great Plains, is an enormous territory that is still relatively empty, lonely, and alive with a wind which never quite ceases. Into this immensity, whose boundaries were the horizon and the sky, moved the last frontiersman—the cowboy. He was a self-reliant, adaptable man, courageous out of the sheer necessity of his environment; his life conditioned by nature and by animals. From his peculiar and arduous existence arose a special culture, one which was manifested in the cowboy's manner of dress, his speech, his humor, and his songs.

The cowboy originated in southeast Texas, in the *brasada,* or brush country, and he learned his trade from Plains Indians and Mexicans. Somehow the original herds of cattle brought to America by Spaniards survived in the flat, dry *brasada,* and multiplied in almost geometric progression. One estimate puts the number of longhorns in 1830 at 100,000. Twenty years later there were 3,500,000, and when the Civil War took Texans off the ranches to fight for the Confederacy, the tough cattle went wild, breeding in such numbers that they threatened to become pests.

After the war a head of beef in Texas brought only three or four dollars; but in the North the demand was such that a mature steer would fetch ten times that. And so the cattle drives began—to take meat, on the hoof, to market. In 1866, 260,000 head were driven up from Texas, mostly to Sedalia and other railheads in Missouri. Unfortunately the longhorns carried Texas fever, and angry Missouri farmers attacked the cowboys, who soon sought other routes to the North. In the summer of 1867 a cattle dealer named Joseph McCoy bought land in a small Kansas railroad outpost called Abilene, built some stockyards, and sent word of the new market to Texas. By 1869, 350,000 head were driven north to Abilene, following a trail up from Brownsville, San Antonio, Austin, Fort Worth, across the Red River and into Indian Territory (Oklahoma). Known as the Chisholm Trail, after the half-breed trader who marked it out, the route led through lush grass and across the Washita, the Canadian, the Cimarron, and the Salt Fork of the Arkansas.

The dirty, exhausting drives were fraught with danger—there were Indians, rustlers, and hostile homesteaders; rattlesnakes, blizzards, and treacherous

Year's "PICTORIAL HISTORY OF AMERICA"

stream crossings; and the worst hazard of all, stampedes. Yet year after year herds moved north in increasing numbers, and rip-roaring frontier towns sprung up out of nowhere. Eventually the Chisholm Trail was replaced by the Dodge City Trail to the west, and between 1866 and 1885, when the open range came to an end, nearly six million cattle were trailed north. Today there are almost no visible remains of the short-lived heyday of the cattle drives. The Homestead Act of 1862 opened the range to settlers; barbed wire enclosed the open range; and the railroad, which came to the rancher, eventually ended the drives. The terrible winter of 1886-87 nearly destroyed the industry, and the cowboy's way of life changed irrevocably as the Wild West vanished from the Great Plains.

Until 1885, when the open range came to an end, millions of Texas longhorns were driven north to wild towns like Dodge City (above), or Abilene, where cowboys cut loose after a long drive.

In a few places like Okarche, Oklahoma, ruts made by wagons which used the Chisholm Trail are still visible.

Near Dover, Oklahoma, is a hollowed depression, hundreds of feet wide, worn by the hoofs of longhorns heading north.

Bat Masterson was Wyatt Earp's best-known deputy.

Wyatt Earp served Dodge City as assistant marshal.

Jesse James' wild career lasted from 1866 until 1882.

Deadwood's Calamity Jane was as tough as most men.

Badmen's West

As the railroads pushed into the Great Plains, one town after another mushroomed up in their wake, some of them cow towns like Abilene, Kansas—tough, rowdy places, open around the clock—where cowboys could find entertainment after the long drives. John Wesley Hardin, a Texas killer who claimed to have forty notches on his gun, came to Abilene in the summer of 1871 and observed: "I have seen fast towns, but Abilene beat them all." Swarming with pickpockets, gamblers, and confidence men, Abilene was like a lot of other towns—short on law and civilizing influences. One reason for this was the Civil War. Men who had fought with Quantrill's guerrillas refused to recognize the fact of Appomattox. Violence had become a way of life, and when Union sympathizers and Texas cowboys who were ex-Confederates met head-on in a Kansas cow town, there was bound to be trouble.

Another factor was the Colt revolver. When the first white settlers ventured onto the Plains, they came armed with weapons of the eastern woodlands— the cap-and-ball rifle and the horse pistol, single-shot affairs which were hopelessly inadequate against Indians on horseback. In the time needed to load one of these guns a mounted Indian could ride 300 yards and shoot twenty arrows—and there were no trees to hide behind out here. But Samuel Colt's revolver, which could be fired six times without reloading, was the perfect weapon for a man on horseback. Texans, the first to settle the Plains in large numbers, were also first to discover the six-gun's merits. Texas Rangers used it for Indian fighting as early as 1839, made it famous in the Mexican War, and plainsmen coined a saying that God made some men large and some small, but Colonel Colt made them all equal.

Out of this West came true stories and a thousand legends of good men and bad, and dotting the Plains from Texas to the Dakotas are monuments of a sort from those lawless days. Over in Missouri, in Excelsior Springs, is the birthplace of Frank and Jesse James, who manufactured a Robin Hood legend to cover their careers of crime, and the one-story house where Jesse was shot in the back by a former gang member, Bob Ford, still stands in St. Joseph.

Most Kansas towns survived the collapse of the cattle boom, but there are places like Wallace which are practically ghost communities now. For a brief period in the 1870's Wallace prospered, then suddenly it was nearly deserted except for the plain frame and stone buildings which are relics of its halcyon days.

What is now the National Hotel in Abilene began life as the Old Gulf House. This flat-roofed limestone building was erected in 1871, when the marshal of Abilene was Wild Bill Hickok. So expert a marksman was Hickok that few men dared comment on his Prince Albert coat and checkered trousers, silk-lined cape, and embroidered vest. With shoulder-length hair and handle-bar mustache, Hickok cut quite a figure as marshal; but he was a little too quick on the draw, and after he killed one of his deputies in the smoky confusion of a gun battle, Abilene let him go. The town was tired of violence and gun-toting marshals, and in 1872 the authorities sent word to Texas that the cattle drives could go elsewhere. Yet one town after another competed for the cattle trade. There was Ellsworth, in which one may still see the White House hotel where Buffalo Bill Cody and Hickok stayed. Here Wyatt Earp first gained prominence before moving on to Dodge City, the wildest town of all. Known as "the Gomorrah of the Plains,"

Deadwood, South Dakota, named for a stand of burned timber, looked like this when Bill Hickok arrived in 1876.

A legendary bad man, Sam Bass had only one success.

Buffalo Bill Cody's fame spread with dime novels.

Wild Bill Hickok was noted as a crack marksman.

John Wesley Hardin shot his first man at fifteen.

it had the dubious distinction of originating the terms "Red Light District" and "Boot Hill"—a cemetery for men who died with their boots on.

For those who found life in the Kansas cow towns growing the least bit stale, a new Wild West developed soon enough. In 1874 General George Custer's expedition to the Black Hills discovered gold, and as soon as the news was out the rush began. By Christmas of 1875 close to 10,000 people had gathered in the new town of Custer, but they found very little that glittered. Today's visitor may see maps of the Custer Expedition, as well as a pictorial history of the Black Hills region, at the Custer State Park Museum just east of Custer. The town itself is one of the region's oldest settlements. Nearby is Gordon Stockade, a reconstruction of the original built by one of the first bands of gold-seekers in the area.

If Custer was a disappointment to the thousands of gold-hunters, they got their real chance in 1876, with the fabulous strike at Deadwood. Within a year over 200 stores, thirty hotels, seventy saloons and gambling houses, and a public bath appeared in town, along with literary societies, dancing clubs, and characters like Poker Alice, Lame Johnny, and Fly Speck Billy. The buckskin-clad Calamity Jane, who swaggered into bars and shattered mirrors with gunfire, was here, as was Sam Bass, a Texas cowpoke gone wrong. This was the place where Wild Bill Hickok, grown a little careless, was shot in the back in a poker game. His grave is on "Boot Hill," beside Calamity Jane's.

Deadwood's Adams Memorial Museum, with its relics of the wild years, is an interesting place, and other remnants of this rowdy era are scattered through the Black Hills. One may find them especially in the ghost towns—places like Rockerville, Rochford, or Silver City, which sprang up overnight and died almost as quickly, when the Great Plains ceased to be America's last—and wildest—frontier.

Sod-Hut Frontier

Near Beatrice, Nebraska, the government has erected a national monument to one of the most remarkable events in American history. Here, in 1862, the first claim was filed under the Homestead Act, a law which expressed the basic, eternal demand of the frontiersman for free land. In no sense was this a charitable handout; it was an arrangement whereby the settler repaid the government by opening up and developing the vast, unoccupied areas of the West. Upon payment of a small fee, the settler could claim a quarter-section (160 acres) of unappropriated public land, which would become his property after five years of continuous residence.

The Homestead Act made land available, the railroad made it accessible, and in sixty years more than a million settlers took advantage of it. Yet few periods in our history have been accompanied by more hardship. The typical homesteader, in a stark land which was still the Indian's hunting ground, found almost no wood with which to build a house, so he constructed a rude, temporary dugout, covered with brush, hay, or sod. After he was established, the homesteader built a "soddy," like those which may be seen at Colby, Kansas, and northwest of Morland. The tightly-matted prairie sod was cut into three-foot bricks, then laid up to form walls. Openings were usually covered with buffalo hides, but some settlers were fortunate enough to have real windows, doors, or a board floor. Although the sod "bricks" might last for forty years, they had their share of field mice and fleas, soaked up rain, and in a heavy storm the entire structure might dissolve in mud. Before 1876, when barbed wire was first used for fences, homesteaders planted hedges of the thorny Osage orange, which can still be seen in eastern Kansas, or put up mud fences—so unattractive that they gave rise to the expression "ugly as a mud fence."

Homesteading was an epic struggle—against economic depressions, foreign competition, exorbitant freight and interest rates, cattlemen, Indians, and above all, against nature. There were freezing winters, prolonged droughts, and fierce summer heat; prairie fires, pesky prairie dogs, and ruinous swarms of grasshoppers. And ironically, the size of the homestead grant was partially responsible for the American farmer's first major defeat. Conditions on the Plains were almost totally different from the rest of the country, and not until agriculture became a large-scale commercial enterprise could it be really successful here.

By 1889 the last unappropriated land was in Indian Territory—now Oklahoma. After refusing homesteaders entry for years, the government finally gave in to the pressure of the railroad interests, western congressmen, and hungry land-seekers, and opened the "Oklahoma District" to settlement "at and after the hour of twelve o'clock noon" on April 22, 1889. Long lines of soldiers did their best to keep the excited homesteaders back of the starting line until noon, when a cavalry trumpeter sounded "dinner call" and the run was on. In the next few years more Indian land was opened to white settlement—some of it by

This historic photograph was taken on September 16, 1893, just after the bugle blew the start of the famous land run on the Cherokee Strip. That day an estimated 100,000 land-seekers scrambled for homesteads on the former Indian land tract.

runs, some by lottery—and on September 16, 1893, the biggest tract of all, the Cherokee Outlet, was opened. That day an estimated 100,000 land-seekers lined up for prairie homesteads, and in the memorable scene shown here men on horses and every kind of vehicle lashed their animals forward through the dust, intent on getting somewhere first.

Only a few of the sod huts are left today. By 1900 most of them had been replaced by houses Willa Cather described as "encircled by porches, too narrow for modern notions of comfort, supported by the fussy, fragile pillars of that time, when every honest stick of timber was tortured by the turning-lathe into something hideous." And yet one cannot help feeling that these buildings were a natural response to the environment—an answer to a deep longing for variety in a land which offered very little.

This 1892 photograph of a Nebraska "soddy" shows how the homesteaders laid up "bricks" of prairie sod for shelters.

233

The Spanish Southwest

Deserted since the thirteenth century, the well-concealed pueblos of Mesa Verde in Colorado remained almost unnoticed until two cowboys happened upon them in 1888.

America's First Dwellings

Nearly every section of the United States bears the mark of prehistoric man, but nowhere is the evidence more spectacular than in the Southwest. Here, 200 years before Columbus' voyage, complex and highly developed societies flourished and then vanished, leaving some of the most fascinating monuments on the North American continent, preserved for centuries by the unique dry climate.

On a snowy December day in 1888 two cowboys named Wetherill and Mason, searching for missing cattle in the wild canyons of southwestern Colorado, rode to the top of a mesa and from a clearing in the junipers and piñon brush suddenly saw a vast cliff ruin nestled in the wall of the canyon opposite them. Above and below the immense ruins, snow fell on the face of the cliff; but the silent city of stone remained untouched by the weather, as it had for centuries. Wetherill and Mason were probably the first men to explore the site in six centuries.

Other men knew of its existence, of course. The Spanish priest and explorer Escalante had seen the ruins and named them Mesa Verde in 1776, but he had not stopped to investigate. The Utes in the region feared these "cities of the dead," and kept their distance. In 1874 a government surveying party led by the photographer W. H. Jackson noted the site of some Mesa Verde ruins, but not until the two cowboys went there was their enormous scope recognized. Since then the 52,000-acre Mesa Verde has been made into a national park where the visitor may see some of the most dramatic and extensive prehistoric ruins ever found.

Ancient men who crossed the 54-mile strait between Siberia and Alaska thousands of years ago eventually worked their way south to Colorado and New Mexico. At Folsom, New Mexico, archaeologists have unearthed chipped dart points near the bones of large bison known to have roamed the region 20,000 years ago. But little is known of the earliest American except that he was a nomadic hunter. About the time of Christ, Indians called Basket Makers settled in the Mesa Verde region, attracted by the fertile land. Their finely woven, decorative baskets of yucca fibre were used for many household purposes, and the Indians lived in caves in which they dug small pits for the storage of corn. The round ceremonial chamber, called kiva, still in evidence in modern pueblos, is an outgrowth of this first primitive reverence for corn.

The next stage in the development of these ancient people is known as the Modified Basket Maker Period, which lasted from A.D. 400 to A.D. 750, an era when the bow and arrow were first used and pottery gradually replaced the basket. At Mesa Verde there are hundreds of pit houses dating back to this period. The next, or Early Pueblo Period, extended from A.D. 750 to A.D. 1100. The pit houses were modified, and became actual stone and adobe houses with vertical walls. Rectangular in shape, and often three or four stories high, they had open courts with circular ceremonial kivas in front. Far View House and Sun Point Pueblo at Mesa Verde are superb examples of the mason's art which was developed at the end of this period.

About 1100 the Pueblo Indians moved into the most advanced stage of their civilization, known as the Great or Classic Pueblo Period, which was to last approximately 200 years. This was the era of huge communal dwellings like Spruce Tree House, Square Tower House, and the remarkable Cliff Palace.

Then, in the year 1276, a terrible 24-year drought began in the San Juan and Colorado River basins. By the start of the fourteenth century, the vast cliff cities had been deserted, never to be inhabited again. Unquestionably many of the Indians perished, while others moved into eastern Arizona, south to Zuñi country, and east to the Rio Grande—areas still occupied by modern Pueblo Indians.

Although Mesa Verde is one of the largest and best-preserved prehistoric pueblos, it is but one of many. Not far from it are Hovenweep and Yucca, also in Colorado, and to the south in New Mexico are extensive remains of two other centers of culture—Aztec and Chaco Canyon. Around Chaco are ruins of eleven great apartment house dwellings, the largest ever uncovered in America, and Aztec has some of the best-preserved ruins in the country. The spectacular Navajo National Park in northeast Arizona includes Betatakin, Keet Seel, and Inscription House, and not far to the east are the sheer red sandstone cliffs of Canyon de Chelly, with its White House ruins. Between Santa Fe and Taos in New Mexico are remains of the last flowering of pueblo culture. The Indians who left the Colorado River basin settled at what is now Bandelier National Monument; but when Coronado visited this latter region in 1550 it was half deserted, and fifty years later the abandonment was complete.

These Indian petroglyphs are at Indian Creek, Utah. Long ago, the White House in Canyon de Chelly (below) was connected to the valley floor by a tower, now destroyed.

ANDREAS FEININGER

ANSEL ADAMS

The Cities of Gold

For Spaniards the sixteenth century was the time of a vision of gold—a vision that drew men toward the western horizon in a search that brought discoveries, conquest, and deeds of courage almost beyond parallel in the history of mankind. In less than thirty years, Spaniards discovered the Pacific, sailed around the world, conquered huge segments of South America and Mexico, found the great rivers of the Americas, and explored the North American wilderness—all a century before England thought about colonizing the New World. Any story about the fabulous lands to the west could be believed—after all, it was but fifty years since men had doubted the very existence of such a world. There were the stories of Cortés, of Cabeza de Vaca, and, in 1539, those of Father Marcos de Niza, who told of the Seven Cities of Cibola.

This was a land "rich in gold, silver and other wealth," where the people were "very rich, the women even wearing belts of gold." As the conquistadors argued over who should conquer this new land, Hernando de Soto set out toward Florida in 1539, while Francisco Coronado, a thirty-year-old nobleman, left Mexico in 1540. In glittering armor, floating plume, and brilliant cape, he led an army of 1,500 (including Fray Marcos and other missionaries) north across deserts, mountain ranges, and deep forests, finally arriving five months later at Hawikuh, a Zuñi pueblo. This, it seemed, was Fray Marcos' Cibola—a few hovels of clay and stone built upon a high rock. No city of gold, it was an adobe pueblo "all crumpled together," with narrow streets, a filthy watercourse, and barren land all around. Perhaps Fray Marcos tried to explain how, from afar, in the light of the setting sun, he had mistaken it for a city of gold, but for Coronado and his men it was a bitter disappointment. So often the dream ended thus. A year later Coronado and his army headed east to search for Quivira, a wondrous land of abundance, only to find a drab settlement of Wichita Indians near what is now Lyons, Kansas.

Although the vision of wealth and glory persisted, it was sixty years after Coronado's expedition before a serious effort was made to colonize New Mexico. In 1598 Juan de Oñate, a wealthy grandee equipped with six complete suits of armor, set out with 130 families, 270 single men, the first wheeled vehicles to enter the region, and 7,000 cattle—the ancestors of a vast cattle and sheep empire. After passing through the Jornada del Muerto, they settled in San Gabriel del Yunque, first Spanish capital of New Mexico. But like other conquistadors, Oñate was no sedentary man, and for ten more years he journeyed through the Southwest, forever hoping to find Quivira.

Thirty-five miles east of Zuñi Pueblo in New Mexico a sheer sandstone butte called El Morro, or Inscription Rock, bears over 500 Spanish inscriptions, many left by disillusioned conquistadors. One states: "Passed by here the Adelantado Don Juan de Oñate from the discovery of the sea of the south, the sixteenth of April of 1605." (Oñate was on his way back from learning that the Gulf of California was not overflowing with pearls). Another message here expresses pointedly the spirit of that remarkable era: "Here was the General Don Diego de Vargas, who conquered to our Holy Faith and to the Royal Crown all the New Mexico at his own expense, year of 1692."

From afar, in the light of the setting sun, adobe pueblos like Walpi looked like cities of gold to the Spaniards.

ANSEL ADAMS

East of Zuñi Pueblo in New Mexico is the towering butte called El Morro, or Inscription Rock, on which more than 500 Spanish writings are carved. The earliest was left there in 1605 by Oñate, returning from the Gulf of California.

RAY MANLEY, *Arizona Highways*

The adobe Taos Pueblo has been occupied continuously by the Indians for centuries. Ladders provide the only access to their four- and five-story community houses.

The Three Cultures of Taos

Seventy-five miles north of Santa Fe, in a small, fertile valley east of the Rio Grande gorge, is Taos —symbol of the Indian, Spanish, and American societies that created the Southwest as we know it. Unlike most villages of this area which lie unprotected in the hot, dazzling sun, Taos is sheltered, remote, almost gloomy in the protective shade of the Sangre de Cristo Mountains, which rise sharply behind it.

The Pueblo, often considered the handsomest of all remaining Indian villages, has been continuously occupied for over 200 years. Behind it looms the sacred Taos mountain, with a lake high on its slopes where "the gods still live." The Pueblo itself consists of two terraced community houses four and five stories high, made of a deep gold adobe. Tall ladders provide the only access to upper stories, and other ladders indicate the presence of subterranean kivas, carefully protected from outside intrusion.

In the days when nomads roamed the Southwest, Taos was visited regularly by Plains Indians, and the Indians of Taos Pueblo—possibly of ancient Kiowan stock—differ from other pueblo tribes. They are taller, handsomer, with sharper features, and the men wear their hair in long braids in Plains Indian fashion. These are people of an independent Indian tribe who have resisted white domination, who have lived next to a non-Indian community without making concessions to the white man's ways. In Taos the Indian leader Popé won his first adherents to the united Pueblo Revolt against the Spanish in 1680; here the Indians rebelled again in 1696; and here they joined the Spanish resistance to American rule in 1847.

In the sixteenth century members of Coronado's expedition decided to settle in Taos, and until the Pueblo Revolt, Spaniards and Indians lived peaceably together. After the Spanish put down the rebellion of 1696 the town grew and prospered as a market center, and long before Americans had seen Taos, traders from all over the West came to its summer fairs. There were French with furs and guns,

Mexicans with silver, Navajos with blankets and pottery, Utes bringing captives to sell as slaves, Comanches offering buffalo robes and booty from their raids.

Sometime around 1730 the Spaniards built at Ranchos de Taos a few miles away the fortress-like adobe Church of Saint Francis of Assisi, whose thick walls and beautifully proportioned apse make it a classic example of strength and dignity. A few years later, mountain men began penetrating the region around Taos, and they found the town the one place west of St. Louis where they could meet civilized women and buy bread, coffee, and sugar. One who stayed to make Taos his home was Kit Carson.

Here one may still see the simple adobe house which was Carson's base for the rest of his life. Carson guided Frémont on two expeditions to the Pacific, led Kearny into California, and conquered the Navajos. He was one of the supreme products of his time and place, and although he died on an expedition to Colorado, it is fitting that he was brought to the simple cemetery in Taos for burial, near the Spaniards and Indians who, like himself, had made this entire section a unique portion of America.

A fortress-like adobe structure built about 1730, the Church of Saint Francis of Assisi combines strength and dignity.

Although the altar is relatively modern, the pictorial reredos of the Taos church probably dates back to its founding.

Spanish Missions

Tumacacori, built in Arizona in 1793

El Santuario of Chimayó, in New Mexico

Santa Barbara, "Queen of the Missions"

Where the sword of Spain went, there went the cross, sometimes following, sometimes leading the way. The armored conquistadors never found their cities of gold, but the men in ragged brown robes with crosses swinging from their waists located the sort of treasure they sought—heathens to be converted for the glory of God. Out of the intense religious fervor burning in Spain came missionary efforts of unmatched magnitude, and all through the Southwest—from Texas to southern California—the landscape is still a space between the missions established there by steadfast, courageous Fathers three centuries ago.

Beginning in 1540, these men endowed the Southwest with some of its handsomest architecture and most interesting historical structures, varying in style from the crudest adobe churches to magnificent baroque cathedrals. Generally speaking, the padres adapted the simple pueblo architecture, adding European touches in the ornamentation. The missions were built of adobe because of the scarcity of wood, and inside the plain façades were brilliantly decorated altars, elaborate carvings, and, because the Indians frequently assisted in the decoration, a conspicuous use of bold, almost pagan symbolism, with strong forms and vivid colors.

Of five missions begun after 1718 near San Antonio, Texas, the most ambitious was San José, which was carefully restored in 1933. Of more than a dozen Arizona missions, only one remains in use today—San Xavier del Bac, which dates from the period of Father Kino, the energetic Jesuit who established 24 missions in the New World. Soaring upward from the sagebrush and cactus-covered valley, San Xavier's luminous white walls create the startling effect shown on pages 302 and 303, like a great, shining mirage in the desert. Forty-three separate missions had been established in New Mexico by 1640, among them the fine examples at Taos, Acoma, and Laguna.

The fourth mission field was in California, along the 500 miles of coast between San Diego and San Francisco, where one can find the largest number of well-preserved Spanish churches. This great chain of missions, begun in 1769 by the remarkable Father Junipero Serra, comprised for half a century the only civilized outposts in that area, and the vineyards, irrigation canals, and farming practices introduced then had a permanent effect on this section of the country. With their red tile roofs, shaded patios, and graceful entrances, the California missions possess a charm seldom equaled elsewhere.

At the rear of San José Mission in San Antonio, Texas, is the arched cloister illustrated above. The beautifully carved figures shown here (above right, and below) are in San Xavier del Bac, the only Arizona mission to survive almost intact.

Of all Texas missions, the most impressive is San José y San Miguel de Aguayo. Completed in 1779, the San Antonio mission is noted for its ornamented façade and beautiful rose window. Allowed to decay after 1794, it was restored in 1933.

No one knows how long Indians have lived at Ácoma pueblo on top of this sandstone butte, but the village was an ancient one when

Ácoma: City

RICHARD ERDOES

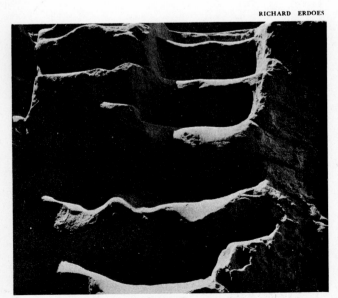

The trails leading up to Ácoma have toe and finger holes cut in the rock centuries ago, worn smooth by moccasined feet.

One of the Southwest's magnificent sights—a scene no visitor is apt to forget—is seventeen miles south of Highway 66 in New Mexico, at the end of a drive across barren, arroyo-cut wasteland. Suddenly one sees, rising out of an immense plain, two enormous buttes whose sheer cliffs tower nearly 400 feet in the air. One is the Enchanted Mesa, the other is Ácoma, city of the sky. No one knows how long Indians lived at Ácoma, but it was already an ancient village when Coronado's men came there in 1540.

From a distance it is difficult to see the 200-odd flat-roofed adobe buildings which seem to merge into the rock itself; and it takes a keen eye to spot the steep trails leading to the pueblo high above. One is the famous "ladder trail," with ancient toe and finger holes cut in the rock and worn smooth and deep by thousands of moccasined feet. In 1540 this was the only access to the pueblo, and it is easy to understand a Spaniard's comment that "no army could possibly be strong enough to capture the village."

Coronado's men saw it in 1540. The only access to the stronghold was by way of steep, narrow trails from the desert floor below.

of the Sky

Yet Ácoma was taken in 1598 by Don Juan de Oñate, whose soldiers found an unguarded pathway up the cliff and slaughtered all but 300 of the 3,000 Ácomas. Not until 1629 was a mission established there, when Fray Juan Ramirez chose to minister to "the most rebellious of all tribes." Alone and unafraid, he walked from Santa Fe to Ácoma, where he was pelted with arrows and stones. On his way up to the summit he is said to have caught and saved the life of a child who fell from the cliff, after which he was welcomed by the Ácomas. Ramirez built the great church of San Esteban Rey which dominates the southern end of the mesa like a huge fortress. Inside it are enormous beams forty feet long, carried on the shoulders of Indians from Mt. Taylor, thirty miles away. The walls are sixty feet high and ten feet thick, of remarkable adobe construction. Today some 1,500 Indians engaged in agriculture and pottery making still occupy the long terraced dwellings of the pueblo and carry on life in the ancient city of the sky.

DAVID E. SCHERMAN, *Life*

The weathered adobe convent at Acoma is described by author Willa Cather in *Death Comes For The Archbishop*.

Santa Fe's Governors' Palace was the seat of Spanish government for 130 years.

The Santa Fe Trail

All the anguish, the struggle, the blood and toil which Spain had put into its New World empire came to naught in 1821 with the success of a revolution in Mexico. Along with their independence, the Mexicans put an end to the old Spanish commercial restrictions, and in 1822 William Becknell left Franklin, Missouri, on his second successful trading mission to Santa Fe. Within a few years the wagon ruts along Becknell's route deepened and became wide enough to be distinguished as the first great western trail—the Santa Fe.

From Independence, out across the Kansas plains it stretched, past Council Grove, Pawnee Rock, and on to Cimarron Crossing of the Arkansas. There the trail divided—one branch continuing west along the Arkansas River into Colorado to Bent's Fort, then southwest across the mountains to Raton Pass, and Las Vegas. The more dangerous southern branch crossed the hot, dry land between the Arkansas and Cimarron Rivers, into Colorado and Oklahoma, down through the northeast corner of New Mexico, past Wagon Mound to Las Vegas, where the two sections of the trail merged and went on to Taos and Sante Fe. This was Indian country—hunting grounds of the deadly Apaches, Utes, Kiowas, and Comanches, whose raids on wagon trains and isolated ranches went on for five decades.

At the strategic junction of the Santa Fe Trail's two forks, in the heart of the Mora River Valley, stood Fort Union, built in 1851 as the largest and most important garrison in the Southwest. Today it lies in the midst of cattle country, row after row of roofless adobe walls jutting up from the prairie, tall brick chimneys piercing the sky like ghostly sentinels of the past. For in 1891, when the Indian menace had been largely eliminated, Fort Union was abandoned to vandals and the weather, its purpose accomplished. Near the deserted ruins one can still see the ruts of the Santa Fe Trail, irregular furrows worn so wide and deep that a century of dust storms have not obliterated them.

From Fort Union it is about 100 miles by modern road to Santa Fe, where the trail ended in the foothills of the Sangre de Cristo Mountains. Along narrow streets shaded by towering cottonwood trees are many old adobe houses and the mission of San Miguel, built early in the seventeenth century by Spaniards for their Tlascalan Indian servants from Mexico. But the most interesting historical structure in this picturesque town is the Palace of the Governors, the oldest public building in the country.

Ten years before the first English colony was founded in Massachusetts, Don Pedro de Peralta, third Spanish governor of the province of New Mexico, moved the capital from San Gabriel to Santa Fe and began work on the presidio. Completed in 1612, it consisted of a rectangular walled fort measuring about 400 feet by 800 feet, enclosing soldiers' barracks, storerooms, stables, parade ground, and servants' rooms; and in the Palace proper, the residence of the governor and his family, and various governmental offices. For seventy years, the community at Santa Fe survived the difficulties of isolation in an unfriendly land; but when the Pueblo Revolt erupted in 1680, the thousand Spaniards were forced to abandon their capital. The victorious Indians destroyed the church and turned the chapel into a kiva for their own use, sacked the Spanish homes, and for thirteen years remained in the town until they were ousted by the Spaniards. For 128 years the Palace remained the seat of Spanish government. Then in 1821 the Mexican Republic took over, and in 1846 General Stephen Kearny's troops marched into Santa Fe to proclaim it U.S. territory.

Santa Fe, the terminus of the Trail, may have been a "ragamuffin capital," but the bustling community was nevertheless one which travelers from Independence looked forward to with unbounded enthusiasm. And even though the volume of trade over the road was never spectacular, its continuation dispelled many

fears about the "Great American Desert," and did much to hasten settlement of the West. No American traveling the Santa Fe Trail failed to notice the tenuous Mexican hold on the Southwest, and the route thus contributed psychologically to the idea of Manifest Destiny.

Few plots of ground in America have witnessed such a variety of history as the Governors' Palace and the plaza in Santa Fe. Warring Indians, proud conquistadors, Mexicans, mountain men, American hunters, traders, trail drivers, and Civil War soldiers —all have made their mark on this small community. And in spite of alterations, and the twentieth-century influx of artists, anthropologists, tourists, and atomic scientists, the plaza is still the place where old men sit in the sun and chat in Spanish, where Indians from neighboring pueblos come, as they have for three centuries, to sell their wares.

Near the deserted ruins of Fort Union, wagon ruts of the Santa Fe Trail are still visible. Built in 1851 to protect travelers and settlers from attack by Southwest Indian tribes, the fort developed into a thriving settlement before it was finally abandoned in 1891.

Tombstone's City Hall has been used since 1882.

The Lawless Years

Today the town of Lincoln, New Mexico, is a quiet, dusty little community in the heart of stock-raising country. A round stone tower called El Torreón, built as a fortification against Indians by settlers in 1852, stands in the center of town, and the old Lincoln County Courthouse offers a collection of frontier relics. In this sleepy town there is little to indicate that it was the vortex of a bitter, all-out frontier feud which reached such proportions that President Hayes ordered General Lew Wallace to establish law and order, with federal troops if necessary.

In the 1870's Lincoln County covered almost one-fifth of the present state and included four of today's counties. Its 27,000 square miles of rich grazing lands lay in a broad valley between the Rio Grande and Pecos River—a remote territory isolated by surrounding desert, into which thieves, murderers, gamblers, and rustlers naturally drifted. The Lincoln County War, which lasted from 1876 to 1878, resulted from an explosive mixture of homesteaders, squatters, farmers, and cattlemen, all vying for land and water rights, thrown into a hopper with as nasty a group of badmen as it would be possible to assemble anywhere.

The wars themselves achieved widespread and unsavory reputation, but this was pale by comparison with that of an eighteen-year-old punk who was right in the thick of them. He was William H. Bonney, or Billy the Kid, and he was already well-launched on a career of crime when he arrived in Lincoln County.

Billy's reputation as the fastest, deadliest shot in the West was second only to Wild Bill Hickok's, and during his short life he conducted a vicious shooting spree that earned him notoriety as the most sought-after desperado in the Southwest. By the time he was 21 he was dead, but his legend persists to this day—sometimes in a form that makes him out to be a sort of Robin Hood, kind to little children and a friend of the poor. In truth, Billy was a mean thief and professional gambler, a fearless killer who had a remarkable genius for saving his own skin while taking the lives of others.

The same year that Billy the Kid rode into Lincoln, a prospector named Ed Schieffelin ventured into the desolate, dangerous hills of southeastern Arizona and put another community on the map. An army scout had warned him: "All you'll find in those hills, Schieffelin, is your own tombstone." So when the prospector stumbled on one of the richest silver lodes ever discovered in the Southwest, he dubbed the site Tombstone.

When news of his spectacular find spread, a great rush began, and fortune hunters descended in droves to build little communities like Bisbee, Galeyville, Contention City, and Charleston almost overnight. But for lawlessness and local color, none of them equaled Tombstone. Like its name, the town's setting seemed an invitation to badmen. In wild, lonely land gouged with arid gulches and surrounded by forbidding desert, it was still a stronghold of defiant Apaches and a perfect hideout for rustlers and murderers avoiding the law. Within a few years after Schieffelin's strike, it had a population of 7,000. As in other boom towns, its main street was a crazy patchwork of hastily-constructed buildings, and at one time there were 110 places licensed to sell liquor. Its most famous attractions were the Bird Cage burlesque theater and the Crystal Palace gambling casino. It had five newspapers—one of them the *Epitaph,* still operating as the state's oldest continuously published weekly journal.

Boot Hill graveyard, an unfenced, desolate plot, provides evidence of Tombstone's wilder days, with epitaphs like "Margarita Stabbed by Gold Dollar," and "George Johnson, hanged by mistake." Among the town's notable early residents were the famous Wyatt Earp and an Episcopal minister, the Reverend Endicott Peabody, who later became headmaster of Groton School.

In 1886 the mines were flooded, and by 1900 Tombstone was nearly deserted. Today it is a quiet community, pockmarked by abandoned shafts, rows of deserted houses and saloons, and enough of the old landmarks to keep alive the legend of those wild days of the 1880's.

An epic Tombstone battle was the climax of the Earp-Clanton feud (above) in 1881. At the O.K. Corral three of the Clanton gang were killed and Wyatt Earp's two brothers were wounded, all within sixty seconds. Below is Billy the Kid, to whom legend ascribes one killing for each of his 21 years of life. At right is Tombstone's notorious Boot Hill cemetery.

ED BARTHOLOMEW

The Indians' Last Stand

As the nineteenth century slipped into its final quarter, a war which had been going on for three hundred years approached its inevitable and ugly denouement. This was the desperate struggle in which nearly all the Indians of North America had been engaged since the Spanish landed in Mexico—the fight to preserve their lands against the fateful tide of white settlement. On a Montana hillside the Sioux and Cheyennes put off the final reckoning by destroying George Armstrong Custer and his Seventh Cavalry troop in 1876. In the Northwest, in 1877, Chief Joseph and his Nez Perces were trying to fight their way to Canada and safety; and in the Southwest, the Apaches were making a last, desperate stand.

For seven centuries the mountains and plains of New Mexico and southern Arizona had been Apache hunting grounds. Marvelous horsemen, capable of astounding feats of endurance, the Apaches waged war as a business and a way of life, and only the Comanches exceeded them in ferocity and brutality. During two centuries of Spanish and Mexican rule, Apache raids helped keep the wild deserts and mountains uncivilized and unoccupied, and this section of the country still looks as if there might be Indians lurking behind the rocks or in steep gullies.

In the southeast corner of Arizona, where the Dos Cabezas and Chiricahua mountains meet, is Apache Pass, once the most dangerous spot on the southern stage route to California. At the eastern end of the pass are the crumbled ruins of Fort Bowie, one of the forts erected in the 1860's to protect travelers against attacks led by Mangas Coloradas, Cochise, Victorio, Nana, or Geronimo, whose names brought terror to settlers for fifty years. There is the grotesquely eroded canyon country of Chiricahua National Monument, ancestral home of the Apaches; and Stronghold Canyon, in the Dragoon Mountains, where the remarkable chief Cochise held out for twelve years.

After the deaths of Cochise and of Victorio, who was the most ruthless of all Apache leaders, Chief Nana took up the struggle against the whites, and in 1881, he and forty warriors conducted one of the most spectacularly successful Apache forays. Traveling as much as eighty miles a day over rough country, he led his men 1,200 miles through hostile territory, pursued all the way by American cavalry. Arriving unscathed in Mexico, he had raided everywhere he traveled, fought eight successful battles, killed up to fifty whites, captured 200 horses and mules, and had eluded more than a thousand soldiers and hundreds of civilians. And Nana was seventy years old, and crippled with arthritis!

By 1882 General George Crook was back in Arizona after the Sioux campaigns, and if it had not been for Geronimo, might have subdued the Apaches immediately. Geronimo, whose real name was Goyathlay, or "One Who Yawns," said that he lived for one reason only—to kill whites. After a string of successes, Geronimo was captured by Crook and brought to the reservation; but within weeks, the chief and 32 warriors slipped away to fight again.

For three years Geronimo rode back and forth across the Mexican border, leaving a trail of death and destruction in his wake. In 1886, Crook again captured him, only to lose him once more. After this escape, Crook asked to be relieved, and was replaced by another famous Indian fighter, General Nelson A. Miles. For five months Miles' troopers combed the countryside for the Apache until finally, worn down by the chase, his supplies gone, Geronimo and his band met Miles and agreed to surrender. Near the present town of Apache, in the rugged, mountainous area of Skeleton Canyon, the centuries of Indian fighting ended at last, on September 3, 1886.

For fourteen years Geronimo and his band of Apaches terrorized ranchers and settlers on both sides of the U.S.-Mexican border. He is shown below (center) with his bodyguard before a conference with General Crook in 1886. At right is a vivid moment in an Apache Mountain Spirit Dance.

The Farthest Frontier

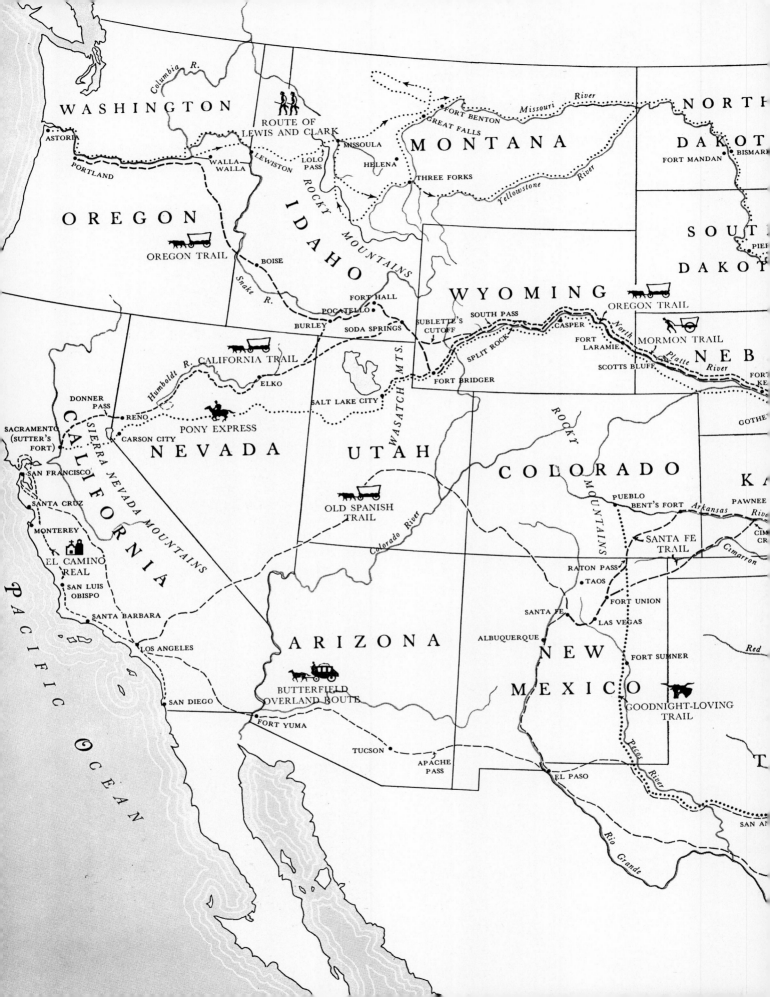

THE GREAT TRAILS

ROUTE OF LEWIS AND CLARK
IOWA
MORMON TRAIL
COUNCIL BLUFFS
NAUVOO
ILLINOIS
PONY EXPRESS
ST. JOSEPH
ABILENE
KANSAS CITY
INDEPENDENCE
ST. LOUIS
TIPTON
MISSOURI
SANTA FE TRAIL
SPRINGFIELD
BUTTERFIELD OVERLAND ROUTE
FAYETTEVILLE
OKLAHOMA
FORT SMITH
ARKANSAS
CHISHOLM TRAIL
ENID
BELKNAP
LOUISIANA
OLD SPANISH TRAIL
NEW ORLEANS
HOUSTON
AUSTIN
SAN ANTONIO
GULF OF MEXICO

At first the Great Plains and the Rocky Mountains were places through which men on their way to a promised land hurried as quickly as possible. For a long time there were no real trails through this country like the Indian and buffalo paths found by eastern settlers. The eyes of America had been opened to the wonders of the West by Lewis and Clark in 1806, yet few men followed precisely the explorers' route.

In 1824 Jedediah Smith led a party through South Pass, the only feasible wagon route across the "Great Shining Mountains," and this pass became the primary objective of the thousands who followed over the Mormon, the Oregon, and the California Trails. These three routes were one until South Pass had been breached. Then the Mormon Trail headed toward Fort Bridger and across the Wasatch; the California Trail went toward Soda Springs, then along the Humboldt into the desert; and the Oregon Trail swung northwest from Fort Hall, and down the Snake River to its junction with the Columbia.

The first great southwestern route, the Santa Fe Trail, began at Independence, crossed the Kansas plains, skirted the Arkansas and Cimarron Rivers, and moved on to Bent's Fort and the Spanish settlements. Starting in the 1820's, these were the highways men traveled to the West, and Americans who head that way today will find that they are highways yet. In time, other trails served men in this vast land, and this map shows most of the important ones.

In spite of the thousands upon thousands of people who have come to live in this area in a century and a quarter, what we have called the Farthest Frontier is still the best place to see a part of America as it was when men first saw it. In this land of the Great Shining Mountains, of forbidding deserts, cascading waterfalls, deep canyons, and magnificent coastline, you can still see some of nature's most wondrous creations, and the limitless space that brought men here in the first place.

William Clark

Meriwether Lewis

255

The Journey of Lewis and Clark

FROM *Two Captains West*,
BY ALBERT AND JANE SALISBURY, SUPERIOR PUBLISHING CO., SEATTLE

On May 14, 1804, William Clark wrote, "I set out . . . in the presence of the neighbouring inhabitents and proceeded under a jentle brease up the Missourie." The photograph below shows the point, ten miles above St. Louis, where the Big Muddy joins the Mississippi. Above is a rebuilt Mandan lodge near Mandan, North Dakota, on the site of a village Lewis and Clark visited. The statue of Sacajawea (left) is in Bismarck.

MARIE HANSEN WESLEY, *Life*

Thirty years after Lewis and Clark visited the Dakotas, Charles Bodmer depicted the interior of a Mandan chief's hut. In his journal Clark describes these lodges as being in a stockade with "the houses round and verry large, containing several families, as also their horses . . ."

Long before the purchase of the Louisiana Territory from France in 1803, men's thoughts had turned toward the land mass spreading west and north from the Mississippi River to the Pacific Ocean—a huge unexplored area about which they knew almost nothing. For twenty years Thomas Jefferson had urged exploration of the territory, but little had come of it beyond the few ships which touched the coastline north of California. To American eyes the most important voyage was that of Captain Robert Gray, who in 1792 discovered the mouth of the Columbia River, gave the stream its name, and thereby provided America with its most tangible claim to the region.

After he became President, Jefferson did not wait long to ask Congress for the sum of $2,500 to finance a journey of discovery. As leader of the expedition he had already settled on his private secretary, 29-year-old Meriwether Lewis, a Virginia neighbor who knew something of the western country from a hitch in the Army. To share his command, Lewis chose a boyhood friend and army superior, William Clark, a

33-year-old Virginian whose older brother was George Rogers Clark, the frontier hero. The two leaders' personalities were almost totally different: Lewis was brooding, melancholy, a man who sought solitude even on their expedition, thousands of miles from civilization; while Clark, or "Red Head" as the Indians called him, was nearly always frank and cheerful; yet in the history of joint commands there are few examples of such mutual confidence, comradeship, or lack of envy. The rest of the party was made up of nine young Kentuckians, fourteen U.S. Army regulars, two Frenchmen, Clark's Negro servant York, and Lewis' Newfoundland dog.

On May 14, 1804, the expedition left the mouth of Wood River, on the Illinois bank of the Mississippi across from the Missouri's mouth, and set forth on what was surely the most thrilling travel drama in U.S. history. It is a journey which Americans may still retrace, because the territory covered by the expedition has changed so little in a century and a half. There is an excitement—a sense of achievement—in

FROM *Two Captains West,*
BY ALBERT AND JANE SALISBURY, SUPERIOR PUBLISHING CO., SEATTLE

Lewis likened the White Cliffs (above) to vast ruins with "parapets well stocked with statuary." Below is the Indian trail over Lemhi Pass in the Bitterroots which the party followed down the western slope of the Continental Divide.

sighting the landmarks they named, following the very trails Lewis and Clark took over wild, rugged stretches unaltered by five subsequent generations.

At first they traveled by boat up the Missouri, making about ten miles a day before their first important stop, some twenty miles north of the future Omaha, where they held their first powwow with Indians. The name they gave this site is perpetuated in Council Bluffs, the Iowa city south of their meeting place. On August 20 Sergeant Floyd died—the only casualty of the two-year expedition—and was buried on a high hill about a mile below the mouth of Floyd's River, near Sioux City.

A week later they killed their first buffalo, and soon afterward sighted an antelope and some prairie dogs, the first known to science. Late in October, 165 days from their start at the Mississippi River, they reached the Mandan villages, thirty miles north of present-day Bismarck, North Dakota, on the north bank of the Missouri. Only two of the old villages that occupied this location remained when Lewis and Clark settled down for the winter. Here they hired a whisky-guzzling French-Canadian halfbreed named Toussaint Charbonneau, who had lived among the Mandans for twenty years and who, as part of his bargain with the two captains, threw in his wife Sakakawea, or Sacajawea, "The Bird Woman," who could row, carry, and stand the beatings Charbonneau gave her. As it turned out, it was the courageous Sacajawea, rather than her unreliable husband, who was of inestimable help to the expedition.

With the coming of spring, the party left the Mandan villages and headed up the Missouri. Crossing country that was loaded with game, they saw herds of buffalo, deer, antelope, moose, elk, and bighorn sheep, not to mention birds of every description. It was Lewis' opinion that two hunters, in this region, could supply a regiment; but they restrained themselves and shot only what they needed for food. Then, on April 26, 1805, they arrived at the mouth of the *Roche Jaune*—the Yellowstone. Although most of the territory traversed by Lewis and Clark was unknown to white men, the Yellowstone had been visited and named by the French explorer, La Vérendrye, fifty years earlier.

On the last day of May Lewis recorded his impression of the White Cliffs, east of Fort Benton, Montana: ". . . a white soft sandstone bluff which rises to about half the height of the hills," which the river had worn down "into a thousand grotesque figures." On June 13 Lewis, tramping on ahead of the boats, came on the Great Falls of the Missouri, which he thought "the grandest sight I ever beheld."

Still following the Missouri, they now headed almost due south until they reached the river's three forks, which they named for Jefferson, Madison, and Gallatin. They went up the Jefferson, largest of the three, to its source in the Continental Divide, and then struck out through the lofty Bitterroot Range which marks the boundary of Montana and Idaho, the roughest and most difficult part of the trip. Often hungry, the party ate nothing but berries for a time, but were providentially assisted by Sacajawea's tribe. The daughter of a Shoshone chief, she had been cap-

The Bitterroots were covered with snow by mid-September, and the expedition nearly starved here on the Lolo trail.

While portaging Celilo Falls at this spot on the Columbia, Lewis and Clark caught sight of snow-covered Mount Hood.

They were astonished to find that the Northwest Indians had been in touch with other white men (along the Columbia they had seen white men's articles, and near the Pacific one Indian astonished them by saying "son of a pitch").

Five miles from Astoria, Oregon, is the careful reconstruction of Fort Clatsop, where they spent the winter of 1805–6; in Seaside, Oregon, is a cobblestone cairn where Lewis and Clark boiled sea water to make salt; and at the foot of the town's main street, a plaque that marks the end of the trail.

This was not, by any stretch of the imagination, the end of the trail for Lewis and Clark. To begin with, there was the first American Christmas in the Northwest, spent at Fort Clatsop, which was a meager affair. "After brackfast," Clark wrote, "we divided our Tobacco which amounted to 12 carrots one half of which we gave to the men of the party who used tobacco, and to those who doe not use it we make a present of a handkerchief . . . our Dinner concisted of pore Elk, so much Spoiled that we eate it thro' mear necessity." The "Musquetors" (fleas) contributed by the Clatsop Indians on their daily visits were "so troublesom," Clark added, that "I have slept but little for 2 night past."

Then there were those thousands of miles to retrace, days and nights of hardship and discomfort, pain and danger. When they finally returned to St. Louis on September 23, 1806, they had been gone for two years, four months, and nine days. They had added immeasurably to scientific and geographic knowledge; they had strengthened the U.S. claim to the whole bountiful area; but above all they had blazed the trail and opened the eyes of all Americans to the rich and wonderful lands which were there, almost for the taking.

Thomas Jefferson, who had finally seen his dream come true, submitted a report to Congress on December 2, 1806: "The Expedition of Messrs. Lewis and Clarke, for exploring the river Missouri, and the best communication from that to the Pacific Ocean, has had all the success which could have been expected, they have traced the Missouri nearly to its source, descended the Columbia to the Pacific Ocean, ascertained with accuracy the geography of that interesting communication across our continent, learned the character of the country, of its commerce and inhabitants: and it is but justice to say that Messrs. Lewis and Clarke and their brave companions have by this arduous service deserved well of their country."

tured by Hidatsa Indians and sold to Charbonneau; and at this time of dire need, among the barren defiles of the Rockies, the expedition was saved by the near-miraculous appearance of the very tribe from which she had been stolen. Her brother Cameahwait was chief, and he gave Lewis and Clark the horses and supplies they needed to cross the Continental Divide.

Once beyond the Bitterroots, they headed down the Clearwater River to its junction with the Lewis or Snake River, then went on to the Columbia. After building new canoes, the party passed through The Dalles of the Columbia on October 24, shot the Long Narrows the next day, and on November 2 slipped through the Cascades. Five days later, on November 7, 1805, they saw for the first time the "object of all our labors, the reward of all anxieties"—the crashing surf of the Pacific Ocean. It was more than eighteen months since the 32 gaunt men had seen civilization, back in St. Louis.

The location at which Lewis and Clark reached the Columbia's mouth in November, 1805, looks much the same today.

BRADLEY SMITH, COURTESY *Time*

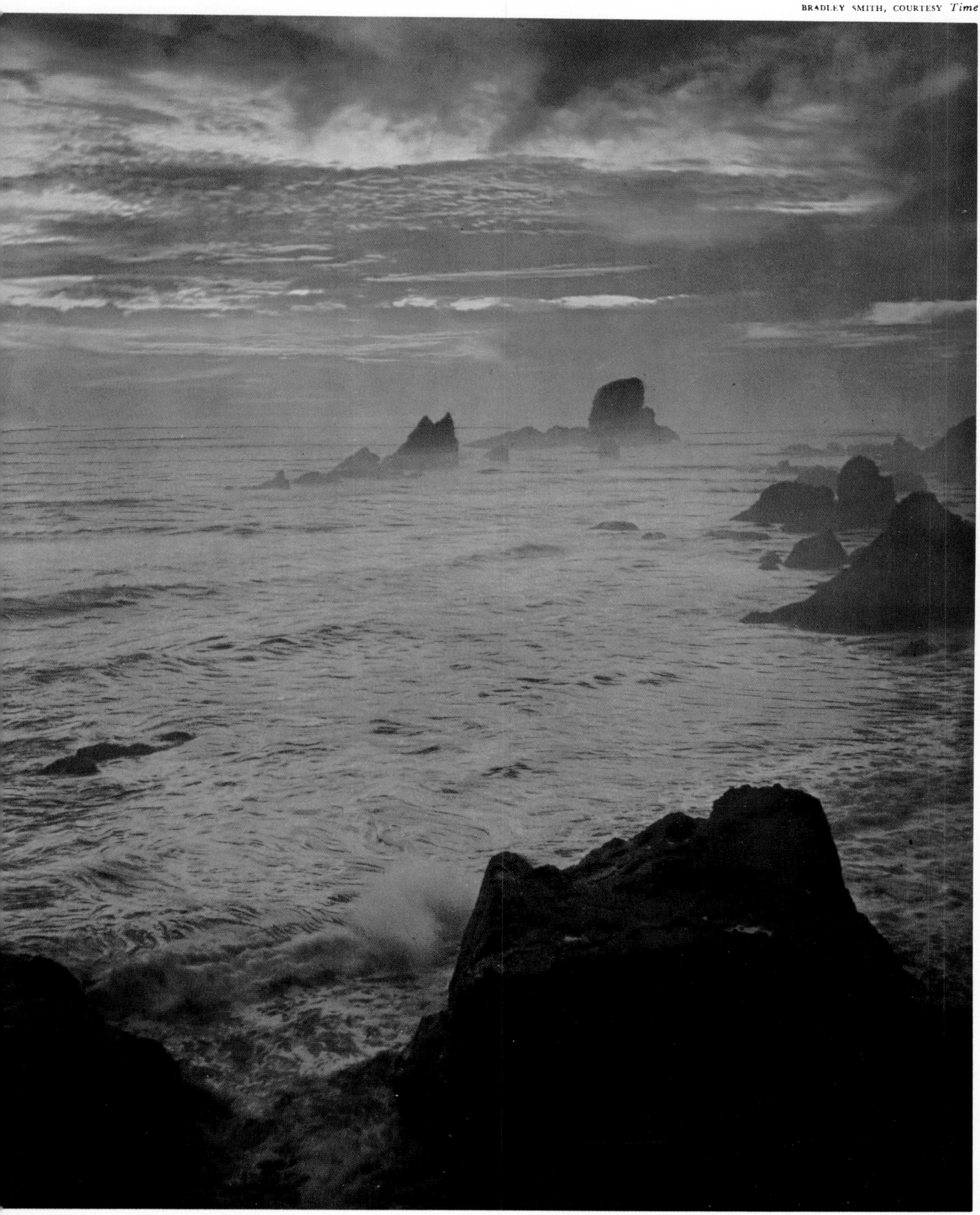

In 1837 Alfred Jacob Miller painted Fort Laramie, showing the colorfully dressed Indians who came to trade there. Above are the ruins of the enlisted men's barracks.

The Way West

In 1849 something like fifty thousand Americans, all of them in a hurry, traveled across the continent by overland routes. That year the procession of caravans on the Oregon Trail was so continuous that the lead wagon of one train frequently was not more than a few hundred yards behind the tail wagon of the group ahead. It was a spring of constant rain—of deep mud, of wet food, blankets, and clothing, of head colds, and of cholera. Perhaps five thousand Forty Niners died of cholera before they reached the high plains, while many more succumbed to the physical strain of the trip itself. A few foolhardy ones, eager to get to California, set off alone with their possessions on their backs, only to go insane in the desert, slit their throats, or end up begging for food along the trail; but most of the travelers were wise enough to stick to the wagon trains.

After they left Mitchell Pass, Nebraska, the route was fairly easy along the upward grade to the way station at Fort Laramie. The ruins of the old fort still guard the fertile, level plain where wagon trains provisioned at exorbitant prices a century ago, but from here on the trail is marked almost entirely by natural landmarks. At the Upper Crossing of the North Platte, alkali salts swirled up to burn the skin, causing ugly sores to form around the mouth and across the knuckles. Here the trail bent to the south again, passing through sagebrush plains dappled with shim-

mering lakes, then on to the Sweetwater River, near Split Rock, Wyoming, and to Independence Rock which lies on the plain like a sleeping Gulliver, tempting emigrants to pause and inscribe their names.

From here the land rises steadily up to South Pass, the unobtrusive gateway through the Rockies, where men suddenly felt unaccountably fatigued, short of breath, and quick to anger. When they arrived at Pacific Springs, the more observant ones noticed that the water flowed west—they had passed the Continental Divide. Now there was a choice of routes: the southern hook past Fort Bridger or the Sublette Cutoff. The trouble with the latter was that it led across

In Samuel Colman's painting, prairie schooners heading west along the Oregon Trail ford a shallow desert stream.

desert, over two ridges of the Wind River Range, and several difficult streams. Even though it was 53 miles longer, most people chose the Fort Bridger route, where there was plenty of water, and some meager provisions at Jim Bridger's ramshackle establishment.

Not far from Soda Springs, Idaho, the more impatient gold seekers branched off to the south, taking the Hudspeth Cutoff through the desert to the Raft River; but the majority went on to Fort Hall. Out in the middle of a bug-ridden flat, and swarming with dirty Shoshoni who came to trade, beg, or steal, Fort Hall was a disappointment—but it was the last way station. Beyond lay the hot, semi-arid bottoms of the Snake River, and a fork in the trail. The northern branch, hardly traveled in 1849, wound on to Oregon. The other took the desert plunge to California.

In the High Sierras, snow piles deep in Donner Pass, named for the party from Illinois which was stranded here during the winter of 1846-47. They were far behind schedule when they were trapped by an early storm.

End of the Trail

No one traveling through the states of Washington or Oregon today can fail to see what drew people to this supremely beautiful section of the country. Parts of it, especially along the Oregon coast, are as wild and untouched as when Lewis and Clark first saw the Pacific; and in the lush Willamette and Columbia valleys one may see the fruits of a thousand pioneer dreams.

Scattered through the two states are a few remains of their earliest days, like the Jackson House in Chehalis, Washington, whose owner used to welcome immigrants from the East. In Vancouver are some of the oldest buildings, dating from the time when Fort Vancouver, the Hudson's Bay Company base, was under the rule of Dr. John McLoughlin, and was the only civilized spot in the Northwest. From 1825 to 1845 Dr. McLoughlin ruled a vast empire which extended from the Rockies to the Pacific, from Alaska to California; and although his first allegiance was to the Hudson's Bay Company, it was he who sent supplies to starving American immigrants, provided passage for them in company boats, and protected them

from hostile Indians. Many of the first settlers owed their survival in the Oregon country to his generous assistance; but as friction increased between the U.S. and Great Britain over claims to this territory, McLoughlin's friendship to the Americans was resented by his employers. In 1845 he resigned and went to Oregon City, Oregon, where he built the square, clapboarded mansion which has been restored and moved to the park bearing his name.

Among Dr. McLoughlin's visitors in the fall of 1836 were Dr. Marcus Whitman and his wife Narcissa, who had come to the Oregon country to establish an Indian mission. Waiilatpu, or "Place of Rye Grass," where they founded the mission, is about six miles west of the present Walla Walla, Washington, and the little community where the Whitmans taught the nomadic Indians agricultural and industrial pursuits became one of the landmarks of the Oregon Trail. As the years passed, there were signs of restiveness among the Cayuse Indians, and in November, 1847, they attacked the mission, massacring the Whitmans and twelve others. The settlement that had begun with such high hopes was destroyed completely, and today the visitor will see only the ruined foundations of the mission buildings, and a few Indian artifacts uncovered by excavations at the site.

It is easy to forget that there was not always a pot of gold at the end of the rainbow, and that for each group that reached the promised land there were some who fell by the wayside, never to glimpse it. Every trail to the West was marked by little mounds of earth containing the bones of the hopeful who had passed that way; and there are memories of dark disasters that still strike terror to the heart.

One of these stories began in Illinois, where the well-to-do Donner brothers read Lansford W. Hastings' exaggerated *The Emigrants' Guide to Oregon and California,* and organized an overland party. Hastings' book glibly advised travelers to reduce time and distance to California by leaving the regular trail at Fort Bridger, and taking a cutoff "southwest to the Salt Lake; and thence continuing down to the Bay of San Francisco." What it did not say was that this led across Utah's Wasatch Range—almost an impossible route for wagons to negotiate—over the terrible Salt Lake Desert, the Nevada desert, and the High Sierras. Against the advice of experienced trailsmen, the Donners took the cutoff at Fort Bridger, and pushed on toward disaster.

After a harrowing trip across the fiery desert, the party was rife with dissension and ill feeling. By the time the Donners reached the Truckee River at the foot of the Sierras it was late October, they were far behind schedule, and as they prepared to climb the 2,000-foot granite ridge of the Sierra the first winter storm came whistling out of the north. Before long the mountains were buried under snow, stalling them completely, and by December the emigrants were reduced to eating twigs and bark. After four men died and one went insane, a party of fifteen of the strongest started for help. Thirty-two days later seven of them arrived at an Indian village, more dead than alive, to tell of having been forced to eat the bodies of companions who died along the way. The first of several relief parties reached Donner Lake on February 18, 1847, where those who had stayed behind had suffered unimaginably. Of the 89 men, women, and children who set out from Fort Bridger, only 45 had survived the awful winter.

Anyone who takes U.S. 40, the winding route that leads up the all but perpendicular wall of lonely Donner Pass, may pause for a moment to imagine what it was like there, not much more than a hundred years ago, when the exhausted pioneers, struggling against the deep drifting snow, started up the cliffs that lay between them and the end of the trail.

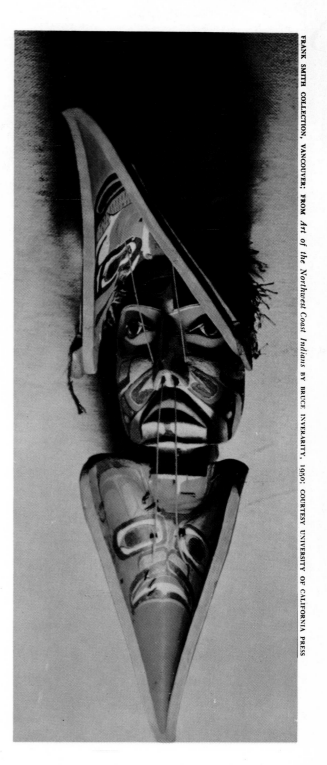

Indians of the Northwest achieved a remarkably high level of civilization, largely because of the bountiful natural resources around them. The Kwakiutl mask shown here is an example of the Northwest Indians' superb craftsmanship. Four feet in height, the wooden mask represents a human head when fully open. When the visor is pulled down, it becomes a raven.

Salt Lake City was laid out on a grandiose scale and, against formidable obstacles, blossomed into a desert metropolis. This early picture shows the multi-gabled house (right) of Brigham Young's wives.

Much of the Mormons' success was the result of Brigham Young's leadership.

This Is the Place

The vision sprang to life in 1827, on a hill near Palmyra, New York, where Joseph Smith said he had found the golden tablets, inscribed with sacred writing. Three years later, Smith and the members of the church he founded felt the hostility and distrust of their neighbors, and in 1831 began a trek which was to continue for sixteen years, transporting Smith's vision to the other side of the continent. It was a journey marked by persecution, bloodshed, hatred, and hardship without parallel in American history, and Joseph Smith was only one of many who died along the way.

In 1831 the handful of Mormons were in Kirtland, Ohio, where one of their temples still stands. Until 1838 the neighbors left them in peace, and then they were forced to move on, this time to Independence and Far West, Missouri. Soon the mobs were at their heels again, the governor announced they must be driven from the state, and they headed east to Commerce, Illinois, renamed Nauvoo. By 1844 they had built a prosperous city of 15,000 on the Mississippi's

Begun in 1853, the Salt Lake Temple was built of granite hauled twenty miles by ox-teams. A figure of the Angel Moroni is on top of the tower. In the background the impressive Utah Capitol may be seen.

banks. That year trouble struck again. Joseph Smith and his brother Hyrum were taken to jail in Carthage, and killed by a mob. Once more the faithful had to decide whether they should stand or flee.

One leader, James Jesse Strang, took a group north to Voree, Wisconsin, and then on to Beaver Island, Michigan, where he became "king" of one of the strangest colonies in American history.

Most of the people, however, decided to follow the 43-year-old Brigham Young, who had decided that the only place they could find repose was in an isolated, unwanted spot far beyond civilization. From John C. Frémont's account of his 1842 expedition, Young knew that such a place existed beside the Great Salt Lake.

Late in 1845 the Mormons began preparations for their migration, and early in February of the following year the first band set out across the Mississippi to Iowa, where they established Camp of Israel, the first of many way stations along the route. Not as a mass migration, but party by party they left, and by June of 1846 Nauvoo was deserted. Brigham Young and a group of pioneers went ahead, establishing way stations like Garden Grove and Mount Pisgah in Iowa. By the time the last covered wagon and handcart had left Nauvoo, Young was at the Missouri, where he laid

out Winter Quarters. That winter food and fuel were scarce and 600 died of a plague, but on April 9, 1847, Young and his pioneer band set off once again.

Beyond South Pass they met Jim Bridger, who directed them across the Wasatch Mountains, and the red-walled cliffs of Echo Canyon. Finally, as Emigration Canyon broadened, they caught sight of the land Brigham Young had promised them. "This is the place," he said; but the brethren could see little to gladden their hearts. It was "a broad and barren plain hemmed in by mountains, blistering in the burning rays of the midsummer sun. No waving fields, no swaying forests, no verdant meadows . . . but on all sides a seemingly interminable waste of sagebrush."

In spite of the overwhelming natural difficulties, in spite of frosts, insects, and drought that killed their crops, in spite of public distrust, government opposition, and attacks by other settlers, they succeeded in carrying through Brigham Young's plan for a Zion in the West. Today, when one visits Salt Lake City's great Mormon Temple, the Tabernacle, the Beehive House, and Brigham Young Museum or any of the quiet old Mormon villages like Toquerville, he can only marvel at the courage which brought life to a desert and substance to a vision.

The Gold Rush

John A. Sutter was a man with grandiose dreams, but in the light of what happened, it is ironic that the discovery of gold did not seem to be one of them. A Swiss adventurer who came to Mexican California in 1839, Sutter had wangled a huge land grant in the lower Sacramento Valley which he christened New Helvetia. At the junction of the Sacramento and American rivers, Sutter built an adobe-walled fort, enclosing a whole village of homes, stores, and warehouses. His fort, which has been restored in Sacramento, was an important trading post for the American settlers coming overland to California, and Sutter said of himself, "I was everything—patriarch, priest, father, and judge."

COURTESY SECOND BANK-STATE STREET TRUST CO., BOSTON

Sutter hired a carpenter named James Marshall to supervise construction of a sawmill forty miles above the fort in a mountain valley the Indians called Coloma, or "beautiful vale," and on January 24, 1848, after the men had done some blasting in the stream, Marshall noticed some yellow particles glittering in the bedrock. He collected them and that night announced to his crew, "Boys, I think I've found a gold mine." No one believed him, but next day the yellow flakes turned up again, and Marshall gathered three ounces of the dust and rode off to the fort. There he and Sutter tested it and, convinced it was gold, did their best to squelch the news. They succeeded fairly well until the middle of May, when a Mormon named Sam Brannan appeared in San Francisco, brandishing a quinine bottle full of gold dust and yelling, "Gold, gold, gold from the American River!" Something about Brannan's antics fused the town into action and before anyone quite knew what had happened, everyone seemed to be off for the river.

San Francisco became a ghost town. By June three-fourths of its population of 800 had departed, business was almost non-existent, and sailorless ships rotted in the bay. As prospectors ranged over the western slopes of the Sierra they seemed to find gold everywhere. What they had come upon was a long, narrow strip of gold-bearing quartz, a mile wide and 120 miles long—the "Mother Lode." By the end of the year, eight or ten thousand men were working the Sierra diggings—one taking out $40,000 in seven weeks, but the majority collecting an ounce a day, or about twenty dollars' worth.

While gold brought riches to a few, it spelled ruin for Marshall and Sutter. As his employees deserted him for the gold fields, Sutter's commercial enterprises collapsed, squatters usurped his land, and he lost his fort through bankruptcy. Miners swarmed over Marshall's claims and appropriated them, and in 1885 Marshall died broke and forgotten, within sight of his discovery. Today a lonely stone shaft on the bank of the American River near Coloma marks the site of Sutter's Mill, and close by is the cabin where Marshall spent many sad, protesting years.

Back East, the initial reaction to the gold discoveries was one of disbelief until President Polk devoted an enthusiastic paragraph of his message to Congress to "the abundance of gold in that territory." This was in December, 1848, and the President's words were dramatized shortly thereafter by the arrival in Washington of an army officer, bearing a tea caddy containing 230 ounces of pure gold. The sensation was

This contemporary etching was an Easterner's acid comment on the attempt of some Forty-Niners to be self-sufficient.

immediate and complete, and from all over the United States—indeed, from all over the world—men pulled up stakes and headed for California. By ship, by wagon train, enduring every conceivable hardship, they came by the thousands to a land where riches lay on the ground, waiting to be picked.

In 1849 the majority of miners worked alone or in small partnerships, using the most rudimentary tools —picks, shovels, and pans. They were too busy seeking their fortunes to worry about cleanliness, and a mining camp like Humbug Creek, Flapjack Canyon, or Gouge Eye was no more than a dusty street, lined with saloons, gambling parlors, and discarded trash, surrounded by the lean-tos or tents of the miners. Some men lived in barrels, and all were beset with fleas, lice, and the various diseases of filth and exposure. Flour sold for $400 a barrel, sugar for $4 a pound, whisky for $20 a quart, but the men objected most to the absence of women.

Decaying, lonely buildings are all that remain of once-booming Melones. The town had a population of 5,000 at the height of the Gold Rush, but less than a hundred live there today. Below, specimens of gold nuggets are shown.

EDMUND B. GERARD, *Life*

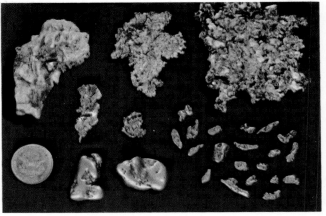

HANSEL MIETH, *Life*

A rough stone shaft on the bank of the American River marks the site of Sutter's Mill, where James Marshall spied flakes of gold one January morning in 1848. Although gold had been found before in California—six years earlier Mexicans had worked claims in Placerita Canyon near Los Angeles—Marshall's chance discovery was the one that provoked the famous 1849 Gold Rush.

By the end of 1852, with as many as 100,000 miners in the diggings, the individual had a hard time making it pay. Gold was no longer within easy reach and soon large companies backed by eastern capital moved in, transforming the gold hunt from an enormous, squalid stag party into an efficient industry. The prospectors began drifting away to seek Eldorados elsewhere—in Colorado, the Klondike, or the Black Hills.

Driving along California State Highway 49, the traveler will see the permanent marks made by the Gold Rush on the Mother Lode country. Some of them are not pretty, like the man-made badlands which have resulted from the hydraulic workings, or the hanging trees where the quick "justice" of miners' courts was executed. But there are many charming old mining villages with their narrow, winding streets to delight the visitor. Off the main road, a few abandoned shanties of the "pick and pan" men are left, but the buildings which have weathered the years best are those which were built to last, like stores and the iron-shuttered Wells Fargo offices. There are towns like Downieville, with its board sidewalks and dirt streets, its Costa Store, and a pioneer museum, housed in an 1852 building. Sonora is another place which is fairly typical of the Mother Lode region.

Placerville is a pretty town that boomed during the 1850's, and El Dorado has a few ruins of the Gold Rush days. There is Mokelumne Hill, Murphys, Angels Camp, and Melones, which was called Slumgullion when Mark Twain and Bret Harte lived there. Best preserved of all these old towns, however, is Columbia, which is now a state historic park. When Columbia was the "gem of the southern mines," 15,000 people lived here—now the population is 200. The Wells Fargo office is a museum, as is the Stage Driver's Retreat, a bar which has a piano brought around the Horn. In the town's firehouse are two 1850 fire engines, and the Pioneer Saloon once contained a bar, gambling parlor, and dance hall.

Downieville, a quiet California town, rests on gravel once so rich that 60 square feet yielded $12,000. Many buildings are remnants of boom days.

Part of the Gold Hill district in Colorado, where a strike occurred in 1859, is visible below from an abandoned cabin.

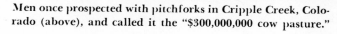

Men once prospected with pitchforks in Cripple Creek, Colorado (above), and called it the "$300,000,000 cow pasture."

Ghost Towns

No one who caught the gold fever ever quite recovered. By the middle of the 1850's, most of the large placer finds in California began to give out, and when the big crusher mills moved in the individual prospector began to seek out more fertile fields. With not much more than a grub stake, a washing pan, and a burro or mule, he roamed from the Pacific to the Rockies, from the Gila north to British Columbia.

There was gold in the eastern Sierras, in Nevada—but not enough water to work the placers. So in 1859 some miners dug a reservoir to hold the runoff of mountain snows at the head of Six Mile Canyon, uncovering, in the process, a vein of bluish rock flecked with gold. At first the "black stuff" was thrown away as worthless; then someone took the trouble to have it assayed and discovered that it held nearly $5,000 worth of silver and $1,600 of gold to the ton. This was the Comstock Lode, and the leading camp in these parts was Virginia City, named for a drunk called "Old Virginny." Today the town has about 1,000 people and a past which is very much in evidence—along A and B streets, the old residential district of unpainted Gothic houses; Piper's Opera House, where Edwin Booth, Maude Adams, and Lily Langtry once appeared; and on C Street, the Crystal Bar, Delta Saloon, and the Bucket of Blood. The *Territorial Enterprise,* again operating, was the first newspaper in Nevada, where Mark Twain served his apprenticeship.

In the spring of 1859 an estimated 100,000 gold-seekers were streaming westward toward Colorado, the words "Pike's Peak or Bust" printed on their packs and on their wagons. There followed, in the next few decades, some of the most spectacular strikes ever made—each creating out of nothing the towns which dot the Colorado landscape today. The list is a long one, and there is no end to the interesting places to see. There is Central City, once known as "the richest square mile on earth," with its famous Opera House and the Teller House, to which President Grant, on his visit in 1873, walked from the stage-coach on a path of silver bricks. Nearby is Nevadaville, a genuine ghost town; and there is Silver Cliff, once the third largest town in the state, but now almost deserted. Leadville, where Horace Tabor struck it rich, is still a mining town; but here you may see the old Wyman Saloon, the former Tabor Grand Opera House on Harrison Avenue, Tabor's Grand Hotel, his house, and the Matchless Mine, where his widow "Baby Doe," forlornly hoping to recoup a lost fortune, froze to death.

All around the Cripple Creek district, behind Pike's Peak, there are abandoned houses and mine workings. Victor was the site of the great Gold Coin Mine, discovered during excavation of a hotel basement. Cripple Creek itself, once known as "the $300,000,000 cow pasture," is a shade of its former self; and towns like Elkton and Gillett are practically deserted.

Another great nineteenth-century bonanza took place in Montana, in Alder Gulch, and the town most representative of that place and era is another Virginia City, also very much worth seeing. Along Wallace Street, the main thoroughfare, are the Fairweather Inn, Rank's Drugstore, an assay office, and the Wells Fargo office, all dating from the days of the big strike in the 1860's.

DAVID E. SCHERMAN

Virginia City, Nevada, named for a drunk called "Old Virginny," was the leading camp of the fabulous Comstock Lode, found in 1859.

FROM *The Old West Speaks*, BY HOWARD R. BRIGGS; © 1956 BY PRENTICE-HALL, INC.

Past Split Rock in the Sweetwater Valley, a Pony Express rider is pursued by Indians. The most dangerous part of the Missouri-to-California route was in Utah and Nevada, but the couriers' horses were so fast that few of them were ever caught.

Passing of the Pony Express

Only one mail bag carried by the short-lived Pony Express failed to be delivered; but in 1861 the service was discontinued after completion of the transcontinental telegraph line. At first the Indians were superstitious of the so-called "talking wires." Later, realizing the significance of the lines, they cut the wires and attacked many of the isolated telegraph stations along the route.

"Away across the dead level of the Prairie a black speck appears against the sky. . . . In a second or two it becomes a horse and rider . . . soon the flutter of hoofs comes faintly to the ear. In another instant, a whoop and a hurrah from the upper deck of our coach, a wave of the rider's hand, but no reply, and man and horse burst past our excited faces, and go swinging away like the belated fragments of a storm."

In *Roughing It* Mark Twain described the thrill of seeing a Pony Express rider one summer day in 1861. It was a sight no one could forget. During its short lifetime—it was discontinued after a year and a half of service—the Pony Express was the object of almost universal respect and admiration. Until it was introduced, twenty days to a month was considered fast delivery for mail from Missouri to California. The Pony Express cut at least ten days off that time.

On April 3, 1860, the freight and passenger hauling firm of Russell, Majors & Waddell, operating out of St. Joseph, Missouri, and Nebraska City, inaugurated its innovation in mail-carrying. In effect, it was a kind of horse-telegraph, like the one Genghis Khan had employed to bind his empire together. The road began in St. Joseph, where the original stables still stand, and ran west to Sacramento, following in general the Oregon Trail to Fort Bridger, then turning southwest. Before sections of the route were replaced by telegraph, there were 190 stations, 420 horses, 400 station men, and 80 riders. The stations were set up at ten-mile intervals, and although few of them remain today, one can see an example of them at Hanover, Kansas, where the Hollenberg Station is the only original and unaltered one left. At Fairbury, Nebraska, is the site of the Rock Creek Station where Wild Bill Hickok was an agent. Nearby, incidentally, is the George Winslow grave, one of the few marked graves on the Oregon Trail. The town park at Gothenburg, Nebraska, has a log fur-trading house that was once a Pony Express station, and at Fort Bridger, Wyoming, one may see some remaining stables.

The typical rider was a young man in his early twenties, light, tough, and inured to the saddle. In Mark Twain's words, "he rode a splendid horse that was born for a racer and fed and lodged like a gentleman"—usually a small, fast California mustang. The rider's daily stint was 75 or 100 miles, and he made two round trips a week. He was expected to average nine miles an hour, and was allowed only two minutes for changing horses. Arriving at a relay station, he received a gulp of water and a bite of bread while the *mochila,* a square leather pad with mail pouches fitted at each corner, was slung over the saddle of a fresh horse. If he arrived to find his replacement sick or injured, he had to keep going. One man, "Pony Bob"

These stables at Fort Bridger, Wyoming, are among the last remaining examples of nearly 200 Pony Express stations.

Haslam, once rode through 380 miles of hostile Indian territory in 45 hours, stopping only for some nine hours to rest.

The station agents' lives were hardly easier. Alone, often surrounded by hostile Indians, they usually lived in shacks, tents, or adobe hovels. One station in the Utah desert was described as a "hole, four feet deep, roofed over with split cedar trunks and with a rough adobe chimney." The most dangerous section of the route was in Utah and Nevada, where the Paiutes were on a rampage of destruction and murder in the early 1860's. Here a number of stations were burned, and agents killed. Because their horses were so fast, few riders were ever killed, but the trips were no less harrowing on that account.

Only the most important mail was carried by the Pony Express. It was always an expensive venture, and unfortunately its returns were never enough to keep it out of the red. To make matters worse, the Pony Express received no financial aid from the government, since the subsidy for transcontinental mail belonged to the Butterfield Overland Mail firm. When Russell, Majors & Waddell had lost an estimated $200,000 in the Pony Express venture they went bankrupt, and received no recompense from the government despite the fact that news of Southern secession, carried by Pony Express, had helped to nip an uprising of California Confederates, and had kept the Far West within the Union.

Beyond any financial failure, however, construction of a transcontinental telegraph brought the end of the Pony Express. Neither romantic nor spectacular, the "talking wires," as the Indians called them, were joined from east to west at Salt Lake City in October, 1861. From that moment on, there was no more need for a cross-country horse-telegraph.

The full story of Custer's last stand at the Battle of the Little Big Horn may never be known. Overwhelmed by a furious Indian assault, his small cavalry force had no hope of escape, and not a single man survived.

Custer's Last Stand

Driving along Montana Route 8, from Lame Deer to Crow Agency, the traveler may pause for a moment high in the Wolf Mountains to look westward, toward the valley of the Little Big Horn, just as Colonel George Armstrong Custer's scouts did near here on the morning of June 25, 1876. The Sioux and Cheyennes were known to be gathering in this area, and Custer was under the command of General Terry in a three-way pincer movement in which the forces of General Terry, General Crook, and Colonel Gibbon were to converge upon the enemy. Custer split off from Terry with a small band along Rosebud Creek.

This three-way attack was all very well on paper, but it did not take into account the rough, untracked country, the deep, swift streams, or the mountain ranges which would have to be crossed before it could be made to work. At the Battle of Rosebud Creek on June 17, Crook was repulsed by a large force of Indians; but neither Custer nor Gibbon was aware of this. All they knew was that a sizable enemy force was gathering somewhere near the headquarters of Rosebud Creek and the Little Big Horn—but exactly where, they were not certain.

Marching south, Custer saw traces of a large band of moving Indians, and without bothering to ask for reinforcements he set off in pursuit. By June 24 the trail was hot, and it seemed probable that the Indians were camped only a short distance to the west, on the other side of the Wolf Mountains.

Shortly after sunrise on June 25, Custer's scouts could see, perhaps fifteen miles away, an ominous blue haze spreading out over the land, the collective smoke of many campfires. Although Custer did not realize it, this was the largest Indian mobilization in

U.S. history, and when his favorite scout Bloody Knife warned him that the odds were too great, Custer replied, "Oh, I guess we'll get through them in one day." About nine o'clock he ordered his dead-tired men forward. Down in the foothills, he inexplicably divided his small force into four parts: Captain Fred Benteen to the southwest to scout for Indians; two detachments commanded by Major Marcus Reno and Custer to the northwest in the direction of the Indian camp; and the pack train to the rear.

Sitting Bull was a power behind the Indian uprising. The 1865 photograph of Custer was taken by Brady.

A little after two, riding through a wide valley where the grass was heat-burned to a dark brown color, Custer and Reno saw their first Indians, some Sioux who rode up close and then dashed away, yelling derisively. Custer sent Reno and his troopers off in pursuit, and across the river they came face to face with a superior force of Sioux, who drove them back with heavy losses.

Meantime, Custer continued northwest, riding along the brown, ravine-gutted bluffs. He had sent a message to Benteen, asking for reinforcements, but Benteen had joined Reno, to help him stave off complete disaster. While Custer waited, he lost whatever time advantage he might have had, and once the Indians repulsed Reno, they hurried to attack Custer's force. With a sudden fury, they must have come at him from all sides, jumping him from the ravines and gullies that crisscross these bare hills. Knowledge

of what happened after that comes only from the Indians who were there—because not one of Custer's 265 men survived. From the position of the bodies it was possible to surmise that the main Indian attack came from the rear, and that Custer's troopers resisted in an orderly enough manner at first, only to be routed by the desperate Indians.

The battle ranged along an L-shaped ridge, and because the Indians had segmented Custer's force, it was impossible for him to organize a concerted stand. The place where he might have made it—on the summit of this ridge—was overwhelmed by the mounted Indians, so Custer's cavalry had to fight it out on the slope under the brow of the hill, and on foot.

The fiercely contested battle lasted but a short time, and must have been over by the middle of the afternoon. In spite of its brevity, and the fact that it was a relatively unimportant incident in American history, few battles before or since have held quite the same fascination for writers or the public.

Anyone who visits the sage-covered ridge and the little cemetery in the heart of the Crow Reservation will have to contend with a variety of legends and facts relating to the battle itself. And anyone who wishes to philosophize about the lightning pace of American history may pause a moment to think that this happened not quite seventy years before the Atomic Age began.

A group of Sioux Indians leaves Sitting Bull's solitary grave in North Dakota's Standing Rock Reservation.

Many of Custer's men lie buried where they made their last stand on a high bluff above the Little Big Horn.

In Joseph Becker's painting, Chinese gandy dancers wave at a Central Pacific train passing through snow sheds in the Sierras. These sheds were built in places where avalanche danger was great.

Spanning the Continent

The discovery of gold in California gave wings to men's imaginations. In 1830 intelligent men were insisting that it would take anywhere from 500 to 2,000 years to settle and develop the country. What happened in 1848 changed the timetable forever, and 21 years later Americans had a railroad all the way across the continent, with settlements springing up along its path. The Civil War and the necessity of binding West to East were decisive factors in bringing it about, but the prospect of riches kept the issue in the public eye for many years.

In California, a man named Theodore Dehone Judah, popularly known as Crazy Judah, had engineered a railroad from Sacramento to the gold fields and by 1855 he was publicly urging a road across the Sierras to the East. Judah was backed by four Sacramento merchants: Collis P. Huntington, Mark Hop-

kins, Leland Stanford, and Charles P. Crocker. In return for financing Judah's survey over the Sierra Nevada, these men later became officers of the Central Pacific Railroad, and later still, four of the wealthiest men in America.

In July, 1862, President Lincoln signed the Enabling Act, which created the Union Pacific Railroad and authorized construction of a "continuous railroad and telegraph line" starting west from Council Bluffs, Iowa. It provided land grants of 12,000 acres to the mile in alternate sections along the line, and bond issues to help finance construction. Upon the same terms, the Central Pacific Railroad was authorized to start building eastward from the Coast.

Hundreds of workmen—many of them Irishmen fresh from the Union Army—began the backbreaking job of grading and laying track west from Council

Bluffs. The route, even at that time, was an historic one—a natural thoroughfare along the rivers which had been followed by buffalo, Indians, fur traders, explorers, Mormons, gold hunters, the Overland stagecoaches, and the Pony Express. First there was the problem of supply—providing the 6,250,000 ties and 50,000 tons of rails and fittings, bridges, and other installations. Until completion of the Chicago & Northwestern Railroad as far as Council Bluffs in 1867, the only means of transporting supplies to the workers on the Union Pacific end of the line was by boat up the Missouri River, or by team. Along the way, gamblers, ex-convicts, and con-men plagued the workers as they moved across the plains and mountains, and always there were Indians, harassing the workmen at every opportunity, seeking to halt this permanent intrusion into their lands. By the end of 1866, 300 miles of track had been laid; the following year saw 240 miles added, and the railroad reached its highest point near Cheyenne, Wyoming. In 1868, 425 miles were covered, and the road was within 125 miles of its proposed meeting with the Central Pacific.

On the western section, the first year's work produced only 18 miles of track, from Sacramento to Roseville. The Central Pacific, like the Union Pacific, had a welter of investment difficulties, and because of the continuing search for gold, there was a shortage of laborers. Finally Crocker, superintending construction, introduced Chinese workers, or Crocker's Pets, as they were called. Many of them were imported from China specifically for this job, and eventually thousands of Chinese pushed the rails through the deep snow and solid granite walls of the Sierra Nevada, using picks, shovels, and wheelbarrows for the enormous task.

By June of 1868 the Central Pacific had reached the California-Utah line, and the race for completion began in earnest, each company seeking the land grants and bonds that came with every completed mile. Finally, the government set the meeting place at Promontory Point, six miles west of Ogden, Utah, and on May 10, 1869, the great day arrived. Shortly after dawn, two cheering groups of workmen met, and later that morning the official parties arrived to see the last section of track laid and to drive the golden spike tying East and West together for all time. Later the road was rerouted across Great Salt Lake, and today only a monument marks the meeting of the rails near Promontory. The original golden spike is displayed in the Leland Stanford, Jr., Museum in Stanford, California. But the meaning of that May day in 1869 will not be lost on anyone who has seen the shining steel rails, stretching to the horizon across the plains and deserts and mountains of the West.

Irish laborers of the Union Pacific joined forces with Central Pacific Chinese as the last mile was blasted out.

Like many railbeds through western mountains, the Animas Canyon passage in Colorado was blasted from sheer cliffs.

When the golden spike was driven at Promontory Point, two engines met, one from the East and the other from the West.

Soon after gold was discovered, San Francisco was practically a ghost town, and sailing ships which had brought the Forty-Niners to the coast rotted in the harbor, deserted by their gold-crazy crews. These daguerreotypes were made about 1850.

Golden Gate

At 5:16 on the morning of April 18, 1906, "the deeps of the earth . . . began to rumble and vibrate." The great San Andreas fault on the Pacific Coast had settled violently, and in San Francisco all hell broke loose. For three days fire raged unchecked through the city, destroying four square miles of buildings, taking over 600 lives, and leaving "a mass of smoldering ruins" in its wake.

Across the continent, a San Franciscan named Will Irwin read the dispatches and sat down to write his classic story of "The City That Was." Before the earthquake, this had been a world center of trade and finance, "the gayest, lightest hearted, most pleasure loving city of the western continent." But the old San Francisco was dead, Irwin concluded, and "if it rises out of the ashes it must be a modern city, much like other cities and without its old atmosphere."

A modern San Francisco did rise phoenix-like from the ashes, but it was never to be like any other place. Instead, it is one which many Americans consider the best their country has to offer, a city of atmosphere and spectacular beauty where one can still catch glimpses of a past as colorful as its present.

There is the Mission Dolores, founded in 1776, and the old Presidio, once a Spanish garrison. There is Portsmouth Square, the Plaza of Mexican days, where Captain John Montgomery hoisted the American flag in 1846. Four years after that event San Francisco was the gateway to the gold fields, and the buildings around Portsmouth Square the heart of a lusty, topsy-turvy town. Fort Gunnybags, on Sacramento Street, was headquarters for Vigilance Committees created to preserve law and order; and what is now the city's financial district was the water front, where scores of ships lay rotting, unable to sail because all hands had run off to the gold fields. Some of the hulks were drawn up on shore, to be converted into stores and homes, and one of them, the Ship Building on Montgomery Street, survived until recently.

In 1860 Pony Express riders came into town after the 10½-day trip from Missouri; and in 1875 the Palace, first great luxury hotel of the West, went up on Market Street where its successor now stands. This was the place that moved Emperor Dom Pedro II to say: "Nothing makes me ashamed of Brazil so much as the Palace Hotel." And on Market Street is Lotta's Fountain, presented to the city by Lotta Crabtree, toast of the golden age.

There is Nob Hill, where financial and industrial giants built their palaces; remnants of the Barbary Coast, once the wickedest section of a wicked city; Chinatown, the largest Chinese settlement outside Asia; and the redoubtable cable cars which have climbed the city's hills since 1873.

Of downtown San Francisco, little but the Montgomery Block survived the fire; but what has been added, like the Bay Bridge and the beautiful Golden Gate Bridge, sum up the magic, the beauty, and the future of a city known as the "Baghdad of the West."

The magnificent Golden Gate Bridge spans the entrance to San Francisco Bay. At its southern terminal is the Presidio.

Acknowledgments

The editors have been most fortunate in the cooperation and suggestions they have received from hundreds of authorities on national and local historic sites. Their gratitude is extended to all the individuals and organizations whose advice and guidance have made this volume possible and to the photographers and artists whose work appears in the book.

Index